The Malays

The Malays

THEIR PROBLEMS AND FUTURE

SYED HUSIN ALI

The Other Press
Kuala Lumpur

Copyright © 2008 Dr Syed Husin Ali

Published 2008 by
The Other Press Sdn Bhd
607 Mutiara Majestic
Jalan Othman
46000 Petaling Jaya
Selangor, Malaysia
www.ibtbooks.com

The Other Press is affiliated to Islamic Book Trust.

Perpustakaan Negara Malaysia   Cataloguing-in-Publication Data

Syed Husin Ali
  The Malays: their problems and future / Syed Husin Ali.
  Includes index
  Bibliography: p.223
  ISBN 978-983-9541-62-5
  ISBN 978-983-9541-61-8 (pbk.)
  1. Malays (Asian people). 2. Malays (Asian people)--Social conditions.
  3. Malays (Asian people)--Politics and government. 4. Malays
  (Asian people)--Economic conditions. I. Title
  305.89928

Cover
People of Naning at the installation of the new *Dato Naning* (chieftain), 1953. Naning was the scene of the first anti-British uprising; *Background*: Kuala Lumpur skyline, symbol of Malaysia's rapid economic growth in the 1990s.

Printed in Malaysia by
Academe Art and Printing Services, Kuala Lumpur.

CONTENTS

Preface vii

Preface to the First Edition xi

1 Who are the Malays? 1

2 From Pre-Colonialism to Post-Independence 9

3 Political History and Process 30

4 Malays and Islam 57

5 Structure and Social Changes 79

6 Wealth, Exploitation and the Economy 100

7 Development Policies: Success or Failure? 124

8 Multi-Ethnic Society 158

9 Conclusion 181

Appendix 201

Bibliography 223

Index 225

PREFACE

This is a revised and updated version of the book that I wrote and managed to publish about thirty years ago while in detention without trial under the ISA (Internal Security Act). The rationale, aim and scope of this book and the circumstances under which it was written have been explained in the earlier preface.

I decided to work on the revision of this book after being persuaded at the end of last year by Haji Koya Kutty, managing director of The Other Press, who wanted to publish it. I immediately set down to work and we planned to have it out in early March 2008. But the date of the general elections was announced before then, and being involved with them quite actively although not as a candidate, the plan was interrupted.

It was only a month after the 12th general elections on March 8 that I managed to resume work and complete it in early May. All the chapters have been modified, some more than others, to make the book more up-to-date. But it needs to be stated that most materials in the original text have been retained almost intact and form the bulk of the present edition.

Three decades have passed since the book was first conceived. During that time many changes have taken place in the country, particularly in the economic, political and social fields. But I contend that the basic problems facing the society, especially the Malays, have remained the same.

The results of the elections were beyond the expectations of many people, even some keen political observers. The Opposition coalition made up of the People's Justice Party (PKR), the Democratic Action Party (DAP) and the Pan-Malaysian Islamic Party (PAS), despite all odds, managed to deny two-thirds majority to the government coalition (BN), obtaining half of the total votes cast and winning 82 of the 222 parliamentary seats (37.3 per cent).

Besides, the state of Kelantan was retained with bigger majority while Selangor, Perak, Kedah and Penang fell to the Opposition coalition (which assumed the name of 'Pakatan Rakyat' – loosely translated as the People's Alliance - after the elections). In the Kuala Lumpur Federal Territory, the 'Pakatan' swept ten of the eleven parliamentary seats.

Finally, the people of Malaysia found courage to change; there was jubilation across the country among all ethnic groups. At the same time the change sent shivers particularly to a section of the Malays in UMNO and their supporters. They immediately sounded the unnecessary alarm that the future of the Malays was under serious threat. Narrow ethnic sentiments and issues were used by them to arouse Malay fear and anger.

A few demonstrations were organised by some shocked UMNO members purportedly to defend the Malay special positions and outdated pro-Malay policies, including the nearly forty year old New Economic Policy (NEP). But they soon lost their steam. Then, a number of exclusively Malay meetings and conferences were organised by some backward looking ex-academics and professionals together with certain outmoded leaders of normally inactive social and cultural organisations. They were held in Penang, Kuala Lumpur and Johor to defend what they perceive as *ketuanan Melayu* (Malay supremacy). It appears they practically ended after the handing over of their resolutions to a sultan, without any serious follow-up plan.

The post-elections responses or reactions of different groups and categories of people, especially the Malays, should make an interesting area of research and writing. But I am unable to deal with them in this book. Here almost everything ends at the close of 2007 when I started revising. Perhaps the post-elections developments require another book.

There seems to be positive sign in these developments. It shows the Malays are rightfully concerned about their own problems and future, but they see different methods and ways of dealing with them. Indeed, there is great need for serious, sincere, critical and creative thinking on all issues. We require more open and rational dialogues or exchange of views. But they must not be dominated by narrow, conservative and ethnically charged approach linked to vested interests that benefit only a small group of Malays with power and wealth that work against the welfare of the large section of ordinary Malays, the majority of whom are still deprived of decent living and a say in their own affairs.

Personally, since this book was originally conceived, I have undergone a lot of internal transformation. But it even surprises me that the basic underpinnings of my ideas and perspectives of looking at various changes and problems in society have not altered very much. I do not think I have to apologise for this. In all humility, I believe my understanding and analysis of them have, hopefully, sharpened and improved.

Admittedly, this book is neither a sophisticated academic exercise nor a committed political treatise. It tries to combine the strength of both and hopefully the weakness of none. It may not be able to satisfy the needs of so-called neutral scholars or the demands of partisan political activists. But I hope it will be able to raise the understanding and awareness of the people at large – irrespective of ethnicity, class, religion and gender – on the fundamental challenges confronting the country now and for the future.

I actually need to express my thanks to many who have helped in this endeavour. But let me confine only to a few. Firstly, my wife Sabariah for her silent encouragement and patience as well as tolerance. Then Haji Koya Kutty for succeeding to trigger and sustain my interest to revise the book and for publishing it; his son Abdar Rahman for editing the book and preparing the index; his daughter Latheefa, who together with Eric Paulsen put together the tables, and others in The Other Press who have made this book presentable. I must also mention Din Merican who helped to go through the first draft. But I take full responsibility for all flaws and weaknesses.

I dedicate this book to all true Malaysians who have struggled at different times in history to establish a genuinely just, democratic, free and united Malaysia. May their dreams be realised in the very near future.

S. Husin Ali
May 2008
Petaling Jaya

PREFACE TO THE FIRST EDITION

The Malay people are now at an important crossroad. Many problems and challenges confront them which will result in different responses and reactions. More often than not they may lose their sense of direction and thereby lose sight of their objectives. Much emotional heat may be generated, which, if not properly managed, will lead to chaos and destruction.

I believe that the majority of people in this country wish to see big changes taking place. The targets they aspire to and the routes they choose may be different. But it is imperative that they have the facts of the situation, and possess clear analyses as well as correct attitudes in order to guide their course of action. They cannot rely on emotions alone.

In this book I shall attempt to analyse various major problems facing the Malay people, covering religious, social, economic, political and other related fields. I shall also try to envisage the possible future. In order to secure a bright future for the country, the people, especially its leaders, must place national interests before anything else, and pay greater attention to the plight of the ordinary citizens who form the majority rather than the fortunes of the small minority in the upper class. I submit this with the most sincere intentions, based on my own field-study and observation on the current position of the Malays. Of course this analysis reflects my own attitudes towards the problems in the first place.

It is relevant to state here that the book was planned and executed under oppressive conditions. I was detained at 2.00 a.m. on 7 December 1974, following a spate of student demonstrations protesting against poverty, inflation and corruption. These demonstrations came in the wake of hunger marches by thousands of disenchanted peasants in Baling, Sik and many other places in the northern part of the country.

On 2 July 1976, after being detained without trial for eighteen months in Kamunting, Perak, I was taken by Special Branch operatives to an unknown place in Kuala Lumpur. For over six months I was in solitary confinement, denied all facilities for reading and writing and decent human life. It was under these trying circumstances that I planned this book. When I was sent back to Kamunting on 13 January 1977, I started writing the original version in Malay and completed it within a month. This translation was done during Ramadan (Fasting Month) in August of 1978. I thank fellow-detainee Abdullah Majid for his help in going through it so meticulously.

I am aware of the many shortcomings in this book. It is written for popular consumption. My main focus of attention is on social, economic and political issues, not only because I feel more conversant with them, but also because I hold that the future of the Malays depends largely on changes in these areas. This does not mean that I am underestimating the importance of other aspects, especially religion, cultural values and education. My only hope is that more competent persons will write on them.

I have no doubt that many will not agree with some, if not all, of the views expressed in this book. Nevertheless, I strongly believe that, in order to seek truth, the differences of views should be discussed openly and dissenting opinions should not be suppressed. I have been detained for nearly four years now as a political prisoner for holding some of the views that I have expressed. But I have no reason to fear. I should be most gratified if this book could stimulate sane and serious discussion and provoke thought on the problems and future of the Malays.

As mentioned earlier, the Malay people are at an important crossroad and they desire major changes in their lives. Let us all make sure that they will be able to proceed along the right path towards progress and freedom from imperialism, exploitation, poverty, corruption and injustice.

Dr. S. Husin Ali
23 September 1978
Taiping Detention Camp, Perak.

1
WHO ARE THE MALAYS?

This book sets out to discuss the changes, problems and future of the Malays. At the outset it is important to define and clarify who the Malays really are. Superficially it is easy to identify them. They are normally brown in skin-colour, of moderate physical build but tough, and often gentle-mannered. We also know that in the Malay Peninsula they are regarded as the 'sons of the soil' (Bumiputera). They live together with various immigrant groups, most of whom were encouraged to come here by the British colonial rulers. According to the 1970 Census, out of a total population of 8,810,348, 4,685,838 (or 53.2 per cent) were Malays. The rest were Chinese (35.4 per cent), Indians (10.6 per cent) and Others 0.8 per cent. By 2007 the total population had risen to 27 million, made up of Malays (54.68 per cent), Chinese (23 per cent), Non-Bumiputera Malays (11 per cent), Indians (6.9 per cent) and Others (1.2 per cent) (*see Table 1.1 and 1.2*).

In different contexts the term 'Malay' has many meanings. Taking a wide social and cultural definition, the term refers not only to those who are settled in the Peninsula, but also includes those in the larger area of the Malay Archipelago, embracing the Malay Peninsula and thousands of islands which today form the Republics of Indonesia and the Philippines. Although they are divided into many sub-groups, and perhaps as many dialects, linguistic and cultural experts always consider them as belonging to the same stock, known as the Malays or Malayo-Indonesians. Indeed the Malay world covers a wide area, and its people constitute one of the major racial groups of the world.

History tells us that there have been ebbs and flows in the old kingdoms which existed in the Malay Archipelago. During the ebbs the kingdoms were small and dispersed, with their jurisdiction confined only to limited areas. But during the flows big empires existed, namely Sriwijaya, Majapahit and lastly Melaka, whose areas of jurisdiction radiated from their centres and throughout the Archipelago. The boundaries of these kingdoms were not clearly marked and often varied according to their power at any particular time. All areas under their domain acknowledged their supremacy and these dominions increased or decreased with each kingdom's rise or fall. Their final disintegration was brought about by the advent of western colonialism.

The arrival of colonialism introduced new political boundaries which divided the peoples of the Malay stock into new nation-states. Portugal was the first western power to set foot in this area, but by the mid-seventeenth century the Portuguese were ousted by the Dutch and the English. Holland took possession of the myriad islands from Sabang to Merauke which today form Indonesia; Britain controlled the peninsular Malay states and formed Malaya, which in 1963 was renamed Malaysia with the inclusion of the Borneo territories of Sabah and Sarawak. Spain and later the United States controlled the many islands which are now the Philippines. It was colonialism which separated the peoples of the Malay stock into groups confined within the boundaries of their new states.

Quite often when we refer to the term Malay, we think only of those living in the Peninsula. Descendants of the Malays in the Philippines are now known as Filipinos, while those in the former Dutch territories are called Indonesians. Our eyes have been shaded by these separate political boundaries to such an extent that we lose sight of the similarities in ancestry, of culture and history which are the common heritage of all the inhabitants of the Malay Archipelago.

The definition of Malay becomes more complex in the context of two other issues, namely, its legal definition and the newly coined term Bumiputera (son of the soil). According to the Malaysian Constitution, a Malay is defined as meaning "a person who professes the Muslim religion, habitually speaks Malay, conforms to Malay custom and: (a) was born before Merdeka Day, in the Federation or Singapore or born of parents one of whom was born in the Federation or Singapore, or was on Merdeka Day domiciled in the Federation or Singapore; or (b) is the issue of such a person." (Article 160). Merdeka refers to Independence on 31 August 1957.

It is not the intention here to challenge the constitution. But let us stop to ponder the implication of this definition. In theory a Malay, from the point of law, can be anybody of any origin so long as he is a Muslim, speaks Malay and practises Malay customs in his daily life. An ex-British Adviser[1] who has embraced Islam, married to a Malay, speaks in the Malay language to his wife and children, and follows Malay customs in his everyday life, can be considered a Malay by virtue of the constitutional provision. Similarly a new Chinese or Indian convert to Islam who lives with a Malay family, speaks Malay and practises Malay customs has the right to be regarded as a Malay too. Of course, many of Muslim Indian and Arab descent have long been regarded as Malay. So there is a difference between the definition of Malay according to the constitution and the historical and socio-cultural definition.

Consistent with the constitution, the Malays are guaranteed a special position, which it is the responsibility of the Yang DiPertuan Agong to protect. It covers recruitment into the civil service, awards of scholarships, opportunities for education and training, and issue of licenses and permits. The Yang DiPertuan Agong has the power to determine the appropriate quota to be reserved for the Malays. As the legal definition of Malay includes such people as the ex-British Adviser and the Chinese or Indian convert mentioned above, does it mean that they too have the right to this special position?

It is not surprising, therefore, that some people have been advocating that new converts into Islam should be regarded as Malays, and granted the same special privileges. However, it may be argued that merely embracing Islam does not fulfill all the conditions of being a Malay. Should the new convert continue to speak his mother tongue, then he has not fully satisfied the constitutional provision. It is quite correct, therefore, to say in this case that 'becoming a Muslim' does not mean the same thing as 'becoming a Malay', although there are some people who tend to regard the two as one and the same. Only if the new

---

1. British colonial officer designated to 'advise' the Sultan in the Unfederated Malay States, following British rule in the country.

convert and his children later speak solely in Malay and follow Malay customs in their everyday life can they be regarded as Malays and have the right to enjoy the special privileges. This must be a *sine qua non* so long as the constitution remains unchanged.

What happens if a Malay takes to another religion? Although this rarely happens, but does happen, especially when recent reports show that some Malay youths have embraced Christianity. By so doing, their position as Malays becomes questionable. In theory the government can deny them the Malay-reserved scholarships, for instance, even if they have the necessary qualifications. But what does belief in Islam really mean? Does it suffice just to be born a Muslim, without taking into consideration whether or not the person knows the fundamental teachings and practises the true faith of Islam? As for the youths who embraced Christianity, should they be regarded as Bumiputera, just as those aborigines who are converts to Christianity?

We now turn to Malay custom. What does this exactly mean? What aspects of Malay custom are we referring to? There are groups of people such as the rustic village folk, who cling tenaciously to old customs; on the other hand there are those members of the urban Malay middle class who lead an entirely Western way of life. A question may be asked: Can a Melaka Chinese (*Baba*) who speaks Malay, sings Malay melodies (*dondang sayang*), wears a *sarung* at home, eats cross-legged on the floor using his fingers, and marries his child according to Malay ceremonies, be called a Malay? Again, what about a Malay officer who has an English wife, speaks English at home, eats at table using fork and spoon, drinks beer, wears pyjamas in bed, and marries his daughter in Western style with a reception at the Hilton? Is he not a contrast to the Melaka *Baba*? Nobody will deny that he is a Malay or question his background if, on retirement, he becomes a politician claiming to champion Malay rights, but uses his special position to get logging permits, business licenses and APs (Approved Permits)[2] for himself, or to get appointed to the board of big local or foreign-owned companies, and finally to be made a *Datuk* or *Tan Sri*. All this becomes possible despite his totally alien (non-Malay) lifestyle and associations.

---

2. These are permits for import of cars. Quite often the permit is given sometimes for as low as RM2.00 each. It enables the import of luxury cars from overseas and sold locally with huge profit.

Now, what happens to the immigrants from various parts of the Archipelago, who by virtue of their history and socio-cultural backgrounds are identified as Malays? There are many ethnic groups in Malaysia such as the Javanese, Minangkabau, Acehnese, Bugis, Banjarese and so forth. Many have lived here since early childhood, but there are also some recent arrivals. Among them there are many who speak only their own dialects but not Malay. In other words, they do not fulfill the language requirement. Does this *ipso facto* mean that they are not Malays and cannot be accorded special privileges? Yet it can be argued that their groups are part of the bigger entity known as the Malay stock, and their dialects belong to the bigger family of the Malayo-Indonesian language. Culturally speaking, they must be regarded as Malays. But this follows the socio-cultural and not the legal definition. There is nothing in the constitution that recognises the Javanese, Minangkabau or Acehnese tongues as being akin to the Malay language. Shall we just categorise all these ethnic groups as Bumiputera? Once again we need to refer to the constitution which states that in Borneo those considered to be Bumiputera are: "(a) in relation to Sarawak, a person who is a citizen and either belongs to one of the indigenous groups listed in Article 7 or is of mixed blood deriving exclusively from these groups; and (b) in relation to Sabah, a person who is a citizen, is a child or grandchild of a person of a race indigenous to Sabah (whether on or after Malaysia Day or not) either in Sabah or to a father domiciled in Sabah at the time of birth." (Article 161A [6]).

It is clear that for the Borneo states those included in the definition of Bumiputera are the indigenous groups, sometimes also referred to as the 'natives' (Orang Asli). In Sarawak there is a list of such groups, but there is none for Sabah. In the Peninsula the aborigines are also regarded as Bumiputera. Those who are not defined under the term are the Javanese, Minangkabau, Acehnese, Bugis, Banjarese and so forth, who speak their own dialects. Their position is not clear. They cannot be regarded as local aborigines because most of them are immigrants or descendants of immigrants, most of whom came not more than a hundred years ago. They are different from the aborigines like the Jakun, Senoi, Temiar and Semang, for example, who have been here for centuries. Nor are these aborigines referred to as Malays because most of them are animists and have their own languages and cultures.

This applies even to those few who have embraced Islam. But on the other hand, there are those of Indian or Arab descent who have been accepted quite easily as Malay or Bumiputera.

The term Bumiputera has gained a special legal meaning, especially since the formation of Malaysia in 1963. Previously the term was generally used in reference to the Malays, to distinguish them from the Chinese and Indian immigrants who are not the sons of the soil. Now the term legally includes the Malays, as defined by the constitution, the indigenous or Bumiputera groups in Sabah and Sarawak, and the aborigines of the Peninsula. Socio-culturally, they and the immigrant groups from various parts of the Archipelago are regarded as belonging to the same Malay stock. But a large number of the indigenous groups in Sabah and Sarawak, like the majority of the aborigines in the Peninsula too, are not Muslims. Many are animists, and there are many more Christians than Muslims among them.

Before Malaysia was formed, only the Malays were guaranteed special privileges by the constitution. For the purpose of according the same privileges to the indigenous groups in Sabah and Sarawak after Malaysia was formed, it was not possible under the constitution to regard them as Malays. There are indigenous Malays in the two Borneo states. The Ibans in Sarawak and the Kadazandusuns in Sabah do not want to be called Malays; they have their own names and identities. The feeling is particularly strong with the Ibans, who historically regarded the Malays as their enemies. However, if the constitutional lacunae is simply because they are not Muslims and have their own language and culture, what about those among them who have embraced Islam and adopted the Malay language and culture? Do they qualify as Malays? The same yardstick should apply to the Muslim aborigines in the Peninsula. Fortunately the discrepancy was rectified when the constitution extended the special position to all Bumiputera. Our discussion up to now has brought to light that: (i) the term Malay as defined in historical and socio-cultural contexts is different from that in the constitution, and (ii) the definition according to the constitution, if closely followed, gives rise to a number of complications, because, by this definition, those who are regarded as akin historically and socio-culturally may have to be legally divided into several sub-groups, while those who do not belong historically and socio-culturally to the Malay stock have to be regarded as Malays merely because they fulfill the conditions laid down in the constitution. Precisely, if we wish to know who the Malays really are, we cannot depend entirely on the socio-cultural or the legal factors alone; instead, both these factors have to be considered together. The Malay stock exists as an entity for the whole of the Archipelago, but as a result of separation and segregation brought about by colonialism and the ensuing historical and political changes, we now have different nation-states with their own identities, viz. Malaysia, the Philippines and Indonesia, each having its own laws and constitution.

In the Peninsula, religion, language and custom have been instituted as the yardsticks for identifying the Malays. If both socio-cultural and legal factors are taken together to determine who should be included or excluded as a Malay, then many of the questions that have been raised earlier can be easily answered. The Javanese who only speaks his mother tongue or the Malay officer with Westernised ways can both be categorised as Malays since they are descendants of the same Malay stock. Similarly, the Melaka *Baba* who has embraced Islam can gradually be assimilated as a Malay, in the same way as descendants of Pakistanis, Indian Muslims and Arabs have been regarded as Malays and accorded the same privileges as the hereditary Malays.

As explained earlier the Malays constitute over half of the total population in this country. They form an identifiable ethnic group. They also form part of what is regarded as the nation. The national question in Malaya (now Malaysia) has long caused confusion among the people, even the leaders. At one time, after World War II, leaders like Dr. Burhanuddin Helmi and even Tan Cheng Lock as well as the coalition of organisations called the PUTERA-AMCJA that drew up the People's Manifesto, advocated that the national identity for the country should be *Melayu* (Malay). Unfortunately, the national political movement that they led failed to gain power at that time. After the Federation of Malaya was formed in 1948, the term 'Malayan' was used to identify the nation. But in reality the Malayan nation never emerged, as the Malays, Chinese and Indians remained separate entities. Even the administration referred to each group as a *bangsa* (nation). In effect, the term Malayan (or Malaysian now) refers mainly to citizenship.

When Malaysia was formed, the term 'Malaysian' replaced 'Malayan' to identify the people. It was merely a change of name, not of substance. Perhaps it was due to the confusion between 'nation' and 'nationality' that Onn Jaafar[3] at one time was reported to have asked: "What is the form of the Malayan nation, is it a dragon or a snake?" The formation of a united nation will indeed take a long time to materialise in a multi-racial or multi-ethnic country. In our case, the struggle against colonialism was never as intense or as heroic as in some other Asian or African countries; hence it did not evoke a sense of pride or arouse a spirit of nationalism which could serve as a strong bond of unity for the people. At the beginning it showed to be multi-ethnic, but after the declaration of Emergency rule by the British colonialist in 1948[4] and truly nationalist political parties and trade unions were banned, the independence movement was very much Malay-based and not fully participated by the various ethnic groups.

Even today there is still a widespread use of the terms *bangsa Melayu, bangsa Cina* and *bangsa India*, which literally mean Malay, Chinese and Indian nations or nationalities. Malays often refer to non-Malays as *bangsa asing* (foreign nation) or *orang asing* (foreign people) in everyday political exhortations. What is referred to as a 'nation' here is no more than just an ethnic or racial group. In fact, the concept of nation in its general sense, which embraces all the various constituent ethnic groups, has not emerged as a reality in this country even now. For an anthropologist or sociologist, each ethnic group constitutes a social entity which regards itself and is regarded by others as having similarities owing to common descent. Members of an ethnic group have the same language, culture and religion, display strong emotional ties with one another, and always want to defend their solidarity as a separate and identifiable group. This will be discussed further in Chapter 8.

The Malays as an ethnic group in this country have undergone many changes and face many problems and challenges. Their ability and degree of success in meeting these will not only influence their future, but will also have a far-reaching effect in determining their relationship with other ethnic groups for the formation of a truly united and progressive nation. ✺

---

3. He was the Menteri Besar of Johor who later became the first President of UMNO.
4. Emergency was declared following the Communist uprising. Actually, until now that declaration has not been lifted.

2
FROM PRE-COLONIALISM TO POST-INDEPENDENCE

We have already examined the concept of 'Malay' from the legal and socio-cultural points of view. It is now necessary to trace the history of the Malays in outline, as a background to understanding the changes that have undertaken and the problems they are facing today. It was Bernard Shaw who said something to the effect that the past reflects the present while the present reflects the future. Therefore, to understand the present problems and the future of the Malays it is imperative that we trace their history. But it is not the intention here to go into the various phases of Malay history in a detailed manner, as a historian would do.

Some people in the past have contended that the Malays have no history. Such people were mostly ex-colonial civil servants and orientalists whose attitudes towards local history (as expressed in their writings) were prejudiced by an ethnocentric and colonial bias. This attitude was common amongst most colonial historians who wrote about the history of the colonies. They usually regarded their own country as being the most advanced and civilised, while the colonised people on the other hand were dismissed as backward and primitive. History to them began only with the arrival of the colonisers, bringing progress and development on their civilising mission. It is this point that is most often stressed in their writings.

Here, as in other ex-colonial territories, orientalists and former colonial civil servants focused their attention on the colonial exploits and successes, not on the changes among the colonised peoples. This trend has now changed. Some indigenous historians, as in other newly-independent countries, have unmasked the shallow views of the orientalists and ex-colonial civil servants. They have successfully advocated that a nation's history should be studied and written from the local point of view, and should not be influenced by colonial or other foreign interests. It is now well established that long before the arrival of western colonialism, the indigenous peoples had their own history which, more often than not, was older and more illustrious than that of the foreign colonialists.

Apart from orientalists and ex-colonial civil servants there are also others, including some local and neighbouring politicians, who assert that the Malays not only have no history, but are also not the 'sons of the soil' and thus have no claim over this country. The views of these politicians have influenced many contemporary political and social scientists, usually from western countries, who normally stay for brief periods to study local society, and then come out with what they claim to be definitive studies. In fact these politicians, like the visiting political and social scientists, do not differ from the orientalists and ex-colonial civil servants in their objectives, which are to undermine and humiliate the indigenous population. Although they are aware of the truth, they deliberately manipulate it in their own interests; these people should be viewed with concern. On the other hand there are others who are genuinely ignorant of the truth, and it is hoped that they will ultimately change their attitude and not continue to propagate their mistaken views.

The Malays have existed as a society for thousands of years in the Peninsula. The evidence is clear from archaeological remains, among the oldest of which are human and animal skeletons and stone adzes from the Stone Age, especially from the Mesolithic and Neolithic periods. Many of the remains from the Mesolithic period have been found in caves, indicating that the early settlers lived in small groups in those caves. At these same sites bones of wild animals believed to have been hunted by these settlers for food have also been found. These small bands of people moved from place to place collecting fruits and plants and hunting wild animals. They did not domesticate animals or plant crops. It is possible that the life they led was quite similar to that of the few Stone Age communities that still exist in some parts of the world to this day.

The most important artifacts from the Neolithic period are rectangular adzes that have been polished. These have been found in open country as well as in caves. In certain sites, believed to have been used for burial, skeletons, well-designed pots made of clay and also remains of cereals, particularly rice have been found. It is believed that the Neolithic communities were not solely cave dwellers, but lived in huts or shelters on the land. Unfortunately their homes have been destroyed by time. It is possible that they had begun to domesticate animals and plant crops, in other words they had already started to master their environment and were not dependent entirely on it as was the case with the Mesolithic people. The size and extent of these communities depended on the amount of crops they could produce. As they became more settled, and no longer had to move from place to place, they had more time for producing more refined artifacts and for expressing their artistic talent. It seems they lived peacefully, as there is no evidence that they fought battles among themselves. Clearly the quality of life during the Neolithic period was better than that during the Mesolithic period.

Many theories have been put forward by archaeologists and anthropologists regarding the origins of the Mesolithic and Neolithic communities in the Peninsula. The most widely accepted theory is that the Mesolithic groups of people came from the Hoabinh area of Indochina. Their southward migration started about 5,000 to 3,000 years ago, and their culture is often referred to as the Hoabinhian Culture. These groups were made up of people with small but tough physique, dark skin and woolly hair. They spread downwards into the Peninsula, and some of them crossed over to Sumatra while others proceeded further south to the Melanesian islands in the Pacific.

More waves of migration of the Neolithic people took place between about 3,000 to 1,500 years ago. There are two theories regarding these migrations. The first is that again they originated from an area in Indochina, flowed down the Peninsula and then crossed to the nearby islands of Sumatra, Borneo and the Philippines. The second theory is that they originated from South China and moved across to Borneo and the Philippines. Both these theories are based on archaeological evidence, especially stone adzes dispersed in these areas. It is possible that both these theories can be taken together, since both migrations could have taken place during different periods. What is important is that, whether the theories are correct or not, for thousands of years there were people living in the Peninsula, and these peoples were undoubtedly the true ancestors of the present-day Malays. The Neolithic groups are often described as proto-Malays.

Besides the stone axes and adzes described above, some other artifacts made of iron and bronze have also been found. One of the most interesting is a drum-like item made of bronze, beautifully and finely decorated, found in the Klang area. There are similarities between this and the bronze drums found in Dongson, an area in Indochina. It is believed that they are the products of what is often referred to as the Dongson Culture. There is a theory that at one time Klang was part of the Langkasuka Empire. There is nothing definite about this historically, but this empire is thought to have existed around the area of present day Kedah.

At the time when these early people were making and using artifacts and trinkets of iron and bronze instead of stone or clay, various other developments were taking place. Proto-Malay communities had already started to settle in big groups along the banks or mouths of rivers. They tilled vast rice fields, domesticated animals, fished in rivers and the sea, and also carried out limited exchanges and barter. In these coastal communities there emerged individual groups who were accepted as leaders, as they had greater power and higher status than other communities.

Indian traders began to arrive at some of these coastal communities, bringing along with them not only commodities for trade, but also Hindu priests whose role was to spread their beliefs. Some of these traders married with the local people, while a number of the priests remained behind. In Java, for instance, Hindu influence was dominant in several kingdoms like Majapahit, as manifested by the many spectacular temples in that region. But in the Peninsula, their influence was more limited. Hindu influence left little trace at the theological and intellectual levels, but expressed itself more clearly in the creative arts, government and in several aspects of social ritual and ceremony. In the arts, especially literature, the stories of Sri Rama are inspired by Hindu epics. In architecture there are temple remains and other monuments that were built to symbolise Hindu philosophy and the belief in the achievement of *nirvana*. One such Hindu-influenced monument is the Candi Batu Pahat in Kedah. As for rituals we find that names of Hindu gods are still invoked in prayers and verses related to traditional rites and ceremonies carried out by peasants or fishermen before going to the rice field or the sea, and also when rulers are installed. In government, the close affinity of Hindu priests to the ruling class and the spread of the belief that the rulers possessed supernatural qualities and must be highly revered strengthened the institution of kingship among the Malays. Hindu influence has seeped into Malay culture and further enriched it. At this stage of development the Malays are often referred to as deutero-Malays.

The Malay feudal system, with its traditional leaders or rulers, reached its apex after Melaka was established. The ruler who founded Melaka was a royal refugee from Temasik (ancient Singapore) who was a Hindu, but who later embraced Islam. Melaka grew quickly as a centre for trade and culture in this region. Traders from the East and West stopped here. In the diplomatic field the rulers of Melaka made contacts with their counterparts in Siam, Java and China. The Malay language spread far and wide as the *lingua franca* for trade and government; it became as important for the region as Latin did in Europe. What is more important in terms of modern Malay social and cultural development is that Melaka eventually became the centre for the spread of Islam.

It can be said that, because of the role played by Melaka at the beginning, followed by other centres such as Bantam in Java and Aceh in Sumatra, Islam became very strongly established in the Archipelago. In contrast with Hinduism, which transformed early Malay society only superficially, Islam can be said to have really taken root in the hearts and minds of the Malays. For the first time the Malays became part of a bigger community of Muslims which dominated Asia Minor and North Africa as well as parts of Europe. Islam, a religion that has a strong rational and philosophical basis, infused its influence into the whole life of the Malays and their artistic expression. In their daily life, Islamic teachings, as well as values consistent with Islam, became important sources of guidance. Inspired by Islam, the Malays of this time wrote many outstanding works of literature, especially relating to Sufism, and the Malay language was enriched by a new vocabulary of philosophical and administrative terms. It is true, as has often been expressed, that Islam introduced a significant process of modernisation among the Malays.

At its height Melaka had an integrated feudal system, extending its jurisdiction over various areas of the Peninsula and large parts of the Archipelago. But this feudal political system gradually disintegrated after the Portuguese captured Melaka in 1511. The era of western colonialism over the Malays had begun. Portuguese influence on Malay society and culture, in spite of its domination of more than one hundred years, was minimal. When the Portuguese were replaced by the Dutch in 1641, the former had left only a few new words in the Malay vocabulary and a small Portuguese community in Melaka. The Dutch likewise did not leave behind many traces. Historically, the main area of Dutch influence was in Indonesia; in the Malay Peninsula the strongest influence came from the British.

In 1786, the British established a foothold in Penang. This island together with what became known as Province Wellesley was sold by the Sultan of Kedah to the East India Company for only $10,000! The British occupied Singapore in 1819 and took over Melaka from the Dutch in 1824. Penang and Melaka together with Singapore formed what was known as the Straits Settlements. For a time the main objective of the British was to trade; they tried not to involve themselves with Malay politics in the Malay Peninsula. The first active involvement began in Perak in 1873. By taking sides in conflicts among the rulers and chieftains, the British were able to spread their political influence. They propped up the chief whom they favoured to become ruler and banished or exiled those whom they disliked. In 1874 the Pangkor Agreement was signed by British officials from the Straits Settlements and the Sultan and chiefs of Perak. Following this agreement the Perak ruler agreed to accept a British official to advise him on political and administrative matters. But the British were not allowed to interfere with matters of Muslim religion and Malay custom. After Perak, the rulers of Selangor, Negeri Sembilan and Pahang signed similar agreements with the British. All these four states were brought together to form the Federated Malay States in 1895.

The four northern states of Perlis, Kedah, Kelantan and Terengganu were under Siamese suzerainty at that time, and every year they had to send tribute to Bangkok in the form of gold leaves. In 1909 an agreement was made between the British and Siamese governments, as a result of which all the four states came under the protection of the British Crown. Not long after, in 1914, Johor concluded a similar agreement with the British. All these five states later came to be known collectively as the Unfederated Malay States. While the Federated States accepted British officials assigned as Residents and Assistant Residents, the Unfederated States had Advisers and Assistant Advisers. Although the designations differed, their function, influence and power were almost the same.

The British entry into the Malay states took effect not without resistance. In Perak, Selangor, Negeri Sembilan and Pahang the main thrust of the resistance came from the Malay feudal chiefs and their followers. In Perak a rebellion broke out, led by Maharaja Lela, who, with his followers, killed a British Resident by the name of W.W. Birch in 1875. In Selangor, Syed Mashur and Raja Mahadi, together with some other chiefs took up arms against the British. In Negeri Sembilan, Datuk Naning led his people to battle against the Indian sepoys sent by the British. The history of Pahang is redolent with the epics of Datuk Bahaman, Tok Gajah and Mat Kilau, who bravely led an armed uprising against the British, and finally found refuge in Thailand.

Almost all the leaders of the resistance movement came from the nobility. They did not want to see the sovereignty of their own states and their own privileged positions being undermined by foreigners of different race and religion. Undoubtedly they were also motivated by personal interests, for, with the coming of the British and the introduction of colonial administration, the noblemen could no longer collect revenues, do much trade and retain their own soldiers in their respective territories. Unfortunately, it is this aspect of personal interest that has been highlighted by many a writer as the main cause for their armed resistance, rather than their determination to defend their power and sovereignty.

Many chiefs who collaborated with the British were rewarded with positions and pensions. But those who resisted were suppressed and severely punished. Maharaja Lela and a few of his followers were hanged. Sultan Abdullah of Perak and his family were banished to the Seychelles. Datuk Bahaman, Tok Gajah and Mat Kilau became hunted refugees; in fact, Mat Kilau was sentenced to death and would have been hanged had he been captured. From these events we can clearly perceive that there was a parallel development of two traditions among the Malay nobility. One was the tradition of collaboration or cooperation with the British colonialists. The other was the tradition of resistance or opposition to them. In the historical circumstances then prevailing the first tradition emerged as victor.

It is an accepted fact that with the coming of the British, many changes took place. The pattern of British rule in the Malay states is often described as indirect, being carried out through the rulers and chiefs. But whether the rule was indirect or otherwise, the fact remains that the British were able to plan and execute their designs as they pleased. Initially, the British stabilised the position of the Malay rulers. Then they set up various departments and appointed British officials for the purpose of collecting revenue, administering land and maintaining law and order. The departmental heads were British; only much later were some Malays taken or recruited from the nobility and given the opportunity for education and for subordinate posts. British officers carried out geological surveys and studied the soil for agricultural purposes. Favourable discoveries led to large scale tin mining and rubber planting later.

British-owned companies were formed to work the world's richest tin field in Kinta. These huge companies existed side by side with much smaller ones owned mostly by Chinese capitalists and some Malay noblemen, who had carried out mining activities long before the British. British companies were established to undertake the opening of rubber estates, some of which are the largest in the world up to this day. Tin and rubber were produced for export and at the same time the import of manufactured goods from Britain was encouraged. To facilitate the growing import-export trade many agency houses were formed.

Concurrent with the development and progress in administration, new towns emerged as a result of these activities. Roads and railways were built to connect mines and estates with towns and ports. As business and administrative centres, these new towns had hospitals, schools and offices. The country appeared to prosper.

But what about the position of the Malays in the midst all these changes? As will be seen in Chapter 6, the big tin mines, rubber estates and commercial enterprises were controlled by British monopoly-capitalists. The medium and small ones were mostly owned and operated by the Chinese. The Malays did not own anything significant. Most of their participation in trade was confined to small sundry-goods shops in the villages. Most of the British-owned mines and estates employed Chinese and Indian workers who were brought in large numbers from their homelands as contract labourers. Some Malays were employed, but not in significant numbers. The Malays continued to live mainly in the villages, pursuing their traditional agricultural and fishing activities. But there was a growing number who did go in for small scale rubber planting. The rapid development of the towns had the effect of widening the economic gap between the urban and rural areas, and within the urban community, between the rich and the poor. The penetration of a money economy to the rural areas resulted in the peasants being more exposed to exploitation both in production and marketing. From the point of view of development, the villages remained largely neglected. In absolute and comparative terms, life among the rural Malays became more depressed.

The myth prevailed that the Malays were protected by the British. But the condition of the Malays became more compromised; their villages and, in fact, the whole country were mortgaged to the colonial power. The rural Malays saw the Chinese shopkeepers and Indian moneylenders growing more affluent, and so looked upon them as a threat to their own future survival. The urban Malays who were mostly middle or lower rung government employees saw how the Chinese, Indians and even Arabs controlled much of the country's economy. This increased their feeling of insecurity which they often expressed in newspapers and magazines and through those organisations which were set up to look after the welfare of the Malays. Malay feelings of discontent were directed not towards the dominant colonial power but towards the Chinese, Indians and Arabs, whom they regarded as exploiters and 'foreigners' (*orang asing*). This is understandable because the simple-minded Malays would see them leading an affluent life, owning big mansions with posh motorcars, and running big businesses. The wealth and power of the British was too remote for them to perceive clearly. Furthermore, the rulers and chiefs, whose positions were propped up by the British, as well as the Malay officials who were given a chance to serve the colonial government, regarded the British as protectors whose position should not be questioned.

But conditions soon changed. In several Muslim countries radical political movements arose which, among other things, regarded colonialism as a great threat to Islam. In the Peninsula there were religious teachers like Sheikh Tahir Jalaluddin and Syed Sheikh Alhady who studied under the Muslim reformists, Jamaluddin al-Afghani and Muhammad Abduh, in the Middle East. Through lectures, writings in newspapers, magazines and books, and teaching in schools, they were able to convey the message of change and nationalism to the Malays. Prior to World War II the waves of national struggle had reached their height in several Asian countries, including this region. The call for independence became louder. The effects were felt in this country.

From among the ranks of the Malay teachers and journalists emerged the *Kesatuan Melayu Muda* (KMM or Young Malays Association) whose aim was to achieve independence within the framework of a bigger entity including Indonesia, known as Melayu Raya. The outbreak of the Pacific War and the short occupation by the Japanese changed the situation. Just as in several other countries, in the Peninsula the Japanese victory shattered the myth of the impregnable West. However, the cruelties perpetrated by the Japanese rulers made people realise how inhuman a colonial power can be, and how important it was for a nation to achieve independence quickly so that it could determine its own destiny.

After the War, national consciousness heightened and the movement for independence gained further momentum. Leaders like Sutan Djenain, who was believed to be an Indonesian Marxist, inspired a number of young people here to fight against colonialism. In the beginning nationalist activities were carried out under the wings of the Malayan Nationalist Party (MNP) led by Dr. Burhanuddin Helmi and Ishak Haji Muhammad. The Women's Section known as AWAS was led by Shamsiah Fakeh, while Ahmad Boestamam led the Youth Section known as API. Many of the leaders of these three organisations were onetime members of KMM. So it is not surprising that most of them leaned politically towards Indonesia, and aspired for the country's independence within Melayu Raya. Their movement was well-received, not only by ordinary villagers, teachers and leading officials, but also by one or two sultans (namely from Perak and Pahang). It is obvious that this movement and its radical demands were not received favourably by the British.

In fact, the struggle for independence within Melayu Raya as initiated by KMM became blurred as a result of a new development when the British tried to introduce some constitutional changes immediately after the end of the second world war. This was the Malayan Union proposal. A colonial official by the name of Sir William McMichael was sent from London to secure the consent and signatures of the nine Malay Rulers of the Peninsular states. Among the provisions of the Malayan Union scheme were: the Malay states and Straits Settlements, except Singapore, were to be placed under the same administration and have a common citizenship; automatic citizenship status was to be granted to Chinese and Indians born in the country; all powers and privileges of the Rulers of the Malay states were to be transferred to the British; and each Ruler was to serve only as chairman of an Advisory Council in his own state, which was to have no power over any matter other than Islam and Malay custom.

The first Ruler to give his signature was the Sultan of Johor. A group of senior officers in the state (including Dr Hamzah Haji Taib, lawyer Sulaiman Abdul Rahman and Dr Ismail Abdul Rahman) rose up in protest and contended strongly that the Sultan had no power to transfer the state to the British or to any other foreign power. They regarded the document signed by the Sultan as invalid. This group formed the Johor Malay Union (*Kesatuan Melayu Johor*), issued a declaration in February 1946 criticising the Sultan for his action, and called upon the people of Johor not to recognise the Sultan anymore. The action of the Sultan of Johor was followed by the Rulers of the other states. The anger of the people grew all over the country and finally the Rulers themselves had to retract and give their support to the movement against the Malayan Union, claiming that they were forced to sign the McMichael documents.

In March 1946, the United Malays National Organisation (UMNO) was formed, following a gathering of 48 state organisations including the MNP. They elected Onn Jaafar as president. Two months later the MNP left UMNO when no consensus was reached regarding the flag and slogan to be used by the organisation; UMNO wanted the slogan *Hidup Melayu* (Long Live the Malays) while the MNP wanted *Merdeka*

(Independence). MNP also wanted the red and white flag similar to that of Indonesia.

From the start the leaders of UMNO were mainly government servants. In August, five months after MNP walked out of UMNO, the Chief Secretary A. Newbolt, on behalf of the British government, gave his assurance to UMNO that government officers would not be disciplined if they participated in politics. Before that the Deputy Chief Secretary had sent a confidential circular to all heads of departments which stated that: "no restrictions should be placed on civil servants and that GO III banning civil servants from calling public meetings to consider any action of government should not be enforced for the time being."[5] So, government officers were free to be active in UMNO. In England a number of senior ex-colonial officers gathered support for UMNO against the Malayan Union.

The cooperation received by UMNO from the various sultans and the support of the people, together with the helping hand of the British government and ex-colonial officers, given either directly or indirectly, all contributed towards the success of UMNO. In February 1948 the Federation Agreement was signed to replace the Malayan Union Agreement. With this new agreement the position of the Rulers was restored, the Federation administration was established to include all the Malay states and former Straits Settlements, except Singapore, with a Legislative Council consisting of 74 members nominated from among British officials, representatives of the Rulers and various groups in the country. The success of UMNO further increased its influence among the Malays.

In June 1948 the British government proclaimed the Emergency Laws, following an armed uprising against the British led by the Malayan Communist Party (MCP). Several mass organisations, trade unions and political parties including MNP, API and AWAS were banned. Many leaders and members of these organisations were arrested and detained for many years. Among those who evaded arrest, a number went into the jungles and many others joined UMNO. It can be seen that the struggles of the MNP and UMNO represented the continuation of the two traditions among the Malays under the leadership of their traditional chiefs generations before. Whereas MNP continued the tradition

---

5. Malayan union/confidential 74/1946, in National Archives, Kuala Lumpur.

of resistance, UMNO can be said to have continued the tradition of cooperation, if not collaboration vis-a-vis the British colonialists.

By their action in suppressing the genuine nationalist movement and leaders at that time, the British opened the door wide to UMNO to monopolise the role of Malay leadership. About three years after the Emergency was declared, UMNO changed its slogan from *Hidup Melayu* to *Merdeka*. UMNO increased in strength. But in the same year there was a split in the party. Onn wanted to open UMNO to non-Malays because he was convinced, perhaps, with the advice of top level colonial officers like Malcolm McDonald, then British Commissioner General in Southeast Asia, that the British government would not agree to give Malaya self-government unless there was cooperation between the Malays and the non-Malays.

When this move was opposed by members of the party, Onn left and formed the Independence for Malaya Party (IMP). The launching pad for the IMP was the Communities Liaison Committee, which was initiated by McDonald with Onn, Tan Cheng Lock and S. Thuraisingam as leaders. This split seriously affected the UMNO leadership, with the majority of the Chief Ministers (*Menteri Besar*) from the different states and senior government servants who formerly supported UMNO leaving together with Onn. A number of non-Malay businessmen and community leaders, including Cheng Lock and Thuraisingam, also supported IMP. But the majority of the middle rung leadership of UMNO and the rank and file members remained with the party. They wanted early independence, whereas Onn believed in the gradual process — *festina lente*. After the split new leaders were elected, headed by Tunku Abdul Rahman and Abdul Razak Hussein.

The rejection of the Malayan Union and also of Onn showed that the Malay leadership in UMNO at that time did not want to share their position with the non-Malays. When IMP failed, Onn formed Parti Negara (PN), membership of which was limited only to Malays with its sole objective to fight for Malay rights and interests. But Onn's tactic was a bit too late and he did not gain much support. On the other hand UMNO eventually came to realise that independence could not be obtained without cooperation between the Malays and the non-Malays. The method they adopted to achieve inter-ethnic unity was not by opening the door of UMNO to non-Malays but by forming an alliance with the Malayan Chinese Association (MCA) and the Malayan Indian Congress (MIC). The first test for the Alliance was the Municipal Elections in Kuala Lumpur in 1952. The Alliance won handsomely and so the cooperation was extended throughout the country. When the first partial general election was held in 1955 to elect 52 of the 74 members of the new Legislature, the Alliance, with UMNO as its backbone, won 51 of the 52 seats.

Following the election Tunku Abdul Rahman was made Chief Minister of the Federation. In December 1955, on British advice, he attempted to end the Emergency by inviting the MCP leader Chin Peng to surrender and end the fighting. He met Chin Peng in Baling but his proposals were flatly rejected by Chin Peng. Later the Tunku led a delegation to London consisting of representatives of the nine Rulers and the Alliance to negotiate Malaya's independence. The British fixed 31 August 1957 as Independence Day. A commission was set up comprising eminent jurists from some Commonwealth countries, headed by Lord Reid, to draft the constitution for Malaya.

Among other things, the Commission proposed the election of a Paramount Ruler every five years from among the Rulers to serve as a symbol of sovereignty; a fully elected Parliament; protection of Malay rights and privileges; a more liberal procedure for enabling non-Malays to become citizens; and determination of the role of the civil service as executors only of the decisions made by politicians in government. Action was then taken to phase out colonial officers and to replace them with local officers through the process of Malayanisation. A large amount of money was paid out in compensation during the process, but it gave local officers wide opportunities for promotion or recruitment into senior positions. In other words, the first group of people who immediately benefited from independence were the Alliance leaders and senior government servants.

Elections were held in 1959 under the new Constitution for the Federal Parliament and the respective State Legislatures. The Alliance again proved that it was still influential, although its popularity had declined notably. In 1955 the Alliance collected 79.6 per cent of the votes cast, while in 1959 it dropped to 51.5 per cent. Two opposition parties emerged with quite a sizeable share of the votes, namely, Pan-Malayan Islamic Party (PMIP or more popularly known by its Malay acronym PAS) with 21.2 per cent of the votes and thirteen Parliamentary seats, and the Socialist Front (SF) with 13 per cent of the votes and eight seats. PAS obtained a majority in the Legislative Councils for Terengganu and Kelantan, and so formed the governments in those two states. The Socialist Front controlled the Municipal Councils of Penang and Melaka, as well as many local councils in smaller townships.

PAS actually originated partly from the Council of Theologians in the UMNO which left the party in 1951. At the beginning it was led by Haji Ahmad Fuad but later the leadership was taken over by Dr. Burhanuddin in 1956. Many leaders and activists from the MNP joined PAS, which expanded rapidly thereafter. The party's platform was to champion Islam and the establishment of an Islamic form of government. It accused UMNO of selling out the Malays and of being controlled by the MCA through the Alliance. The clarion call of PAS received support from the Malays particularly in areas of traditional economy where the position of Islam was strongly entrenched, in states such as Kelantan, Terengganu, Kedah and Perlis.

The Socialist Front (SF), formed in 1957, was made up of the Malayan People's Party (Partai Rakyat Malaya, or PRM) and the Labour Party of Malaya (LPM), the former led by A. Boestamam and the latter by Ishak Haji Muhammad. The support for LPM came mainly from the urban Chinese, while the PRM received limited support from the Malays. Right from the beginning the Socialist Front based its platform on socialistic principles and on the cooperation between the lower classes of people of all races, championing the interests of the poor and disadvantaged people who formed the majority.

Following the 1959 election victory, the Alliance formed the government with Tunku Abdul Rahman as Prime Minister. During his tenure of office, which lasted until 1970, four major events took place, namely: split with Lim Chong Yew, President of the MCA, and later with Abdul Aziz Ishak, the Agricultural Minister and senior UMNO leader; the Confrontation by Indonesia; merger with Singapore and the May Thirteenth Incident. These episodes had a tremendous effect on the Malays. The first one weakened UMNO for a while. Regarding the second, Tunku first advocated the concept of Malaysia at a luncheon address to the Singapore Journalists Union in May 1961; it was evident that he was inspired by none other than Malcolm McDonald. Confrontation took place soon after the formation of Malaysia in 1963 which incorporated Sabah, Sarawak and Singapore together with Malaya.

The Malaysia concept was opposed internally by PAS and the SF and externally by Indonesia, which considered it a threat to its politics and security. PAS and SF, while recognising the evil intentions of the British imperialists, also thought that this new grouping could cause several problems, namely: (a) it might upset the population balance and give rise to more acute communal politics, (b) it could cause economic difficulty to the Peninsula because much of its revenue would have to be channeled to Sabah and Sarawak for their development, and (c) it could result in grave political and administrative complications since the level of development of the various states was varied and unequal. Demands were made for referendums in Sabah and Sarawak to determine the will of the people.

Opposition from PAS and SF together with Indonesian Confrontation led to the mass arrests of many of the leaders and members of the opposition parties, among them ex-minister Abdul Aziz Ishak, who by then headed his newly-formed National Convention Party (NCP), which joined the SF. A number of them were accused of planning to form a government in exile to undermine the Malayan government. As usual they were detained without trial under the Internal Security Act (ISA). Following these repressions, the SF split; among its component parties, the LPM 'closed its shutters', the NCP decided to wind up, and the PRM decided to continue. In the midst of this crisis and the widespread allegations that the arrested leaders were conspiring with Indonesia to topple the government, an election was held in 1964 resulting in a landslide victory for the Alliance. As predicted by the opposition parties, many problems arose between Malaya and Singapore which exacerbated communal tensions. This eventually led to the ousting of Singapore from Malaysia in 1965. Confrontation came to an end following the failure of the Gestapu coup attempt in Indonesia, the ousting of President Sukarno and the counter-coup led by General Suharto, who eventually succeeded as President; diplomatic relations were renewed, and most of the detainees were released.

The May Thirteenth Incident took place a few days after the 1969 elections. The results showed that the opposition parties managed to gain more than half of the popular votes cast, although in terms of seats they only managed to deny the Alliance two-third majority. In the states of Perak and Selangor, the UMNO hegemony and the positions of the Alliance-backed Menteri Besar were seriously threatened. Largely due to these circumstances, communal clashes erupted in Kuala Lumpur, with many lives lost and much property destroyed. A large body of people believed that the carnage was sparked by certain UMNO leaders who wanted to preserve their own position in the state leadership of Selangor, in particular. In this connection many accusations were leveled against the Selangor Menteri Besar then.

Following the May Thirteenth Incident, some government leaders, among them Dr Ismail Abdul Rahman, declared that democracy was dead. Parliament was dissolved and a National Operations Council (NOC) was formed with Deputy PM Abdul Razak Hussein as Director. The Tunku was sidelined. Many UMNO members and the Malays blamed the Tunku for the incident; they accused him of being too liberal towards the Chinese and as a result the influence of UMNO began to decline, and it lost out to the PAS. Because he strongly opposed Tunku and wrote an open letter criticising him, which was distributed widely to the public, Dr Mahathir Mohamad was expelled from UMNO. Dr Mahathir and many Malays believed that it was due to Tunku's indecisiveness and liberalism that the Chinese became more outspoken in their demands. The Democratic Action Party (DAP), which claimed to be a socialist democratic organisation, was alleged to be strongly pro-Chinese and racialistic owing to some of its actions and policies, and was able to cut the ground out from under the feet of the MCA, especially in urban centres.

The tide against Tunku Abdul Rahman was so strong that he finally resigned as Prime Minister in 1970, but only after it was agreed that a handsome pension would be paid to him – rather ironic for someone regarded as a nationalist fighter. Abdul Razak, who was elected as the new UMNO President, became Prime Minister. Parliament was reconvened in January 1971. Many laws were passed to prohibit open discussion on sensitive issues, such as the position of the Malay Rulers, Malay privileges, the national language and so forth. The new leaders exhorted that politicking should be reduced and full attention to be given to development.

In this connection, the government introduced the New Economic Policy (NEP) aimed at promoting national unity through a two-prong objective, namely eradicating poverty without regard of race and restructuring society by removing racial identification to economic activities. At the same time, Razak together with Dr. Ismail tried successfully to integrate opposition parties like PAS, Gerakan, PPP, SUPP and SNAP into a broader coalition called the National Front (NF) – or Barisan Nasional (BN) – to replace the Alliance. Under its banner and using the scale as a symbol, the BN achieved a tremendous electoral victory in 1974.

Not long after the elections, there was a hunger march in the district of Baling by about 25,000 peasants who were protesting the fall of rubber price, the increase of allowances of the elected parliamentary representatives and the rumoured death of two children who were believed to be driven to eat a poisonous tuber *(ubi gadung)* owing to the poverty of their family. The peasant demonstrations gained the support of students in various universities and colleges, which led to a huge protest in Kuala Lumpur. The government acted with a heavy hand, arresting more than a thousand demonstrators and finally detaining nearly fifty students and lecturers under the ISA, ranging from about a month to nearly six years. The protests were significant in two ways; firstly they were led and participated mainly by Malays, and secondly, they were also supported by non-Malays, mainly because the issues raised were economic ones that appealed to various groups and cut across the ethnic divide. It was the first protest of its kind during the UMNO rule.

Soon other problems were brewing within UMNO. Harun Idris, the Selangor MB was perceived as trying to challenge Razak the Prime Minister. Harun was alleged to be involved with corruption and legal actions began to be instituted against him. It was only after Razak died in 1975 and succeeded by Hussein Onn as Prime Minister that Harun was tried and convicted. Meanwhile Mahathir was reaccepted into UMNO under Razak and moved up quite rapidly to become third Vice President and later chosen, albeit quite reluctantly by Hussein, to become Deputy PM. In 1976, there were arrests of two Deputy Ministers, prominent editors of newspapers and some leaders of the opposition parties. They were accused of being involved in pro-communist activities. There was also an attempt to implicate DPM Mahathir with such activities, coercing and torturing some detainees to admit the same. The man behind the conspiracy was the Home Minister Ghazali Shafie, who felt that he was denied to become Deputy PM, although PM Hussein favoured him to Mahathir.

All this created some crisis within the UMNO leadership which affected its membership as well as the Malays in general. But it was not serious compared to what happened after Mahathir apparently managed to outmaneuver the ailing Hussein behind the scene and succeeded him to become PM in 1981. In the following general assembly of UMNO after he became PM, Mahathir was challenged for the position of President by Tengku Razaleigh, who was then a senior vice president of the party. The latter lost by a mere 43 votes, the validity of which was actually challenged. A split occurred within the party, with Tengku Razaleigh and his supporters leaving the party to form Semangat Melayu '46 ("the Malay Spirit of 1946"). The split went down the line in the Malay community, from the palace to the rural village. UMNO was challenged in court and subsequently declared illegal. Very soon Mahathir was able to revive his party as the New UMNO. He led the party in a number of general elections and remained as Prime Minister for about 22 years.

During his long premiership, Mahathir promoted a number of new policies and programmes. He introduced modernisation plans, but more in the physical sense by undertaking major constructions, building mega projects and carrying out industrialisation, which included the national car industry. He encouraged leaders of his party to be involved in various forms of business and contract work, consistent with the objective of achieving bigger Malay parity in business and industries. Consequently, he paid less emphasis on agriculture, which was the main basis of the Malay traditional economy. He was also critical of the traditional mindset and the feudal political structure that constrained the Malays. Probably owing to this, at one stage he opposed quite strongly some of the Malay beliefs and practices as well as the institution of the sultanate. In terms of foreign policy, he showed strong leaning towards the Third World countries, and critical of new forms of colonialism and capitalism practiced especially by the United States to the disadvantage of especially the third world countries.

The large scale and fast pace of development stimulated under the leadership of Mahathir – which was actually in the form of building capitalism for the country as a whole and the Malays in particular – undoubtedly resulted in impressive economic growth and development. At the same time it also created greater capitalisation and concentration of wealth that caused wider regional, inter- as well as intra-ethnic socio-economic inequity. The effects on the political and social spheres were adverse and caused much concern. Politically, there was a tendency for power to be concentrated on one man, and increasingly Mahathir was seen as being more authoritarian and less democratic. Socially, wasteful spending came together with the practices of corruption, nepotism and cronyism. Other social problems also raised their ugly heads, especially the increase in crime rate and moral decline.

Around 1997, the Southeast Asian region was hit by a serious economic downturn. Among others this led to the downfall of Suharto's regime in Indonesia. Mahathir was fearful that the same fate might fall on him. Incidentally, Anwar Ibrahim, his deputy, was perceived as being in a hurry to succeed him. A number of Anwar's youthful supporters became overly critical sans any clear or well-thought out plan against Mahathir and for Anwar. The former had enough reason to sack the latter after Anwar, who was for a long time regarded as the anointed successor to premiership, refused to admit the allegations of corruption and sodomy on him which he regarded as blatant lies. His sacking from both the government and UMNO leadership caused great public anger; a series of huge public rallies were held all over the country in his support. Later, when Anwar was found guilty and convicted six years for alleged corruption, *Reformasi* demonstrations took place and continued. During that time an NGO, known as ADIL (lit. 'just') was formed which was later transformed into Parti Keadilan Nasional (National Justice Party). It later merged with the Malaysian People's Party (PRM) to become People's Justice Party (Parti Keadilan Rakyat or PKR).

After completing the corruption sentence, Anwar was acquitted of the allegations of sodomy by the highest court of the land. It so happened that the acquittal took place after Abdullah Ahmad Badawi became Prime Minister. Actually, Abdullah who was then Deputy PM, succeeded Mahathir when the latter resigned. Abdullah was touted as 'Mr Clean' and someone who was more democratic and religious than Mahathir. He was a welcome change and there were high expectations from him. In the ensuing general elections that he called in 2004,

Abdullah led the BN coalition to a trouncing victory, winning 65 per cent of the popular votes and disproportionately grabbing about 90 per cent of the parliamentary and state seats.

But soon it became clear that Abdullah was a disappointment. He was not as firm a leader as Mahathir. He promised to fight corruption, but hardly did anything effective about it; on the other hand corruption and cronyism increased and came very close to him and his family. He gave the impression of wanting to battle against the social problems bugging the society, but instead almost allowed these problems to become more serious. More and more he has proven to be no less authoritarian than Mahathir, controlling the media much more, repressing public dissent, condoning police brutality against peaceful public gathering and continuing to use draconian laws like the ISA, the Police Act and the Printing and Publications Act. His true face became exposed, particularly after a spate of street demonstrations that took place towards the end of 2007. These will be discussed in later chapters.

3
POLITICAL HISTORY AND PROCESS

Some of the aspects of Malay political development and problems outlined in the last chapter will be examined in greater detail here. The basic questions relating to the politics of the Malays in particular and the country as a whole will be stressed. Before doing so it may be useful to examine first the Malay traditional political system, for this will provide the background necessary to understand many of the present day problems faced by the Malays and the nature of political changes which have taken place, especially as a result of colonialism and then independence. These changes and problems can be perceived with greater clarity if viewed against the traditional political system and its later transformation.

The political system during the Mesolithic and Neolithic periods was very simple. Local communities then were small and did not require a complex politico-administrative structure with a large number of personnel to keep them going. As mentioned earlier the leaders in each community were the older members; each group chose its own leaders but these leaders were not connected with one another in any form of centralised structure. The elders were respected and influential, for it was taken for granted that wisdom came with age. They had gathered knowledge and experience on various customs and beliefs, and knew how to live and maintain security within a threatening environment. These leaders seldom exercised their function by use of force; in fact in this kind of society, in particular amongst the men, there was a great deal of consultation and discussion. This form of government seems to continue within some of the simple communities that still exist in this region.

With further development these small political units merged into bigger communities under a chief or even a ruler. Each component unit continued to have its own chief known by various names, such as *batin, ketua* or *penghulu*. These local chiefs continued to function as leaders of their own units, but besides that they also began to serve as subordinates to their more powerful superiors, and very often had to carry out the commands of these overlords. The overlords could wield influence because they had gathered into their hands political and economic power and had their own fighting men. With the power they had, these chiefs could easily collect taxes and gifts, which further strengthened their positions economically. Increasing wealth enabled them to expand their fighting forces and their areas of jurisdiction. Some of the chiefs eventually became powerful rulers.

As explained earlier, in the Peninsula, Melaka marked the zenith of the old Malay kingdoms. By then the political system had become quite complex. The Sultan of Melaka was powerful and respected by many smaller kingdoms. He had many minor rulers under him, who were often linked to him by blood or marriage ties. Besides this, there were also several chiefs who could be categorised as: (a) those who had well-defined functions, such as *Bendahara, Laksamana, Shahbandar* and *Temenggung*; and (b) those who were appointed by their ruler to lead the people and represent them in the outlying areas. Through these chiefs the Sultan ruled and maintained contact with the people.

It can be said that, in the hierarchy of that time, the Sultan of Melaka, the various rulers under him, the chiefs and their relatives, constituted the upper class of society. Their respective positions were determined by tradition. They were acknowledged leaders in whose hands all political, economic and military power was concentrated. Obviously at the apex of all power was the Sultan himself. The chiefs were in a slightly different role. Although they exercised authority in their own area as middlemen between the ruler and the people, they also served as a kind of cog in the administrative machinery. If the political system is represented in the form of a pyramid then we get the following picture:

```
            S
          /|\
        SS | SS
        /  P  \
      PP /|\ PP
      / SS|SS \
     R   R R   R
```

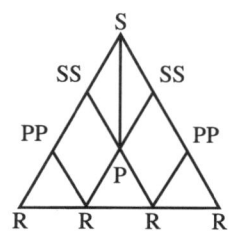

In this figure, *S* is the Sultan and *R* his people. Between them are *SS* who were rulers subjected to the main ruler *S*; *P* and *PP* are chiefs. The Melaka Sultan (*S*) and the subordinate rulers (*SS*) had their own chiefs, namely *P* and *PP*. The relationship between *S* and *P* was direct while the relationship between *S* and *PP* was through *SS*.

The political and administrative system of Melaka can be regarded as an integrated feudal system. This system disintegrated after the fall of Melaka. Subsidiary kingdoms and provinces became fragmented, each with its own ruler and chiefs. There were also communities subordinate only to their own chiefs. Their structure can be represented by a series of smaller pyramids which are independent of each other, as illustrated in the following figure.

The three pyramids represent three political structures that existed. *Figure I* shows a rather big kingdom but not as big as Melaka, for example the Johor-Riau Sultanate, which had its own Sultan (*S*), chiefs (*P* and *PP*) and people (*R*). *Figure II* presents a much smaller kingdom, and *Figure III* shows a small community led only by a chief.

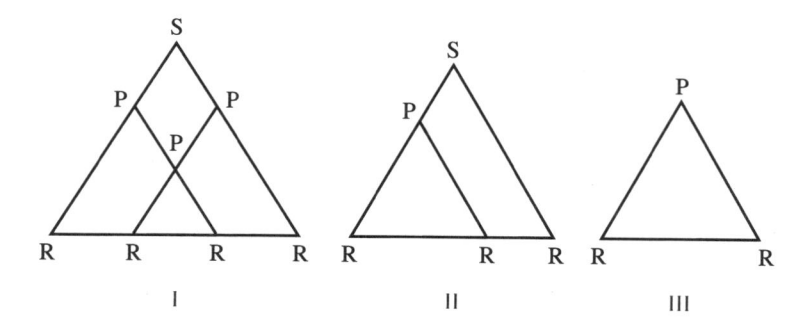

```
        S                    S                   
       /|\                  / \                  P
      P | P                P   \                / \
     /  P  \              /     \              /   \
    / / | \ \            /       \            /     \
   R  R R R  R          R  R  R  R           R       R
        I                   II                 III
```

Between different governments, states or social groups there could be a relationship of harmony or conflict, resulting in integration or disintegration. There could be a situation when a state or group – often the latter – might be completely isolated and so did not have any relations, either of harmony or conflict, with another. Harmonious relations could occur between two kingdoms when there was an agreement or a kinship tie between their rulers. They mutually visited each other, sending delegations and presents, and arranging marriages between members of their families. But a ruler need not be subordinate to another ruler. The superior-subordinate relationship often occurred between rulers and chiefs. A chief who recognised the legitimacy of a sultan might place himself willingly under a sultan. So he became part of an integrated structure, however small.

Relationships of conflict occurred more often between sultans, but could also happen between a ruler and his chief. The conflict between rulers could arise from competition over political and economic power and resources. The conflict between a ruler and his chiefs often took place when the latter did not recognise the legitimacy of the former; or, there might also be a chief who felt strong enough to challenge a weak ruler. Although in the disintegrated feudal system the scope and area of jurisdiction was small and limited, nevertheless each ruler or chief played an important role and had great influence over political, economic and military matters.

What happened after the coming of the British? As indicated earlier, the British destroyed all opposition and removed all sultans or chiefs who rose against them. The sultans recognised by the British were given some power over their own states, whose boundaries were then clearly demarcated. Because the chiefs and kinsmen of the deposed sultans had been stripped of their powers, the position of the rulers who were propped up by the British became more stable. Some degree of peace and order was also maintained through colonial administration. But the real power of the sultans had been removed. Politically they began to serve only as symbols of Malay political sovereignty, but without any authority to make their own decisions or have them carried out, because they always had to refer matters to the British Residents or Advisers.

Economically, they could no longer collect revenues from their own people, for such collections were already made by specific departments in the administration. They only received salaries and allowances paid from part of the revenues collected. Furthermore, they did not have their own fighting men because police and military forces were formed to maintain security and defence, which were no longer the responsibility of the sultan to provide. Finally, most of the rulers did not have many other economic resources, as these were beginning to be controlled by foreign traders or capitalists.

Real power, such as that which was in the hands of the sultans in the past, is no longer theirs. They function as symbols only during state ceremonies. The fate of the chiefs was worse. Only their titles remained with them; the rest had been removed. Nevertheless, some of them were given pensions in place of the revenues that their ancestors used to collect for themselves. For instance, in 1903 it was reported that 2,876 chiefs and members of royal families were paid a total of $939,722 annually.[6] Their role was limited to attending state functions, unless of course they were absorbed into the new administrative structure set up by the British.

In the new administration the most important officials of the Federated States were Residents and Assistant Residents, while their equivalents in the Unfederated States were Advisers and Assistant Advisers. At first colonial officers were assigned to one particular state, but after 1895 they were transferable from one state to another. The highest officer for all the Malay states was the High Commissioner, while his equivalent for the Straits Settlements was the Governor, but in fact he was one and the same person until 1942.

In 1909 a Federal Council was formed under the chairmanship of the High Commissioner, whose members consisted of the Resident-General, the four Sultans and the four Residents of the Federated States, and four persons appointed as unofficial members representing plantation and business interests. In the first Council there were nine Europeans (British), six as official and three as unofficial members, four Malays and one Chinese. The arrival of the Rulers was usually accompanied by pomp and ceremony, after which they returned home and the Council proceeded to meet. In 1927 the places of the Rulers

---

6. Puthucheary, M.C., 1973:20.

were taken over by unofficial Malay members. The function of the Federal Council was mainly to advise the High Commissioner on the introduction of new policies and regulations. Clearly, in matters of legislation the British were the most influential; at the level of administration or implementation of policies and laws the senior officers were also British. Obviously British rule was carried out not indirectly, as often claimed, but directly.

As administration increased in volume and became more complex, there was a shortage of British officers. The Malayan Civil Service (MCS), from the beginning, was confined only to British citizens or their offspring. The positions that were open to the Malays were in the Malay Administrative Service (MAS), which was lower in status and salary than the MCS. MAS officers could be admitted into the MCS, but this could be done only after crossing several barriers and serving more than ten years in MAS. Thus the possible time served by Malay officers in MCS was always ten years shorter than that served by their British counterparts; there was only a remote possibility for them to reach the top-most positions. A Malay could never be a Resident. Most of the Malay officers in MAS and MCS were recruited from royal and aristocratic families. The Malay College of Kuala Kangsar (MCKK), opened in 1905, was established to train and educate Malays to be recruited to these services. But later the door to MAS was opened to commoners.

British officials combined political (making policies) and administrative (implementing policies) functions. This was especially true of the senior officers such as the Residents or Advisers. Within the administrative hierarchy they came under the Secretary of State for the colonies and carried out his orders; however, they had quite a free hand in making political decisions in the places where they served. Furthermore, the Residents were also members of the Federal Council and so participated in the formulation of policies.

On the other hand, Malay officers functioned only to implement policies and directions from the top. Their role in determining policy was practically nil but this was to be expected because they were always subordinate to the British. Only in 1927 did some change occur when the four Sultans were replaced by non-official Malays members in the Federal Council. Since the Malay administrative officers were the most able and educated group among the Malays, it was from this group that the four members were nominated. One of the most outstanding members of the Legislative Council was Raja Sir Chulan. Unlike British officials, these four Malays were not official members of the Council.

Between 1937 and 1939 several Malay associations were formed in the Malay states, led mostly by government officers. The main objectives of these associations were not political but welfare; they aimed to advance the interests of the Malays in various social fields, especially education. It is believed that most of these associations received encouragement from the British. After the Second World War these associations were galvanised into political organisations such as MNP and UMNO. As already explained in Chapter 2, there were many MCS and MAS officers who participated in UMNO as leaders at the state and national level to fight against the Malayan Union scheme. They were given unrecorded leave to attend UMNO meetings. These government officers played a major role in Malay politics at that time.

When the new Legislative Council was established following the Federation Agreement of 1948, many officers who had been active in UMNO became influential members of the Council. Out of 75 members of the Legislative Council, 25 were official and 50 non-official members. There were 33 Malays in all: nine official members who were Chief Ministers representing the Sultans and 24 unofficial members; out of the 33 members, 25 were from the civil service. Then in 1951, when steps were taken by the British to introduce the Member System, three leading Malays were appointed to hold portfolios, all from the civil service.

The Malay officer corps participated not only in political organisations and legislative bodies but also in competitive inter-party politics. This started after Onn left UMNO, an event which precipitated a split among these officers. Then in 1954-55, when the local and national elections were held, competition among them became more intense. The most acute competition was between the supporters of UMNO and Parti Negara. Many resigned from the civil service to stand as candidates in the 1955 election, and out of 103 Malays who stood, 53 were ex-civil servants. More than 80 per cent of UMNO candidates were from this category. UMNO won 51 of the 52 contested seats, capturing about 80 per cent of the voters.

Direct involvement of civil servants in politics ended after independence. The civil service had increased in size and number. With Malayanisation, many Malay officers were promoted to take over the places vacated by expatriate officers. At the beginning many of the Malay officers had connections with upper class families, but after independence there was a greater intake of graduates with middle and lower class backgrounds. The constitution adopted after independence stressed the importance of restricting the function of civil servants to administration only; they should execute the decisions made by the politicians in the government; however, civil servants could remain as ordinary members of political parties.

The politicians now took over the former role of the British; some of them became ministers, members of Executive Councils and parliamentarians. At first quite a few of them were members of the royalty or ex-civil servants, but slowly the participation of professionals and others from the middle class increased. The most important function of these politicians was to determine the policies which had to be implemented by civil servants. At the same time the armed forces were also expanded to ensure peace and security. Although the army and police were under the control of the government, under normal circumstances their professional competence and specialisation caused them to be regarded as immune from interference by administrators and politicians.

The thing to be stressed here is that politics, administration and the military (including police) have now become separate, having their own functions and officers. Before the coming of the British, all three spheres and their functions were under the control of the sultans and chiefs; but after independence the groups controlling each of these spheres have become quite distinct from one another. Nevertheless, at the very top level there is very close cooperation between these groups. This happens not only because they are all Malays; they also have a common background and school ties, and among some of the senior officers and politicians there is also a common royal or civil service background. The bonds among some of them are further strengthened by blood and marriage relationships as well as membership in certain exclusive clubs.

It must be noted too that as UMNO became more established and almost hegemonic in its control of the country's politics, its senior leaders became very powerful politically. When they began and succeeded in acquiring wealth for themselves, their close family members and cronies, they also became powerful economically too. Through their position in government, especially as Prime Minister or Deputy PM, they also had strong influence, if not control, over the military. So, the tendency grew when political, economic and military power began to be converged in one person or a very small and closed group of persons. Being so powerful, they could also control the second rung of political leaders at the state level and the third rung at the district level.

Political subservience and economic dependence of the lower to the higher rungs are now strong. Most of those at the third and second rungs are beholden to the most powerful at the top, and they easily become middlemen or brokers who can easily be controlled, sometimes almost absolutely, by the powerful top leader or leaders. The structure of political control that develops within UMNO becomes almost similar to that of the traditional feudal structure described above. It is not surprising that the feudal system, process and psychology seem to prevail in Malay politics until now.

But at the lower levels, especially between the administrators and the politicians, misunderstandings and conflicts are quite common. At this level there are fewer of the ties and relationships which are found at the higher levels. Furthermore, political pressures are more strongly felt. Party leaders or 'people's representatives' (*wakil rakyat*) who have promised land or licences to their supporters, for example, are sometimes disappointed because they find administrators tend to be slow and bogged down by rules and procedures. On the other hand, the administrators often feel that the politicians always interfere with their work and show little respect for these rules and procedures.

Some conclusions can be drawn from the development of political leadership after independence. As already indicated, at the beginning many of the senior politicians were ex-civil servants who had links with the royal households. The nobility and civil service groups have a history of cooperation or collaboration with the British colonial rulers. Furthermore, the leaders who received independence from the British were mainly educated in the West, and so tended to be westernised in their lifestyle and outlook. They knew more about the glories of the British Empire than about the rise and fall of the Malay kingdoms, and they enjoyed horse-racing or a round of golf more than kite flying or top spinning. Many among them had confidence in their ex-colonial masters as friends, nay, even as protectors of the Malays.

It is this category of leaders who followed the tradition of cooperation with the British. Their backgrounds and attitudes were reflected in the political philosophy and policies that they chose for the country and the people. They were extended versions of the tradition of cooperation or collaboration which became manifest when the British arrived towards the end of the last century. The group which continued the tradition of resistance, or at least non-cooperation with the British, was drawn mainly from the MNP, API and AWAS – organisations which later were weakened through the mass arrests of their leaders or by being banned following the start of the Emergency in 1948.

In politics, the leaders who held the reins of power at the beginning of independence were pro-Western. This was the result not only of their confidence in Western political systems, but also because they felt pressured by the Communist insurrection, which gave them a *raison d'etre* for taking a pro-Western stance, at least for the purpose of getting economic support and military aid. In the economic field the *laissez-faire* or free enterprise system was continued. This system acknowledges the importance of the private sector and foreign investment. This explains why British economic interests in the country were left untouched, leaving British control in three quarters of the big estates, two-thirds of the mines and more than one-half of the commercial houses of the country. The development of the private sector was further encouraged and wide opportunities were given not only to foreign concerns but also to local capitalists, especially the Chinese.

The political line taken by UMNO leaders on certain major issues caused discontent among a large section of the Malays. From the beginning some Malay teachers were unhappy with the government's policy on language and education. They wanted a higher status and an economic value for Malay language and education, consistent with the nation's independence. Not long after independence much noise was made about the importance of the national language and local education, but the position and economic value remained inferior to the English language and education. There was a strong divergence of views between the government and the Persatuan Guru-Guru Melayu Semenanjung (PGMS), a major teachers' union at that time. When the Minister of Education then, Mohd Khir Johari, who was regarded as not being too sympathetic to the Malay cause, announced a policy that was unacceptable to them, the union finally decided to advise all its members to leave UMNO, or at least to resign from their positions in the party.

The 'revolt' of the Malay teachers indirectly strengthened the position of PAS, which was unhappy not only over the question of the Malay language and education, but more so over the Muslim religion. They held that UMNO, through the Alliance, had sold out to the Chinese; time and again they raised the complaint that UMNO had been too liberal in granting citizenship to non-Malays. They argued that the plight of the Malays compared to other communities had deteriorated; a saying often quoted was "They were like ducks dying of thirst in the pond." Actually the sentiments voiced by PAS were widely shared among a large section of the Malay population which was disenchanted with *Merdeka*, for it did not bring substantial changes as promised.

The disenchanted shifted their support to PAS and to a lesser extent to some other opposition parties. This could be seen from the results of the 1959 election. The Alliance collected only 51.5 per cent of the vote and 74 out of 104 seats (71.2 per cent), while PAS collected 36.2 per cent in the areas they contested, or 21.2 per cent of the total vote, and won 13 seats (12.5 per cent). There were also expressions of dissatisfaction from other quarters. The Socialist Front emphasised economic issues and criticised the Alliance policies which favoured foreign and local capitalists while neglecting the lot of the local poor. At the same time, the Malay voice in the SF grew stronger through the Partai Rakyat, although the Front received more urban Chinese support through the Labour Party. Nevertheless, it cannot be denied that there was latent discontent among the Malays, centred on the economic and political issues affecting the poor as a group rather than appealing to narrow communal sentiments. The SF managed to get substantial Malay support. In the 1959 elections it collected 34.8 per cent of the vote in the areas they contested, or 13 per cent of all the votes cast in the whole country, winning eight seats in Parliament.

Two interesting points emerged from the results of this election. First, the influence of the ruling elite in UMNO (or the Alliance) was beginning to be challenged, though only slightly, and UMNO had lost much support to PAS in particular. Second, there were two trends in the opposition against UMNO policies: the first trend with an Islamic basis was led by PAS, and the second, with a socialist basis, was led by the SF. Both these trends could be offset and contained by UMNO and the government, particularly during the Indonesian Confrontation that began in the early 1960s. During the Confrontation both PAS and the SF were accused of conspiring with Indonesia and this was followed by mass arrests of opposition leaders. At the time, a split occurred between the Partai Rakyat and the Labour Party owing to differences of views on language and education as well as dissatisfaction over the allocation of seats and resources during the 1964 election. The problems became more serious because the leaders who could have solved them had been detained.

After Confrontation communal politics became more rampant. PAS became more outspoken in expressing Malay disappointment with UMNO and the government. At the same time the DAP voiced Chinese disgruntlement with greater audacity. Obviously, the MCA also took strong pro-Chinese communal posture, to ensure survival. Thus, one community was always blamed for the backwardness or difficulties faced by the other. By that time the Labour Party had become ineffective as an open party because many of its branches and divisions had closed down, following demonstrations and the *hartal* launched in connection with the currency devaluation in 1967. The Malays were talking about the need for Malay unity, while at the same time the Chinese expressed the need for unity within their community. Communal feelings reached their zenith just before and during the 1969 election. After the election, as described earlier, UMNO became strongly aggressive because the Alliance that it led nearly lost power in Selangor and Perak. With so much heat generated by public utterances about emotional issues it was not surprising that the May Thirteenth Incident erupted.

As we already know, following the disturbances, Parliament and political activities were suspended for about 18 months and the National Operations Council (NOC) became the highest and most powerful body governing the country. It is interesting to note how the NOC brought the political, administrative and military elite into close cooperation, although the leading roles in it were played by politicians. In the traditional political system, administrative and military powers were concentrated in the hands of the traditional ruling elite with the sultan as its apex. Now, when the government was faced with a crisis the three groups were united under the NOC, which comprised the new ruling elites with the Director as its apex. There seems to be some continuation of the traditional structure in the new format when facing a crisis situation. This becomes more significant when we examine the roles played by members of the bureaucracy.

As could be seen in another crisis situation, namely the opposition to the Malayan Union, the British who were then in political control allowed Malay administrators to be involved in politics. At that time a large number of Malays thought that their political power and future were threatened by the changes brought by the Malayan Union, which could open the door wide for non-Malays to participate freely in the political life of the country. After the May Thirteenth Incident the ruling elite also felt that their position was being threatened; this was interpreted as being a life and death matter for the Malays themselves. The ruling political groups took steps to strengthen themselves by incorporating the administrative and military groups into the NOC. This interesting development is a good indicator of how the ruling political elite might react in facing any future crisis, namely by suspending the parliamentary process and seizing power with the help of the administrative and military (including police) elite.

After the NOC was dissolved and Parliament reinstated, some of the administrative officers in the NOC began their careers as UMNO politicians and were given high positions in government or important posts in statutory bodies which were established with the objective of improving the Malay economy. This was a cause of great concern to UMNO rank and file and Malays in the opposition parties. The leadership of UMNO itself changed hands. Tunku Abdul Rahman and some of his stalwarts who were accused of being too lenient to the non-Malays and not firm enough in carrying out pro-Malay policies were 'removed'. The Tunku's critics emerged as the new power group in the UMNO leadership led by Abdul Razak Hussein, who was feared at the beginning by a large section of the Chinese as being too pro-Malay.

Actually the changes that were taking place in the UMNO leadership were not entirely due to the challenge from PAS or the May Thirteenth Incident. In fact, they were signals of transformations that were taking place within the society itself. After independence political changes gave greater opportunities to the Chinese to participate in national politics and the government. In terms of statistics the change might be perceived from the increasing number of new citizens among the non-Malays who were given the franchise. For instance, during the 1955 election, out of 1,280,000 voters, 84.2 per cent were Malays and only 11.2 per cent were Chinese. But by the 1959 election the number of voters increased to about 2,144,000, with the Malay proportion shrinking to 56.8 per cent and the Chinese expanding to 35.6 per cent. Non-Malay political parties like the PPP and the DAP were set up to fight for the interests of the Chinese. Inside and outside UMNO this development was seen as a threat to the Malays.

Economically, independence had also opened more opportunities for some people to become rich quickly. Development projects carried out in greater numbers and on a bigger scale incurred large expenditures. For a long time timber was and is an important source of revenue in many states. Opportunities to get contracts and tenders were almost unlimited. But many at that time felt that these opportunities were monopolised by a few people, mainly non-Malays. There were some Malay entrepreneurs who obtained contracts and concessions, but in a great number of cases they farmed these out to non-Malays, following what was termed as the 'Ali Baba' arrangement. Through political influence, and the use of money and women in corrupt ways, several Chinese businessmen quickly seized the chance to make wealth quickly. The expanding Malay middle class managed to get some of these opportunities, but in most cases they felt that they were outbidded or outplayed by the more powerful Chinese capitalists. Malay failures in the face of Chinese competition led to widespread dissatisfaction and they blamed the government for not implementing effectively the constitutional provisions regarding Malay special privileges.

From the social point of view, in addition to the new middle class groups involved in trade and industry, there also emerged a professional group including lawyers, doctors, accountants, executives and administrators. Most of them had graduated from local universities, and a large number originated from the villages and were well aware of the Malay rural situation. They had a strong desire to improve the lot of their own people. Some of them, correctly or not, regarded the non-Malays as a threat, or at least an obstacle to the progress of the Malays in the economic and business fields.

Many of them became or were already members of UMNO. There were some who really wanted to bring about changes in UMNO, but there were others who had more opportunistic motives and saw UMNO as the quickest means to reach the top. The pressure from members of this new middle class who wanted power, or at least a share in the political and economic leadership, was one of the main factors which caused the change in UMNO. They strengthened their position by mouthing pro-Malay slogans, for they knew this could attract wider support and would cause them to attain more influence among the lower strata of people and society as a whole.

It was stated earlier that, through the NOC various members of the Malay elite were brought together. It was hoped that this new basis of organisation and politics could give a greater boost to UMNO's becoming a much stronger and bigger Malay political party. No doubt cooperation and integration already existed among the elites themselves, but there were several differences and even conflicts of interest among leaders inside and outside the government, particularly as regards UMNO and PAS. These political differences and conflicts of interest were regarded by government leaders as the main cause for disunity among the Malays. Hence immediate steps were taken to find a basis for cooperation and integration between the two big Malay political parties.

As mentioned already, after the NOC was dissolved and Parliament revived, several new laws were passed to restrict public discussion of issues that were regarded as sensitive – such as the position of the Malay rulers, Malay special privileges, Islam and the national language – because these issues could arouse strong communal sentiments. These were also some of the main issues raised by PAS in their election campaign in 1969. The new laws restricted the movements of PAS and threatened to weaken its position. Further, PAS, which controlled Kelantan, was faced with serious financial difficulties. Allocations from the central government were greatly needed not only for carrying out development projects, but also to pay the salaries of the state's government servants. The new laws as well as the financial difficulties of Kelantan were effectively used by UMNO as leverage to pressure PAS into giving its cooperation and, finally, into joining the BN. But more important was the personal commitment of the president of PAS then, Asri Muda, who did not have any choice but to join the BN government in order to forestall possible government action on alleged corruption within the PAS leadership.

There were other factors as well. It is possible that UMNO leaders were successful in convincing PAS leaders that UMNO was already undergoing policy and leadership changes that would make it more acceptable to PAS. Further, the continuation of the decade-long political conflict between UMNO and PAS would only threaten the present political power balance as well as the future of the Malays, about which PAS was supposed to be most concerned. It was also stressed that politicking should be reduced so that more attention could be paid to development and security. Of course the lure of participation in government as ministers, deputy ministers and parliamentary secretaries must have attracted some of the PAS leaders too. In 1973 PAS agreed to join the government at the state level and in 1974 became a component member of the BN.

Malay unity has been the hope and dream of many people, especially the politicians. Almost every predominantly Malay party even now talks about the necessity of Malay unity under its own leadership. There are many reasons for this. First, there is the belief that now all that the Malays have left is their political power. The number of Malay voters at present exceeds that of the non-Malays. There are many constituencies with Malay majorities. So, within the framework of the parliamentary democracy now in existence, UMNO (or more exactly the BN) can remain in power only as long as the Malays are united in supporting it. That is why many UMNO leaders always remind the Malays about the unity achieved previously when opposing the Malayan Union, as an inspiration for Malay unity today. The question of Malay unity has often been associated with Malay power, which is often referred to as *ketuanan Melayu*. UMNO continues until now to talk about it.

Second, political power is considered to be of vital importance in determining policies in other spheres such as economics and education, which are believed to have great potential to enhance or at least to maintain the special rights and interests of the Malays. UMNO, for instance, strongly believes that only with united Malay support will it be able to carry out programmes designed for Malay interests. If the Malays are disunited and their support is divided among the different opposing parties, their power and influence will be reduced, with the result that the policies and programmes that they claim will benefit the Malays cannot be carried out. So runs the usual argument.

Third, from the point of view of security, which is closely linked to national politics and economics, it is often stressed that the country is constantly faced with the danger of communist insurrection. The government hopes that the Malays, with their strong belief in Islam, will serve as a bastion against communism. Some government leaders and security officers often stress that "the communists are Chinese and Chinese are communists". Such views are more often expressed at small, closed-door meetings, deliberately aimed at arousing Malay feelings so that they will stand united against the communists. Although the Malaysian government signed a peace agreement with the Communist Party of Malaya and the latter has already laid down arms and so no longer constitute a security threat, yet the communist bogey continues to be raised especially over television.

Various tactics and strategies may be employed to promote Malay unity for Malay power. One way is by arousing fear of other ethnic groups. Another is by using government and non-government organs to bamboozle the Malays concerning the importance of unity for the purpose of promoting the economic, political and security interests of the country as a whole, particularly for the Malays. But the most common method is by cajoling and convincing the Malays that policies and programmes are for their interests alone.

It is recognised that religion, race, language and culture are issues that can easily arouse the emotions of particular groups of people. That is why some political parties, be they Malay or non-Malay, often exploit such issues in order to gain popular support. During the movement against the Malayan Union, the question of the Malay's survival as a race was raised as the magic slogan to mobilise united Malay support. Not long after independence, language and education became hot issues. Now the question of religion is exploited to the full as a means of achieving unity and maintaining security. Whatever the issues – religion, race or culture – all are open to political manipulation and exploitation. But this does not deny the fact that there are some individuals and groups who are sincere in their intentions over these same issues.

As a political objective, Malay unity and power is indeed laudable. Nevertheless, a number of basic questions have to be satisfactorily answered first. In the first place, unity for whom? Quite often the call for unity ultimately benefits only the leaders and not the common people. Malay 'unity' which successfully aborted the Malayan Union and later gained independence did not change the basic colonial economic structure, although it opened up opportunities for businessmen, contractors and capitalists to become rich. It gave more power and influence to senior politicians and better positions to civil servants, but gave little cause for happiness among the Malay school and religious teachers, for example.

As for peasantry of Kelantan, Kedah, Terengganu and Perlis, they were by and large disappointed because the earnest support they gave to the call for unity and independence did not bring the socio-economic improvement which they had hoped for. The disenchantment and frustration felt by an increasing number of people manifested itself in the increasing support given to PAS and declining popularity of UMNO, which was reflected by the reduced percentage of votes it obtained in 1959, for example. One can shout all kinds of slogans in the name of Malay unity, but this is a futile effort if ultimately it only promotes self-interest and perpetuates the ruling elite.

The next question: what are the bases of unity and what effects will they have on the country and people? It is necessary to ensure that any move to unite a particular ethnic group will not result in dissension or conflict with other ethnic groups. Political and economic issues can cut across ethnic or racial lines and positively contribute towards unity within a group and also with other groups. But even these issues can create tension and cause dissension if they are influenced by ethnic or racial considerations. We have seen during the May Thirteenth Incident how racial politics could cause bloodshed among innocent people, destruction of property and social dissension.

Fourth, we must define what type of leadership will hold the reins of Malay power. There are leaders who shout slogans about national independence and sovereignty, but who actually sell out the country to imperialists, neo-colonialists or big capitalists. This type of leadership is certainly unacceptable. Nor do we want leaders who talk only about poverty and development, while at the same time encouraging policies whereby the rich can freely exploit the poor and plunder the wealth of the country. Similarly the people do not want leaders who merely mouth honesty and integrity, but who are corrupt, swearing readily in the name of Allah, but constantly living in sin. "Power to the people" must have more meaning than just being able to vote once in five years. That phrase must signify the people's ability to determine the nature of leadership in the country. Malay power must be based on the power of the less-privileged and the poor.

Actually, total unity within a particular ethnic group or between different ethnic groups cannot be easily achieved. Under normal circumstances there will always be differences and conflicts of view. When referring to Malay power, it has often been alleged by certain groups, inside and outside the country, that the Malays monopolise political power which they use to benefit their own community. These allegations are based on the fact that the sultans and most ministers and civil servants are Malay, and also on the fact that the constitution safeguards Malay privileges. In fact there are even a few among the Malay ruling elite who make similar claims, just to appeal to the Malay masses in order to ensure the success of their policies. But not all those who are in power are Malays.

In traditional society the sultans and chiefs were in power and they were Malays, but they constituted only a small fraction of the total Malay population; therefore this fact did not mean that all the Malays held political power. Today, the majority of the ruling political elite are Malays, but they constitute a minor fraction of the Malay society. Most of them are in the upper class or upper-middle class. They provide many opportunities to the non-Malay economic elite to share power with them too. The ideology that they promote has an inherent quality which protects and furthers their own class interests, and the policies that they carry out are often for their own advantage, not for that of the masses of people in the lower classes.

From the above discussion it is clear that the political objectives of promoting Malay unity and power are meaningless unless they are oriented to the type of ideology, politics and leadership that can really benefit the common people, especially the poor. Nor should they serve to strengthen the position of foreign monopoly-capitalists together with local capitalists so that they can continue to exploit the country and the poor. The politics of Malay power can only be meaningful if they are directed towards achieving genuine unity based on the unity of the less privileged lower class who form the majority of the population, not to cause dissension and bloodshed; they can be meaningful only if used genuinely to safeguard national independence and not to encourage monopoly-capitalism and neo-colonialism to persist in new forms.

We have seen that after four years in the BN, PAS left the coalition. The latter's position was getting untenable. PAS entered the coalition mainly on the strong persuasion and influence of the then premier Abdul Razak Hussein over Asri Muda, who was PAS leader and Kelantan Menteri Besar who was later appointed federal minister with jurisdiction over the Felda[7] land schemes. After his death, Razak was succeeded by Hussein Onn, who appeared to be less tolerant of PAS, its political stand and demands, and apparently not so willing to concede important roles to Asri and the other PAS ministers and deputy ministers. Further, a large body of PAS membership and also leadership were not so happy with the coalition because it constrained propagation of their Islamic political agenda. They were also getting more dissatisfied with the leadership of Asri. In some states PAS found it lost much support to other parties, for instance to PRM in Terengganu. As relationship became more strained, PAS finally pulled out of BN. Thus an effort to forge stronger Malay unity and power was undermined.

Apparently due to ill-health Hussein was forced to retire and he was succeeded by Dr Mahathir Mohamad. Unlike the previous three prime ministers, who were all lawyers, Mahathir came from the medical profession. While his predecessor Hussein was seen as being slow and undecisive, although much appreciated for his straightforward attitude and clean image, Mahathir ruled with a strong and firm hand. He soon showed authoritarian tendencies over UMNO and the country. Owing

---

7. Federal Land Development Authority, established in 1956 under the Land Development Act. Among its objectives is to develop new land for plantation.

to greater involvement of party leaders or associates with business ventures and the introduction of more mega projects, there were a lot of contracts to give to his close relatives and friends. Consequently corruption as well as money politics became more widespread.

Internally, not long after Musa Hitam left his post as Deputy PM, Tengku Razaleigh Hamzah, a senior minister and vice-president of UMNO, challenged Mahathir for the position of president but lost by a very narrow margin of 43 votes. Soon after, UMNO was challenged in court for illegal practices during the election and declared illegal in 1987. Subsequently, after Mahathir succeeded to revive and control UMNO, Razaleigh and his followers left UMNO to form Semangat Melayu '46 (The Malay Spirit of '46). At that time Malay society seemed to have split right in the middle from the palace to the *kampung*.

Almost around the same time inter-ethnic tension was rising mainly because of conflicts over the position of Chinese language and education, as well as the move that was seen by the Chinese as government attempt to control national type Chinese schools. There was much protest by a significant section of Chinese through their organisations, both political and educational. The UMNO youth movement that was led by Najib Abdul Razak together with the then Menteri Besar of Selangor, Muhammad Muhammad Taib, led a rally at the TPCA stadium in Kampung Baru, Kuala Lumpur. They hoisted the *keris* and banners which showed blood flowing from that weapon. When tension really ran high, the government used the ISA to arrest political leaders from DAP, PAS, PRM, even some from UMNO as well as NGO activists.[8] Most of them were not at all involved in spreading ethnic hatred. But the real culprits, especially Najib and Muhammad, were spared. They played the necessary role of rallying the Malays by creating hatred of the non-Malays but were not acted upon although they exacerbated inter-ethnic tension.

To face the elections in 1990, Razaleigh formed electoral pacts with the other opposition parties – PAS, DAP and PRM – to fight UMNO-BN. There was an interesting development – the emergence of two coalitions that appeared to be multi-ethnic in composition – and this promised well for a multi-ethnic politics in the Malaysian scene. But it

---

8. This ocurred under what is well-known as *Operasi Lalang* in 1987, when 87 persons were detained under the draconian ISA.

was shortlived. Although the opposition coalition led by Razaleigh was popular at the beginning, it crashed a couple of days before voting.

Razaleigh went to Sabah to meet the Kadazandusun leaders there, and on his arrival they donned him with a traditional headgear known as the *sigah*. On the *sigah* was a motif of the shoot of a plant, but since it looked like a cross, the BN spin doctors successfully accused that by having the cross symbol on his head, Razaleigh was promoting the Christian cause. A day before the votes were cast, a document purported to be from the Pope that praised Razaleigh and the opposition was widely spread overnight in mosques all over the country timed for the Muslims' Friday congregation. Immediately the Malays turned against Razaleigh and the opposition. UMNO was able to mobilise Malay support by using this emotional religious issue that succeeded in returning them with a trouncing victory, especially over Malay candidates in the opposition who stood in Malay-majority constituencies.

After succeeding to unite a large section of the Malays behind him, Mahathir as a stronger PM became more authoritarian in his exercise of power. At the same time he accumulated greater control of the economy when many among his families and friends were farmed out with big projects and contracts. To ensure he stayed as leader of UMNO, he introduced new procedures, which allowed him to collect bonus votes for his nominations and to deny anyone to stand as President and Deputy President who failed to collect 30 and 20 per cent respectively of the total number of nominations from the various divisions.

But soon his popularity began to decline. Things came to a head when there was a financial crisis in the region, beginning 1997, which also affected Malaysia. Owing largely to this crisis Suharto fell from power in Indonesia. Mahathir feared that he would follow suit. He read signs of his deputy, Anwar Ibrahim together with his youthful followers possibly mounting a challenge against him as premier. Mahathir moved speedily to remove Anwar from his party and government positions. He accused the latter of committing corruption and sodomy, in order to completely destroy him politically.

Before he was arrested, Anwar managed to hold public rallies nationwide to explain his position and accuse Mahathir and his government of practising nepotism, cronyism and corruption; these soon became household words. Huge crowds attended to hear him. The night he was arrested under a criminal act, he was beaten up very badly by the inspector-general of police (IGP) Abdul Rahim Noor. Since Anwar's condition was really bad and could not be produced in court, there was a change and he was detained under the Internal Security Act (ISA), which allowed him to be held by the police without trial. A number of his followers were also detained under the ISA.

There was public outcry within and outside the country. So it was back to criminal charges against Anwar, so that he could be produced in court. He appeared in court a week later with a black eye which was for all to see. This created greater anger amongst the people. But Mahathir claimed that Anwar had inflicted the eye injury himself. A series of demonstrations under the name of Reformasi were held. With the media, police and court being controlled and orchestrated, the conspiracy to jail Anwar and to destroy him politically was for a time successful. He was convicted to six and nine years imprisonment for corruption and sodomy respectively.

The Reformasi demonstrations were stepped up. The government and police moved with iron fists. Hundreds were attacked with water cannon, the water spiked with chemical, sprayed with tear gas, beaten up and arrested by the police. A non-governmental organisation, named ADIL was soon formed, led by Dr Wan Azizah Wan Ismail, Anwar's wife, with a number of activists and professionals as members of its committee. ADIL was later transformed into a political party, known as National Justice Party, which was founded in April 1999 and also elected Wan Azizah as leader.

Public anger continued to be strong and this translated itself somewhat in the results of the 1999 elections. The opposition managed to muster about 45 per cent of the popular votes and won 42 of the parliamentary seats (or 22 per cent). In August 2003, Keadilan Nasional together with Parti Rakyat formalised their merger as Parti Keadilan Rakyat (People's Justice Party) with a public launch in 2003. The pressure against Mahathir was still strong, and perhaps partly because of this he realised his days as PM were already numbered. He announced his intention to retire in an UMNO general assembly. Although there was strong opposition among some party leaders, in November 2003 he finally withdrew and was forced to give way to his deputy, Abdullah Ahmad Badawi, although his own stated preference was for Najib Razak.

In November 2004, about a year after he came to office, Abdullah called the eleventh general elections. He presented a different image from Mahathir; all the government controlled electronic and printed media were well orchestrated to promote him as a humble religious person and a "Mr Clean". During the election campaigns he promised to fight against corruption and to open wider space for democracy. His popularity was rising and UMNO-BN was stronger; the prevailing favourable economic condition also helped. On the other hand the opposition parties were facing problems of unity, with DAP leaving BA[9], the opposition coalition, before the elections. There was a general swing, of both Malay and non-Malay votes, towards Abdullah. As a result the BN won a trouncing victory. This time the opposition could muster only 35 per cent of the popular votes and managed to win only 20 parliamentary seats, which constituted around 14 per cent. In other words, with 65 per cent of the votes, the BN collected nearly 90 per cents of the parliamentary seats.

But it was not all plain sailing for Abdullah. Soon he was in stormy waters. He was severely attacked by his predecessor Mahathir from all fronts – for weak, corrupt and "half past six" leadership – as well as being responsible for the decline in the Proton car industry and the ensuing AP scandal. Abdullah chose to remain silent. Mahathir stopped only when he was admitted to hospital for heart surgery. Besides that, Anwar had reappeared in the scene on being released from prison after the Federal Court freed him from the sodomy charges. He held road shows all over the country, his public rallies drawing from 500 to 50,000 people at a time. Unlike Mahathir, who was often given wide media coverage, Anwar has always been almost completely blacked out by the UMNO-BN-controlled media.

Without attacking Abdullah pointedly, as Mahathir did, Anwar exposed that the PM continued on almost the same – if not bigger – scale the practices of corruption and cronyism, thus rendering meaningless his election promises to fight against them. He also accused Abdullah of controlling and manipulating the media in a worse manner than ever

---

9 Barisan Alternatif (Alternative Front), a coalition of PAS, Keadilan, DAP and PRM, formed prior to the general elections in November 1999. The DAP left the coalition in September 2001, citing differences with PAS.

before and keeping a blind eye on police violence against peaceful public gatherings to continue. Cracks began to appear in UMNO and to certain extent this affected the unity of the Malays, many of whom were beginning to be disenchanted with UMNO and Abdullah's leadership.

During the last quarter of 2007, three major events took place. The first one was Anwar's exposure of a video tape showing V.K. Lingam, a prominent lawyer close to Mahathir, talking to a senior judge, promising to work for his promotion to become the Chief Justice. During the conversation the lawyer explained that he would get a politician, Tengku Adnan and a businessman, Vincent Tan, to lobby Mahathir, who was then PM. Lingam had been exposed earlier for going on a holiday in New Zealand with one of the former Chief Justices, Eusoff Chin. Although it was claimed that the holiday was not pre-planned, tickets and documents were supplied to show that it was all planned and acts of corruption were committed. Yet no action was taken on either the lawyer or the Chief Justice.

Anwar's partial exposure of the Lingam tape at the beginning was given only limited publicity in the government-controlled media. But it was enough to spark anger among the lawyers that led the Bar Council to organise about two thousand lawyers to go to the street in protest. The government was dilly dallying and appeared reluctant to investigate. At first Deputy PM Najib appointed a panel, but it proved to be a lame duck in that it failed to produce a report that could be made public. Finally, PM Abdullah reluctantly announced the formation of a Royal Commission of Inquiry, chaired by the same discredited judge who chaired the panel. A few days after, when Anwar exposed the full contents of the 18-minute video, there was hardly any report on this in the media.

The second event was a public rally organised in Kuala Lumpur by BERSIH to hand over a memorandum to the Agong. BERSIH was a broad-based coalition of over 70 organisations including political parties and NGOs, set up to ensure free and fair elections. The rally was to be held in the centre of Kuala Lumpur but it ended up with a mass gathering in front of the palace where the memorandum was handed to palace officials. It was estimated that in all those who gathered in front of the Agong's palace and elsewhere in Kuala Lumpur totalled about

50,000. The gathering as a whole took place peacefully. But government leaders later spun all kinds of stories to discredit the rally.

The third event was a rally organised by the Hindu Rights Action Force (HINDRAF) which planned to submit a memorandum to the British High Commission, claiming compensation for the sufferings of the Indian labourers who were brought into this country to work especially in estates and their families. The police suppression of this rally was brutal. A number of people were detained in the early hours of the morning and later accused of attempting to murder a policeman. They were initially denied bail and jailed. But later, as a result of political pressure, they were released on bail of only RM500 each and the murder charge against them withdrawn by the Attorney General. More than the BERSIH rally, news of which the media appeared to deliberately suppress, the HINDRAF issue and actions were given wide exposure by all electronic and printed media in the country and outside. In a way, the rally was used to submerge the story of corruption and judge fixing that had come to be exposed.

The way the Lingam tape and the HINDRAF issues were handled proved Abdullah was indeed a weak leader with no clear direction and lacking vision. The credibility of his government was undermined. His position as leader was weakened. Abdullah realised he was losing support from non-Malay voters and so he tried to concentrate on winning them again. To ensure he remained in power, those around him especially the likes of his son-in-law adopted several methods of mobilising and increasing support, especially from the Malays.

Firstly, they accused those who participated in the different rallies of causing riot, although they were organised peacefully and became restless only after the police used force. They misrepresented these rallies as being disruptive to efforts on development, which they claimed were aimed mainly to help the Malays. Secondly, they declared that the government would adopt pro-Malay policies, and this declaration was given the widest publicity by their controlled media. In this connection, for example they vehemently voiced their commitment to defend the New Economic Policy (NEP), which they claimed was for promoting the interests and future of the Malays. Thirdly, they attacked and discredited any party or leader whom they could brand as being against the NEP. Anwar was a convenient target because he called for the NEP to be replaced by a "Malaysian Economic Agenda" that is multi-ethnic in approach. Anwar wanted to focus more on the poor and marginalised at large irrespective of ethnic origins and not to give a racial twist to development efforts. He stressed on what he called "concern for the people" which is effectively encapsulated in the Malay phrase *"kepedulian rakyat"*.

Finally, the government leaders and their controlled media would grab any issue that could be manipulated to arouse Malay emotion and anger. This opportunity presented itself, for instance when HINDRAF came to the fore. Following the mass demonstrations organised by HINDRAF and their demands, which were accused by some UMNO leaders as being anti-Malay, even the top UMNO leaders went all out to use them to rally Malay support. They spread lies that the opposition parties and leaders, in particular Anwar, supported riots and the HINDRAF demands, and therefore, anti-Malay. This was done deliberately in order to undermine Malay support for the opposition. In other words, to mobilise Malay support and unity behind them, these UMNO leaders would not stop short of using narrow ethnic sentiment and threats. This method had been used in the past and now continued to be used during critical times when Malay support for them and their party were waning. Even the Deputy PM in an official speech in Sabah at the end of 2007 went as far as to raise the ghost of the May Thirteenth Incident to create fear and drive away support for the opposition.

The media that they control would be fully manipulated to spin all kinds of untruths against those whom they oppose. The call for Malay unity and *ketuanan Melayu* (Malay power) serves as a convenient ethnic weapon for mustering political support for UMNO, notwithstanding that it could threaten national unity. Politically we observed that Abdullah had become more authoritarian and together with his cohorts became more blatantly self serving, vis-à-vis the use of narrow communal methods in order to remain in power. Thus Malay unity is promoted not so much for the salvation of ordinary Malays as for increasing the wealth and power of a small coterie of leaders together with their families, friends and cronies. ❀

4

MALAYS AND ISLAM

In this country almost all Malays are Muslims. Although Hindu beliefs were widespread in this part of the world many centuries ago, we do not often hear of a Malay being a Hindu today. This is quite different from Indonesia where the spread of Hinduism and its culture have left many adherents, particularly in East Java and Bali. The influence of Islam on the Malays is very deep-seated; from the time they discarded their animistic beliefs and embraced Islam during the days of the Melaka kingdom, the Malays have never changed their religion. Before and after the coming of the British, Christian missions were active especially through schools. Initially, Malays were reluctant to send their children to English-medium schools for fear of their being converted to Christianity; but eventually they became wiser and adopted English education. No Malay pupil became a Christian. Not so with the Chinese and Indians, many of whom left their faiths to embrace Christianity or at least adopted Christian names. But recently there have been reports of some Malays embracing Christianity and causing controversy.

Any Malay who tries to change his religion will face strong sanctions or downright condemnation from his family and community. The fact that we never hear about conflicts within the family or the community over this issue, except for a very small number of cases recently, proves that the Malays hold to the Muslim faith very firmly. However, the attitude of an individual toward his religion differs from person to person; there are those who believe deeply and practise it fervently and there are those who hardly practise it at all, whose faith is only skin-deep, despite the fact that they have been born Muslims. We have seen many Malays, who seldom pray or fast as required by Islam, but become emotionally upset when Islam is criticised, especially by a non-Muslim. At the same time there are Malays who may not know even the ABC's of Islam, who literally live in sin, but who, when asked about their faith, will proudly say, "I am a Muslim". The constitution does not allow others to induce Malays to leave Islam; the consequences are serious when a Malay leaves his religion, even of his own volition.[10]

Although Malays are Muslims, the influence of traditional beliefs is still strong among them. Manifestations of these beliefs can be seen in all aspects of Malay life – social, economic political, in health practices and even in love. These traditional beliefs, widespread among the Malays of today, are the continuation of the belief systems which existed before the spread of Islam in this region. It is difficult to reconstruct the old belief systems which are based on what is called animism. In animism it is believed that there exist many types of supernatural powers which inhabit or protect everything surrounding man – the mountains, hills, even molehills, lakes, rivers and streams, the sea and sky, trees, and even a worm-eaten tree trunk. Man makes all kinds of requests to these supernatural powers through persons who have expertise in supernatural affairs, and who resort to all kinds of ritual in which members of the community concerned sometimes participate.

At a glance it is clear that animistic beliefs are opposed to Islam. But how is it that they persist until today in Malay society? Why do the Malays, with their faith in Islam, hold on to these traditional beliefs? These questions can be answered if we look at this system of belief or religion from three aspects: (a) ritual, (b) functionaries, and (c) doctrine. These three levels are not isolated from but are related to one another. At each level one can perceive the processes of conflict and accommodation between traditional beliefs and religion.

At the ritual level we can see many forms of activities carried out in Malay society. Let us take three examples, namely, marriage (social), cultivation (economic) and curing the sick (medical). In marriage there are many rituals such as "sounding out" (*merisik*), asking for the hand in marriage (*meminang*), delivery of expenses (*hantar belanja*), the ceremonial sitting on the dais (*bersanding*), eating face to face

---

10. Constitution, Article II (4).

(*makan beradap*) and so forth. These rituals have been carried out for generations as part of the cultural heritage of the Malays.

There is nothing in Islam that expressly states whether these should or should not be done. If ever there is anything that seems to go against the spirit of Islam, it is the lavish expense of some of these rituals, which creates waste (*membazir*) and encourages haughtiness (*riak*). But generally speaking if they are performed in a moderate manner, they are permissible (*harus*). It should be remembered that even if all the traditional rituals are carried out in the best manner possible, the marriage is not considered legitimised until and unless all the conditions of marriage according to Islam – such as the utterance of the marriage contract (*ijab kabul*) in front of witnesses – are faithfully fulfilled by the bride and groom. Among the Malays we can see the integration of both the traditional rituals and Islam. As in the case of marriage, the demands of both tradition and religion are met.

In cultivation there are also several rituals that have become part and parcel of the traditional belief system associated with economic matters. There are rituals for every stage of cultivation: during planting, during the interim and during harvest. For example, in certain places, when the time comes for planting rice seedlings, the peasants collect some leaves, yellow rice and a handful of *paddy* to be blessed by the magician (*pawang*). The leaves are planted in the nursery beds with the following utterances: "Praise be to you. O my Father, the Sky and my Mother, the Earth, please take care of our gems."

The yellow rice is scattered over the beds followed by three invocations (*salawat*) to Prophet Muhammad. The *salam* and *salawat* are Islamic elements that have been integrated into the traditional ritual. But the ritual itself can lead to belief in powers other than God (*shirk*) if the help sought for protecting the plants is made to the spirits of the land and not to Allah. Perhaps the *salam* and *salawat* signify that the ritual is subordinated to the Islamic faith, as will be discussed later.

So also is the case with curing illness. According to traditional belief, illness is caused by spirits or devils entering a person as a result of sorcery. The way to cure the illness is by chasing away the spirits, and only a magician or "medicine man" (*dukun*) has the supernatural power to do this. He carries out his own rituals when treating the sick person. Usually incense is burnt and the medicine man chants his verses; sometimes he goes into a trance, and it is during such a state that he treats his patient. A piece of yellow or black cloth, according to the individual choice or practice of the medicine man, is used to flog the body of the patient and drive away the spirit that has caused the illness. In some of these rituals the only elements of Islam found are the invocation of praise to Allah (*Bismillah*) and the names of God and His prophets in the magical verses. In some other cases the prayers may be in Arabic, sometimes quotations from the Qur'an, and the element of supernatural power induced to drive away the spirits is the Muslim jinn.

The second aspect concerns the functionaries who play the leading role in the various rituals explained above. For cultivation there is the specialist who invokes the prayers and for treating illness there is the medicine man. They are actually the functionaries in the belief system, and the most important among them are known as *pawang* or *bomoh*. They have acquired this specialised magical knowledge and supernatural power in various ways, from their elders, or through dreams or by living in seclusion *(bertapa)*. This magical knowledge holds guarded secrets and has very little to do with Islam. The prayers and verses that are invoked and the symbols that are used on a talisman are sometimes based on quotations from the Qur'an or various appellations of Allah. Some may not know much about Islam, but a few are quite religious and claim that their source of knowledge is Islam, particularly the Qur'an.

Between those who rely on the Qur'an and those who do not, there exist differences and conflict regarding their source of power, ability and the type of medium they use. Those relying on the Qur'an are easily accepted at village level by such religious functionaries as the prayer leaders (*imam*), religious teachers and others; however, those who do not base their practice on Islam are looked upon with suspicion. Whatever the religious functionaries may think of them, the *pawang* and *bomoh* retain a special niche in the hearts and minds of the Malays, especially amongst the village folks. The functionaries of traditional beliefs exist side by side with the religious functionaries, each playing his role in his own area of expertise. In fact there are some religious functionaries who also have roles as functionaries in the traditional belief system.

Although there seems to be some integration of traditional and Islamic elements, in addition to some coexistence between the religious and traditional functionaries, the relationship is quite different from the third aspect of doctrine. According to the principal doctrine of iIslam, Allah is One and Omnipotent, and He is the source and cause of everything. He gives life and causes death; He creates and destroys. Any contrary belief to the effect that there is another power which makes plants grow well or causes a man to be ill or die is against Islam.

In the traditional system there are beliefs in supernatural powers that can cause certain things to happen: ghosts, satans and evil spirits. There are the functionaries who claim that they can make use of these powers as mediums to perform their will for good or evil. Quite a few Malays strongly hold to these traditional beliefs and have great faith in their functionaries. How do they allow these beliefs to exist side by side with Islam? And how do traditional functionaries rationalise their position and role?

There are two explanations. First, they contend that it is indeed Allah who causes everything, while the ghosts, spirits and satans are only the means. Therefore, if someone wants to hurt anyone he dislikes by using spirits and ghosts, he will not succeed unless Allah wills it so. In other words, the powers that the spirits and ghosts possess are limited, and whether they are effective or not depends on the Power and Will of Allah.

Second, whatever help is sought from traditional functionaries is considered merely an initiative (*ikhtiar*). So when the *pawang* or *bomoh* carries out his functions, he is just acting on his own initiative. Whether the initiative succeeds or not depends entirely on Allah. It is clear therefore that traditional beliefs are subjected to the belief in Islam. But whether the ordinary Malay really puts his faith in the *pawang* or *bomoh*, or places his faith in the Will of Allah, or whether he is conscious that he is only making a personal initiative when he resorts to traditional belief, is hard to say. It is entirely up to the individual.

Although there is a trend that allows for traditional rituals and their functionaries to exist on the basis that they are subjected and do not exist as alternatives to the Power of God, there is also another trend that calls for the elimination of the traditional belief system. Ghosts and spirits do not exist within the context of Islamic doctrine, and believing in them is against Islam. Of course the Qur'an speaks about such supernatural beings as angels, jinns and devils (*iblis*), but their forms, origins and functions are not the same as those held within the traditional system. Furthermore, since belief in Islam is not really very deep among the common people, there is always the possibility that their beliefs in ghosts and spirits will supersede their belief in Allah, which is tantamount to polytheism (*shirk*), a cardinal sin in Islam.

But why do traditional beliefs still persist in Malay society? Probably they have become part and parcel of Malay life, part of the Malay cultural heritage. They are related to social and economic values and to the activities of the Malays, and as long as these exist so also will traditional beliefs remain. Although there are counter trends to traditional beliefs, they have not become very strong or effective. At the village level not many religious people really understand or can effectively argue that traditional beliefs are contrary to Islam and should be rejected. At the supra-village level, although there are authorities like the religious departments and movements like the missionary groups, they have not been able to eradicate traditional beliefs from Malay society.

As traditional beliefs are still strongly rooted in Malay society, it may not be wrong to imply that Islam as generally practised among the Malays is only skin-deep. The roots lie in the history of Islam itself and in its development in the region. Islam was spread in this region in an informal and rather unsystematic way. During the peak of the Melaka kingdom, the position of Islam was closely linked with the power of that kingdom. The upper class, particularly the sultan, played an active role in spreading the teachings of Islam. Some teachers and religious men were brought all the way from Arabia or India, and, under the sultan's patronage, taught the fundamentals of the religion to the aristocrats and chiefs. The common people merely followed and thus never gained a sophisticated understanding of the laws and philosophy of Islam. This pattern of development also took place during the time of the Acehnese sultanate. But after the decline of these kingdoms, following the expansion of colonialism, the situation changed. Nevertheless Islam has become an integral part of Malay life and culture. It has been passed down through each generation and has gathered a large following among the people.

An important channel through which the teachings of Islam are transmitted is, of course, the family. It is a well-known fact that the family is an important institution for the perpetuation of culture in society. The transmission of cultural elements from parents to children takes place through the process of socialisation. Through this process the children observe, imitate and participate in the activities of the parents. There are social controls in the family and society to ensure that the children will not deviate from what is practised by the parents. Islam makes it incumbent upon the parents, especially the father, to advise and teach their children who have come of age to perform all the compulsory religious rituals. Instruction on the practice of the important rites, especially those pertaining to the five daily prayers and fasting, takes place at home. When the father prays the little children will follow, and during fasting month they share in the joys of breaking fast. The elder children participate, either through conviction, out of respect or because they have no choice. There are some family heads who are knowledgeable about the fundamentals of Islam, and so are able to enlighten their family members as to the whys and wherefores of performing certain rituals. But their number is relatively small. Most of them just follow blindly (*taklid*) and for them performing the prayers and fasting is merely to avoid the criticism and sanctions of other members of society. For some, these rituals have even less significance.

The common tendency is for Islam to spread as a cultural trait, emphasis being placed more on the rituals which are performed, without full understanding of their significance. Islam has become an important factor for promoting social relations, and its significance in maintaining unity and solidarity at the village level cannot be underestimated. Usually the village mosque or *surau* serves as an important centre for religious as well as social activities. Even those who do not normally perform the daily prayers will attend the mosque on Fridays, and particularly so in the case of the Eid congregations. For them the prayer is nothing more than mere ritual. So, when they perform it occasionally in public, members of society will take note that they are faithful to Islam. In other words prayer serves a social purpose. It becomes a way of identifying oneself with and not isolating oneself from existing social values. But then this devalues the real significance of Islam itself. Due to the lack of knowledge and understanding of the philosophy behind prayer, its social aspect is made paramount.

This is also true with regard to the non-compulsory aspects of Islam. For example, when a death occurs in the village, all the villagers will visit the family and pay their respects to the departed. The family of the deceased, who may not be the praying type, and may be quite ignorant of the fundamentals of Islam, will usually insist on reciting the *tahlil*. A feast will follow, and they will feel disappointed if it ends too soon, as if the ritual has not been satisfactorily performed. Rituals and again rituals. They are always uppermost with most Malays. The true essence of the teachings of Islam tends to be ignored. But villagers may not be the only guilty ones. The lavishly organised, annual Prophet's birthday celebrations and the Qur'an recital competitions have become part of the national life and amply demonstrate that the leaders themselves, who ought to know better, also lay greater stress on ritual and ceremony rather than on the essential teachings and philosophy of Islam.

When Islam, or for that matter any religion, is thus degraded to the level of ritual, what then can really distinguish it from the traditional beliefs? How can it be asserted over and above the traditional beliefs which are contradictory to Islam? The day may come when Islam, like the traditional beliefs, may be regarded as nothing more than just one aspect of the total culture. As a "cultural aspect" it can exist side by side with other aspects of the cultural milieu. It will be a sad day indeed when the status of Islam is downgraded to the level of traditional belief, regarded as nothing more than another aspect of Malay culture.

Lest I may be misunderstood, it must be emphasised that it is not my intention here to put forward the view that religion is no more than ritual or ceremony. The point is that among a large proportion of Malays the ritual or ceremonial aspects are often more emphasised than the true doctrine and philosophy. In other words, the social rather than the theological significance of religion is of greater concern to them. It would be misleading to say that efforts and institutions for the spreading of Islam are non-existent in the village. In fact we can find in most villages, especially in Kedah and Kelantan, the traditional centres for teaching and learning Islam have been long established. These are the *pondok* schools. One cannot miss seeing this picturesque institution, an interesting residential teaching system in which the students live in a cluster of huts around the house of the *guru* or the main "school building". These schools are mostly in the rice-growing areas. The *pondok* institutions are usually situated in predominately Malay areas. This is understandable since these institutions and their *guru* have to depend on tithes (*zakat*) of paddy in order to sustain themselves.

Some of the religious teachers and elders in the *pondok* schools are well-known for their extensive knowledge of Islam and a few have written noteworthy religious tracts. Many are also highly respected as Sufi mystics. But unfortunately these institutions do not seem to be progressive if viewed from the methods and content of their instruction. In fact, many of those who have completed their studies at such schools have a narrow view of the world. For a long time the *pondok* communities have been closed to the outside world and not very much involved with many of the happenings around them. The method of teaching and learning is by rote which does not encourage critical thinking. What is emphasised are the rules and laws pertaining to Islamic practices. This is necessary, of course, but at least it should be balanced by some studies in depth of the history and philosophy of Islam, in comparison with other religions and also with knowledge of science and other modern subjects.

As was explained earlier, when the British came it was agreed that all matters of administration in the Malay states, except those pertaining to Islam and Malay customs, would be taken over by the British. According to the agreement, religion was clearly separated from secular matters such as politics, administration, law, economics, education and so forth. Islam and Malay customs were under the jurisdiction of the sultans while the rest came under the British. There were two implications from this agreement as far as the position of Islam in the country was concerned. First, development in all matters other than religion was to be implemented along lines determined by the British and according to their own models. The effect of this on Islam in Malay society was negative. I shall elaborate. Second, under the sultan the management and administration of Islam was organised according to modern lines. Superficially this sounds attractive, but what really happened?

One of the first steps taken was the formation of Islamic Councils or Departments in all the Malay states. Melaka and Penang did not have similar councils until after independence, probably because it was not thought possible without a sultan; the British governors for both these states were not appropriate authorities to symbolise the protection of Islam. In the Malay states the religious councils became the administrative centres for all religious affairs. They administered the collection of religious tithes which were the main source of their income. Each religious council had its own treasury to collect revenue and disburse expenditure. From the tithes the councils financed the building of mosques, religious courts and schools; officials of the councils and subsidiary bodies were paid from the same sources.

For the administration of its day-to-day affairs, the religious council has a head or president, secretary and several officials. They need not be religiously qualified or educated, for they act only as ordinary administrators and so need no such qualification. For them the council is no more than an administrative structure and they are the staff responsible for its smooth running. The person responsible for all religious matters in the states is a *mufti*. Sometimes the *mufti*'s department is situated in the council building itself and sometimes not, but the important thing is that he and his department are both under the Religious Council. His appointment is made by the sultan. He is responsible for giving religious edicts (*fatwa*) and views on various problems, and he is the source of advice and direction on all religious matters in the state.

Under the *mufti* is a *kadi* who is head of religious administration in the district and a judge for the religious court. There is usually a *kadi* for each district, and his office also serves as the court. To administer the office there are often some officers and clerks. Under the *kadi* is the *imam*, whose normal duties are to lead group prayers, read sermons to Friday congregations, officiate in Muslim marriages, and serve as the tithe collector. In the mosque, under the *imam* is the *bilal* whose special duty is to make the call for prayers and also occasionally bathe the dead. Below him is the *noja*, serving as caretaker to look after the cleanliness of the mosque.

The religious functionaries from the *mufti* and the *kadi* right down to the *imam*, *bilal* and *noja* are holders of positions that have been bureaucratised. They have become government servants who are paid monthly salaries, appointed on the basis of selection and merit, and can be promoted or demoted, depending on circumstances. It is not surprising, therefore, that some of them have become mere tools of the government in the name of religion, and are not courageous enough to criticise the various anti-religious practices that are widespread in society, especially if such criticism would reflect badly on the government. But the bureaucratisation process has not reached the villages fully.

Most of the old village mosques and prayer houses were built by the villagers themselves or by their forefathers, from their own collections, and it was only after independence and the introduction of the rural development schemes that mosques were built with government aid. Except for the state and district mosques, until this day only some of the village *imam* and *bilal* are regarded as officers of the Religious Council, and thus do not receive fixed salaries although their letters of authority are issued by the same body. Nevertheless they take orders from and abide by the decisions of officers from the Council.

Nowadays there is a growing tendency for mosques at different levels to be controlled by the ruling party. In Kelantan, ruled by PAS, the party has a strong grip on these religious institutions. In the other states, the ruling party UMNO has become increasingly active in its effort to control them through the mosque management and various mosque officials who are appointed by the Religious Council.

All states have their own *muftis*, *kadis*, mosques and and even *suraus*. At the same time there are also *Syariah* courts, which co-exist beside the Civil courts. The former is based on Islamic jurisprudence and meant to hear cases involving only Muslims. They have jurisdiction especially over family and property matters. But not every state has schools administered under the religious councils. Among the states where religious schools are well organised are Johor and Kelantan. In Johor the religious school sessions are held in the afternoon using the same premises used by the Malay schools in the morning. Religious education lasts six years, and the curriculum covers various aspects of Islam – its doctrine, law, economy and so forth. After the sixth year promising pupils attend another extra year when classes are held on Saturdays; those who pass will have the chance to become religious teachers.

The situation is quite different in Kelantan. Besides the *pondok* schools, there are the more formal *Sekolah Agama Rakyat* (People's

Religious Schools), and as the name suggests, they are financed and administered by the people, as opposed to the government. There are also schools built by the religious council, which are often referred to as *Sekolah Majlis* (Council Schools). In these schools, although the core of education provided centres around Islam, subjects like mathematics, history and geography are also taught. There are not many of these schools, and now they are slowly being replaced by the new national and national-type schools under the Ministry of Education. In Johor the religious teachers are paid by the state government, while in Kelantan, they are paid by the religious council. In other words they have been absorbed into the bureaucracy.

We turn now to the first implication of the agreement between the sultans and the British. As has been mentioned above, all non-religious or secular matters were administered under the British along the British model. Various departments were established to administer land, education, law and order, security and other civil matters. These departments and their serving officers far outnumbered the religious departments. The expenses of all of them were met from revenues collected by the states. These state revenues in the form of different types of taxes, totalled much more than the religious tithes collected by the religious departments. The financial basis of secular administration was therefore always more firm and secure.

All the laws and regulations introduced were taken almost *in toto* from the British, and they were separated from the Muslim laws, which were used only by the relevant religious departments to deal with matters affecting Muslims. Courts of all levels were established and magistrates and judges were appointed. None of the civil and criminal laws and codes adopted by these courts contained any element of Islam. Furthermore, under the British a strong educational system was established from primary to university levels; the buildings were bigger, the equipment better and the teachers better qualified than those in the religious or council schools. The secular schools used the English medium and certificates issued by them were valued more than those from the religious schools.

The point to emphasise here is that, although religious administration appeared organised, and in theory should have been stronger, in practice it was limited in scope and not firmly based. The religious and secular administrations existed side by side, with the latter having wider jurisdiction, more staff and better finance. Secular administration was based entirely on the British model. Although it appeared that religious administration was strengthened under the sultan, it was actually weakened by the competition from the secular administration, which was always strongly supported by the government. Elements of Western colonialism have resulted in the weakening or even obstruction of Islam and its administration in the country.

Turning from administrative organisation to its personnel, we also find that developments in various fields also had some negative influence on the level of religiosity among members of society. As was explained earlier, towards the end of the last century and at the beginning of the present one, many towns sprang up. The process of urbanisation naturally has had its effects on the Malays. There is a tendency for religious values not to be strongly adhered to by urban people. Sometimes, owing to the wide generation gap, a family becomes ineffective as an institution for carrying out the process of religious socialisation. At the same time life in the town is more individualistic and often even neighbours do not know or care about one another.

Unlike those living in the rural areas, urban people normally do not impose strong sanctions on those, for instance, who do not pray. A person in the town feels more free to do whatever he likes, whether walking hand in hand with a girlfriend into a cinema during the time for Friday prayer, drinking beer or stout in a coffee shop or consuming one glass of whisky after another in a hotel, gambling in a small way in an amusement park or on a big scale in Genting Highlands. But of course they form only a very small minority.

There are many places for doing all kinds of things that are considered to be sinful by Islam. The position of Islam being what it is in this country, it has no effective control over all these activities. Besides that, the kind of job and working hours in some factories or departments make it difficult for workers to perform regular prayers, and only those who are deeply religious will replace the prayers missed when they return home. Furthermore, the influence of secular education makes youth cynical towards the role of religion and its functionaries.

The discussion hitherto has shown that in the villages and among people of the lower class Islam has been diluted by traditional beliefs, while in the towns and especially among the upper and middle classes it has been weakened by the style of life associated with the more modern West which came in with colonialism and which still persists today. The capitalists, who are strongly motivated by the desire to make quick money, are ever willing to build hotels, tourist complexes and even gambling centres, all of which also provide facilities for prostitution and other kinds of vices. But none of this matters according to them; after all, more tourists can be attracted, state revenues will increase and naturally people will become richer.

In the same way different kinds of attire, which attract youth especially, flood the market. Various patterns of trousers and shirts are advertised by exploiting sexy pictures of young girls, in order to entice the young. Indeed the Coca-Cola and dungaree culture is widely disseminated here by the West. Through the mass media a way of life and values that are actually opposed to Eastern lifestyles and religious morals are widely propagated. The process of cultural subversion is widespread. All this helps to weaken morals and religious convictions.

A deep sense of unease about the negative influences of traditional beliefs on one hand, and the evil effects of sensual imperialist culture on the other, has long been felt by some groups, including religious leaders. At the turn of the century there emerged people like Syed Sheikh Alhady and Sheikh Tahir Jalaluddin, who desired to see progressive changes among the Muslims here. They started movements which were inspired by Muslim reformists such as Jamaluddin al-Afghani and Muhammad Abduh, whose ideas – among them against imperialism – were beginning to be influential in the Middle East. Likewise both Syed Sheikh and Sheikh Tahir also regarded Islam as being opposed to colonialism and wanted to see the Malays rise and modernise on their own strength by following the tenets of Islam. They also maintained that traditional beliefs weakened the spirit of the Malays.

Syed Sheikh and Sheikh Tahir published books and magazines, opened schools and carried out polemics against what they considered to be wrongful practices among the Malays. They were often referred to as reformists (or *Kaum Muda*). The modernist movement was widespread not only in this country but also in Indonesia, where a number of such leaders accused of opposing the Dutch were arrested. In the Peninsula there were no known arrests, but the movement was obstructed, especially by the patrons and leaders of the new religious institutions which were encouraged by the British right from their early colonial intervention. The sultans, as head of Islam banned it in their states. A number of religious teachers or preachers from Indonesia, who were accused of bringing revisionist ideas of Islam, because of their modernist approach, were sent back to their own country. Probably the reformist movement was considered dangerous because it was beginning to challenge the *status quo*.

Partly as a continuation of this movement a political organisation orientated towards Islam was formed after World War II, known as Hizbul Muslimin. It was centred mainly in a religious institution of learning in Bukit Semanggol in Perak. The head of this institution by the name of Abu Bakar Bakir also became the leader of that organisation. Hizbul Muslimin cooperated with other political parties already in existence then, like the MNP, to fight for independence. When the Emergency was declared in 1948, Abu Bakar was detained with other independence fighters by the British and his organisation ceased to function.

But later its struggle was continued by PAS. A splinter group which split from UMNO also helped the formation and strengthening of this party. It managed to build its strength on the many religious institutions, especially the *pondoks*, *suraus* and mosques which existed in the rural areas in the states of Kelantan, Terengganu and Kedah. But at the same time strong association with these institutions made it rather conservative. Although after Merdeka Dr Burhanuddin Helmi, who was regarded as a modernist, took over the leadership of the party, it did not manage to shed its rather conservative orientation.

PAS participated in the struggle for independence; its aim then and now is to set up a government based on the principles and values of Islam. Although its constitution does not state explicitly the aim of forming an Islamic State, yet some documents produced by the party and statements issued by its leaders from time to time have resulted in the party being implicitly linked to that aim. It may be noted that around that time, the idea of an Islamic state was already much discussed among Muslim scholars, politicians and commentators in many parts of the world, particularly in the Middle East and South Asia.

Beginning the 1970s a new wave of development towards what appeared to be a religious revivalism among Muslims was discerned in this country. During the one or two decades prior to this, many Muslim countries (i.e. those with majority Muslim population) have been holding summit meetings in order to organise themselves as a united force. The struggle of the Palestinian people against Zionism and for their birthright had also given rise to a new consciousness among most Muslim states that they should be united in support of this struggle.

Some of the Arab states emerged as economic powers that could not be underestimated owing to their control over huge oil resources. Earnings from petrol enabled these states to help other Muslim and Third World countries, and also to support the Muslim missionary movements in various parts of the world. In many of these Muslim states there emerged organisations which carried out research and missionary activities that they considered to be essential to meet the ever-growing challenges of what they regard as destructive and decadent Western culture.

External developments have also had some influence over developments within the country. But even here conditions had already existed which encouraged religious missionary activities. There was a large body of people who were dissatisfied with the position of Islam in this country, even though it had been given official status by the Constitution. They saw that the new secular developments had weakened Islam among the Malays. They did not want to see Islam continue to decline and the Malays become more ignorant of its tenets. They were also unhappy over various influences that were undermining morality, especially among the young. There was growing opposition and revulsion against the influences that they associated with westernisation.

An interesting phenomenon was that the process of religious revivalism became active, particularly among young people and students in institutions of higher learning as well as graduates from these institutions. The outward manifestations of the turn to Islam could be seen in the adoption of attire that is considered to be more in line with Islam. Among the women the use of the headscarf (*tudung*) became more popular, while among some men the use of the Arabic coat (*jubah*) and the turban became more fashionable.

Other aspects of this movement were not entirely religious in nature, but had social and political implications as well. The increase in missionary (*da'wah*) groups and activities in this country had risen dramatically, especially after the May Thirteenth Incident. This traumatic event caused many people to revert to traditional beliefs which were felt to possess the potential for uniting the Malays, wherein unity is regarded as strength.

As we have seen earlier, it was during the National Operations Council (NOC) administration that PAS, which was regarded by many Malays as a champion of their rights and of Islam, cooperated with the Alliance in the National Consultative Committee (NCC), and later in 1974 joined the Barisan Nasional government. The move by PAS was looked upon by some of its followers as a betrayal of the original party policies. Following the NOC rule, issues such as the national language, Malay privileges and citizenship, which had often been raised by PAS before, were banned from public discussion. So, PAS was left only with religion through which to take up cudgels with the government. It was not surprising that some groups later raised the issue of religion to criticise the PAS leadership and the BN, and by so doing they claimed they were championing the cause of Islam.

Another factor which further strengthened the religious trend was the encouragement given by the government itself, which wanted to disseminate Islamic teachings among the Malays as a shield against what they warned as the threat of communist ideology. The Third Malaysia Plan expressed this succinctly in the passage that read: "An additional source of strength is that Islam and the other religions practised in this country continue to provide a strong bulwark against insidious communist propaganda. The youths in both rural and urban areas of the country have an important role in this regard".[11] According to government sources, even the communists at that time were adopting religion in order to gain influence.

Clearly the encouragement and motivation for the widespread religious activities and missionary movements of today were many and varied. The activities encouraged by socio-political factors could not have a lasting effect in the long run on the development of Islam within society or in the creating of a true Muslim. Those who were involved

---

11. Malaysian Government, 1976:101.

usually conceived of religion only as a political issue; as long as religion could draw support and votes, it would be exploited to the full. But after political success was achieved, what they could implement in the religious field was limited, limited by their own political stand and by the consideration of losses and gains if religious issues continued to be whipped up.

We have seen how PAS, in spite of its earlier claim to be the champion of Islam and the Malays, was not able to bring many significant changes consistent with Islam when it achieved power in Kelantan. Admittedly, under its administration certain open centres where immoral activities had been rampant were closed or brought under control. But obviously there was little it could do about those activities carried out behind closed door. The degree of religiosity among the people had not really been raised except in rituals. Criminal activities and drug abuse in the state are widespread among the Malays, although the sale of liquor to Muslims in the state is strongly and effectively prohibited. For about four years PAS was as a member of the BN government at the federal level, but this did not destroy its credibility as an Islamic party.

The problem was quite different for groups which carried out missionary activities with the idea of disseminating Islam without any involvement in party politics. Their activities had two objectives. The first was to strengthen religious convictions among Muslims who were encouraged to study Islam more deeply, to carry out its teachings, and as far as possible, to follow the path of the Prophet in their daily lives. It is true that among highly-educated youths and those in the upper and middle classes who used to be influenced by materialistic and western values, there was increasing number of those who turned to religion in a serious way.

But among many of them most of the activities were concentrated at the ritualistic and ceremonial level. Real knowledge about Islam was still lacking. That was why some of them were easily misled into extreme postures. Some mistakenly believed that a good Muslim must pray all the time, isolating himself from all worldly things, even leaving behind his responsibilities to family and society, and rejecting all the pleasures bestowed by God on this earth, in order to do missionary work in faraway places as encouraged by such movement as the *Tabligh* (which means missionary). This trend was then not widespread yet and many felt that it should not be encouraged by any religious movements today.

The second objective dealt with questions that were external to the self. Among many Muslims there exists the desire to establish an Islamic social system, and a state power based on the principles laid down in the Qur'an and the Hadith (Traditions). The groups which try to achieve this objective must first of all overcome the two problems which tend to weaken Islam: the negative influences of traditional beliefs and of westernised culture. Besides that they must be convinced that their objective is not merely a beautiful dream but actually something that can be achieved politically. What is meant by Islamic social, economic and political systems must be clarified, and the concept of the Islamic state must be explained thoroughly. It is not easy to wipe out the internal and external influences which weaken Islam. But it is more difficult to establish an Islamic social system and an Islamic state. This objective cannot be achieved merely by fervent missionary work, attractive ways of influencing people, or persuasive methods of winning over the minds of those in authority. It also needed power.

We saw that after leaving the BN coalition, PAS returned to its original path of fighting for Islam. But a large body of *ulama* (religious scholars), most of them more elderly, and the youths, were not particularly happy with the leadership of Asri Muda and his close associates who led the entry into the BN. They were considered not fervent enough. Furthermore, the effect of the Iranian revolution of 1979 was already felt in the country and it inspired a significant group within PAS to follow a more revolutionary and strictly Islamic path. Soon Asri was removed and replaced by a comparatively more radical Islamic group. When some of the leaders raised strictly religious issues that were associated with the Shariah, the party appeared to many as transforming more into a missionary rather than a political organisation.

Towards the end of the twentieth century and during the beginning of the twenty first, more young professionals joined PAS and soon they were elected into influential positions within the party. They were able to set a new direction that was consistent with the change that was already taking place within the party. PAS began to adopt some wider political issues, it was willing to tactically submerge the demand for the formation of an Islamic state in order to appeal support from non-

Muslims as well as the more secular-orientated Malays. It undertook organisational efforts to attract and accommodate supporters from the non-Muslim communities.

At the same time, there was also some change happening among the more well-known Muslim youth organisations, such as ABIM (Muslim Youth Movement of Malaysia) and JIM (Jemaah Islah Malaysia). The former had Anwar as one of its early founding leaders and most of its leadership consisted of local trained graduates, while the latter had foreign trained graduates – most of them professionals – as its leaders. When Anwar was sacked by Mahathir, ABIM which saw it as an unjust punishment appeared to give full support to Anwar, ADIL and also Keadilan later. JIM gave its support too but in a more limited way. Anyhow, a few leading ABIM and JIM figures continued to be in the leadership of Keadilan, even after these organisations resumed almost fully its long standing missionary and educational activities, as almost independent NGOs not involved in party political issues. I say almost because ABIM seemed to be showing more leaning to certain pro-government positions on an increasing number of issues, although it certainly has shown more commitment to Islam than UMNO of course.

Owing to pressures from PAS and some Muslim NGOs as well as the increasing groundswell support for Islam among the certain sections of the Malay populace, UMNO took the tactical political measures of integrating some Islamic values and programmes into the government and administration. Especially following Mahathir's success of enticing Anwar into UMNO and after the latter occupied many positions of influence, government servants were encouraged to study and practise Islam; Islamic secondary schools were set up that taught various aspects of Islam as well as the normal school subjects, the International Islamic University was set up in 1984 and Islamic banking and insurance were introduced.

Finally, Mahathir declared that Malaysia was indeed an "Islamic state", without explaining what it meant and on what basis he declared the country to be so. Afterwards, not long after he convincingly won the 2004 elections, Abdullah introduced his concept of 'civilisational Islam' which he called *Islam Hadhari*. This concept covers ten aspects that are normally within the scope of good governance, which Abdullah aspired to introduce under his rule, but it did not show clearly strong Islamic characteristics, let alone clear underlying Islamic principles.

After the 9/11 attack on the United States, Islam became demonised and Muslims were branded as terrorists. The war against terrorism, mainly so-called 'Muslim terrorists', spread all over the globe. This is not to deny that there were small groups of very radical Muslims who were turning to terrorism, some of them in order to counter state terrorism of the US and their own authoritarian states. In the Southeast Asian region, a number of radical Muslim groups were identified and some of them were linked with terrorist acts such as bombing of public places. In Malaysia, a number of individuals have been detained under the ISA on allegations that they were involved with so-called terrorist activities. None of them has been clearly and justly proven as having really committed any terrorist act.

These political responses to Islam by UMNO actually did not result in any positive basic changes that could be appreciated as being genuinely Islamic. Many anti-Islamic values and practices continue to prevail, in fact, in some cases have worsened. A few examples may be provided. Firstly, Islam does not allow for detention without fair trial, but the draconian ISA continues to be used, purportedly for maintaining order and security, but often more clearly to ensure the government continues to be in power. Secondly, corruption is condemned by Islam but it is increasing, and getting more rotten from the top downwards.

Thirdly, interest taking and greedily accumulating wealth through methods not considered consistent with Islamic teachings are forbidden by Islam. But all these immoral and un-Islamic practices and many more have been increasing, especially after Mahathir declared Malaysia to be an Islamic state and Abdullah pronounced his *Islam Hadhari*. Besides these, criminal acts of all kinds, like drug abuse, robbery, rape, murder and so forth have become more widespread, especially among the Malays (*see Table 13*). Ironically, these have increased almost directly as the government proclamations of commitment to Islam became louder.

In the final analysis it is clear that political power, although essential, is not sufficient for ensuring the establishment of Islam and the Islamic state. Those with power must have the full knowledge and commitment to it, besides possessing clear vision of exactly what ought to be done, especially in the context of a multi-ethnic and multi-religious society like Malaysia. It is at this point that the Muslim politicians and missionary activists would be faced with a dilemma. Do the missionary activists want to participate in politics? If they do, how and when should they begin? Is it by themselves or by affiliating with existing parties? As for the Islamic political parties, they must be clear as to what extent they can go. What should be the nature of their political philosophy? If based on Islam, what form should it take? Which model should it follow out of the various states which claim now to be based on Islam? Saudi Arabia, Iran or Pakistan? It is not possible to follow all at the same time. But which one should be chosen? If none of them should or could serve as a model, what then?

The Qur'an and Hadith provide only the foundation. But what sort of structure is going to be built upon it? All the above questions need to be analysed and answered. Unfortunately, different types of Islam propounded by different parties and other groups have caused much confusion among the ordinary Malays or Muslims. It is necessary to give clear and convincing answers and to demonstrate firm stands. These stands will determine the future positions of the missionary groups and the Muslim political parties in the country. The Muslim or Islamic politicians as well as the *da'wah* activist cannot afford to play hide-and-seek with politics much longer. Like the others, they have to think not only of their own interests and future but more so the interests and future of the people and the country at large.

5
STRUCTURE AND SOCIAL CHANGES

According to social scientists there are at least four important social groups in human society, each based on the following factors: (a) family, (b) locality, (c) ethnic background, and (d) shared interests. The family group is determined by sanguineal (blood) and affinal (marriage) relationships. There are small nuclear families comprising husband, wife and children, and there are big extended families consisting of husband, wife, children, parents, grandparents, grandchildren, siblings, in-laws and so forth. In some societies it is the family group that is most important. The family members carry out their socio-economic activities together, and if they do not have a fixed place to stay they move from one area to another without breaking up.

Groups based on locality factor (b) usually take the form of communities with fixed places of residence. They are much bigger than families and have more members. In any community there may be some who have family ties within the community while others do not. In addition, there may also be those who have relatives in different localities. In these cases it is the locality or place of residence that is the most important binding factor and which serves as a basis for social, economic and political activities.

Groups based on factor (c), which are based on common descent, are known often as ethnic or communal groups. They consist of members from different families and locality groups. Group members as well as non-members believe they have a common ancestry. They have strong group feelings, not only because of the common descent but also they inherit a common culture, religion and language. These common elements are often a pride to them and readily defended.

If an ethnic group can take a vertical form, an interest group (d) may be pictured horizontally. A society with different interest groups may be perceived as being stratified according to different status ranking. Economic and political power as well as social prestige are different from one group to another, and more often than not these factors are concentrated more in the higher than the lower strata. So, differences in interests may exist between different social strata, and similar interests may exist within the same stratum. Any society with different interest groups which can be ranked hierarchically is often said to be a stratified society.

In this chapter we shall turn our attention to groups (a), (b) and (d), concentrating mainly on their transformations and problems. The discussion on group (c) will follow in Chapter 8.

Before any misunderstanding arises it may be well to emphasise that each group need not exist separately. It is also untrue to say that only one factor determines or forms the basis of one group. For example, there may be locality groups whose members have close family relationships, and there may be locality groups that have economic, political and social differences existing to such an extent that we can clearly see its stratification system. A village society, for instance, is based on common locality, and whereas its stratification system may not be clearly seen or crystalised, more often than not its members have close kinship ties. In the same manner it is possible to have certain members in a particular interest group who form only one stratum in society having family ties. Furthermore, although it is common to have people of the same interest group living in a common locality, it is also possible to have them staying in different localities.

The point is that the type of group is categorised according to which factor is most dominant in determining its form. If the family factor is most dominant, and there is no basis for social stratification, then we say that the group is primarily a family group. But on the other hand if the factor of interest overrides all others in determining group formation, or if factors of kinship and locality further buttress the position of interest groups, then we say that the society has a stratified system where each stratum constitutes an interest group.

In the old Malay society, family and locality groups tended to dominate. During the Mesolithic age, for instance, it is believed that the social groups were in the form of extended families made up of a number of smaller families. But during the Neolithic period, these groups became bigger and more settled, forming communities by the rivers or coasts and in the middle of agricultural areas. Economic and social cooperation was carried out by members of the communities based on different factors, the most important being family ties. Differences in interests led to the formation of a stratified system. Therefore, there began to be members of the community who were looked upon as being of higher status or class than other members. This situation was clearly seen during the Melaka kingdom and also in other Malay societies before the arrival of British colonial rule. To facilitate discussion, the type of Malay social system existing before this colonial intrusion may be referred to as the traditional system.

The traditional Malay society may be said to have been feudal in form; it was strong and integrated at the height of the Melaka kingdom, but later weakened and disintegrated after the kingdom's collapse. Under the feudal system there existed two main strata of society, the ruling or upper class (*bangsawan*) and the ruled or lower class *(rakyat)*. The upper class was made up of the sultan, his family and chiefs. This group was rather small, but as already explained in Chapter 3, it had extensive political and economic power. Socially it was highly respected and a refined form of language was used for addressing its members. The lower class was made up of common people, including slaves. They lived outside the palace compounds, or in villages where they undertook agricultural or fishing activities. They did not have any political power and economically they often owned only enough land and equipment to provide for their own needs.

Between the upper and lower classes there was a wide social gap. The two groups did not mix. They lived separately, with the sultan and his family living inside the palace compound. Marriage occurred only among those of the same status, and usually these marriages further strengthened the social links among members of the upper class. Men from the upper class could take a wife or concubine from among the lower class women, but it was impossible for a lower class man to take a wife from the upper class. This was to preserve the royal descent, and it was this factor that determined the position inherited by a person, because status was ascribed.

Achievement was not important. But it was possible for a person from among the lower class to be presented with a new attire (*persalinan*) and appointed as chief because of the services he had rendered to the sultan. Upward mobility was difficult although it sometimes occurred. But downward mobility was more common. For instance, a once powerful ruler might slide down in prestige and power should he be defeated in battle, forcing him to live as a common refugee or even a slave to his conqueror. This uncertain situation was quite a common feature of the Malay sultanates, especially when they started to decline after the fall of Melaka.

Although it was clear that society was stratified, with the upper class having and controlling economic and political interests quite separately from the lower class, the family and locality factors still had some role to play. But these roles were different for different classes. For example, among the upper ruling class there existed strong family ties between its members, and these strengthened the solidarity of the class. But these family ties never cut across the social boundaries to reach the lower class. Likewise, among the lower class there was an important locality unit in the village, which indicated close kinship ties between some of its members.

On the basis of these social ties many activities were carried out by members of the same village, such as mutual assistance and feasting, and various forms of cooperation in the economic field. Besides that, they also participated in rituals that were organised amongst themselves. For example, before the fishermen went to sea or the farmers began a new planting of the rice fields or in order to drive away evil spirits believed to be the cause of illness, certain rituals would be performed by village members. With these social ties and mutual participation in ritualistic and economic activities, the relations among members of the village were further consolidated.

What about the position of women in society at that time? On the whole their status was low, but there were distinct differences in the context of the upper and lower classes. In the royal court a woman served merely as an adornment or as a source of entertainment. Members of the upper class, especially the sultan, always had an unremitting desire for beautiful women, whom they had the power to obtain. The queen usually had to share the ruler's love with his legal wives and numerous concubines. Some of them were presented to the ruler either as a sign of friendship or reverence, while others were forcibly taken away from their parents or husbands the moment they caught the ruler's eyes. Palace maids and servants also were forced to provide constant companionship and pleasure.

Among the lower class the position was somewhat different. Women played a key role in the family, serving their husbands and children and undertaking many domestic duties. They also helped in economic activities, such as planting paddy or harvesting. In certain communities which carried out small-scale trade, women participated actively. It cannot be denied that women were subordinate to, and dependent on men. As a group they had lower social status; by tradition they had to accept a lower status than their menfolk, but women in the lower class were, in many ways, nearly equal to the men in spite of the fact that they could be easily divorced by their husbands. The upper class ladies – including the sultan's wives sometimes – were treated as mere chattels and could be given away as rewards. There were, nevertheless, outstanding figures such as Permaisuri Tun Fatimah, who asserted her position in the face of her weakling consort.

Many changes took place after the coming of the British. Several factors influenced these changes, among them (a) urbanisation, (b) industrialisation, (c) administration and politics, and (d) education. Although these factors began to appear long before independence, all four played bigger roles after that period. Their effects on the social structure were many and have continued to this day. In the following pages these factors and their influences in society will be discussed without distinguishing between the pre- and post-independence periods. As we know, the process of change has been one of constant momentum and what exists today is, in fact, the climax of changes which have been building up till now.

I have explained earlier that, with the expansion of economic administrative activities under British rule, old towns grew and new ones emerged. Some Malays were drawn to these towns, attracted by new job opportunities there. But on the whole the percentage of the Peninsular Malays in the towns has not been large; in 1911 it was 17.8 per cent, in 1947 it was 17.4 per cent and in 1957 it was 19.3 The percentage of urban Malays for the whole of Malaysia are as follows: 21.7 per cent in 1970, about 40 per cent in 2006 and over 41 per cent as projected for 2008. Although at the beginning the percentage increase is small, recent figures show that the Malay urban population has increased quite substantially. The current government policy following the New Economic Policy seeks to open new towns in order to expedite the process of urbanisation among the Malays.

The British introduced rubber and further exploited the tin mining industry. But most of the workers employed in these industries in the early days were imported from other countries. In spite of the participation of some quasi-government bodies like State Economic Development Corporation (SEDC) and Permodalan Nasional (National Corporation) or PERNAS, the number of Malays working in mines has been small. Today, tin mining has almost stopped. Although rubber production is still important, it can be said to have been outstripped by oil palm. In estates, Malay workers made up only about 25 per cent of the total number of workers but they formed the majority in the small holdings.

Manufacturing activities were encouraged and many factories were opened during the last few decades in or near the towns of Kuala Lumpur, Georgetown, Ipoh, Seremban and Johor Bahru. Now they are situated in many smaller towns. These factories have opened up new opportunities for employment of Malay workers, and their relocation to their places of work also constituted a process of urbanisation. Malay women were also employed in some of these factories, especially the electronics and textile. Petro-chemical industries have also grown in importance.

Turning to the third factor, the new system of administration was introduced during British rule, and this also provided many job openings for the Malays. Many members of the upper class were recruited to be administrators under the British. Many more were taken into the clerical services. But the biggest number came from the lower class, recruited into the uniformed services of various types, from office boys and postmen right up to policemen and soldiers. Since the towns also served as administrative centres, the job-seekers in the administration became town-dwellers.

After independence the elite civil service (now known as Administrative and Diplomatic Service) was filled largely by Malays; there were further openings in the other services and the lower echelons. Now the administrative and diplomatic services, especially the upper echelon, may be said to be monopolised by Malays. But the most important element in the post-independence Malay society has been the emergence of new politicians. Political leaders of the governing parties hold high positions at the federal and state levels.

Finally, there is the factor of education. The British recognised that schools were needed to provide some education for those to be recruited into government service. Naturally priority was given to English-medium schools. Among the earliest schools that were set up was the Malay College at Kuala Kangsar (MCKK), the aim of which was to educate and train children from the upper class to become government servants. When the suggestion was made that the College, patterned after Eton, should open its doors to the common people, the dominant upper class opposed the idea, for they felt that each place given to a commoner would rob one of their own children of the opportunity. Of course there were other institutions of equal importance, i.e., Victoria Institution in Kuala Lumpur, King Edward VII in Taiping, King George V in Seremban and Clifford in Kuala Lipis.

The University of Malaya was established in 1949 in Singapore, and the University played a key role in producing graduates needed to fill the places left vacant by the expatriate officers. The Malay language began to take a more important place as the medium of instruction in the schools. More universities and colleges were built in the late sixties and early seventies; at present there are about 20 state universities and almost the same number of private universities or university colleges. All of them contribute to the pool of administrators, technicians and other professionals required in various spheres. At the same time graduate unemployment has also increased. There are at present about 100,000 graduates who are unemployed, a large number of them Malays.

As for the newly-emerging politicians, most of the early leaders received their education in Arabic or Malay. As the independence movement gathered momentum and UMNO was formed, a number of English-educated Malays, especially those who had received higher education in England, left the civil service which they had joined earlier, to take up its leadership. Later, particularly after the May Thirteen Incident, many graduates of local universities were encouraged and entered politics. Some of them have now become leading politicians either in the government or opposition parties. Most of the Malay- and religious-educated were pushed back to serve as middle-rung leaders. But a good number of the Arabic-educated, especially those graduating from the Middle East, have provided leadership for PAS.

Changes that have taken place can be examined from three aspects, namely, (a) transformations in the traditional social structure, (b) social problems that have arisen, and (c) new social groups that have emerged in contemporary society. Regarding (a), attention will be paid to the position of family groups. As for (b), a close look will be taken at the problem of slums, unemployment and crime; and regarding (c), new groups that have emerged and altered the stratification system will be examined.

Let us focus our attention now on the changes occurring in the traditional society. As has already been explained, the family and village groups were important in that society. In fact the influence of these groups is still strongly felt even now, especially among rural Malays. The reason is that the process of social transformation has not seeped deeply into the villages. But for the rural Malays who have migrated to the towns, the forms of family have changed somewhat. Among the urban migrants there are those who went alone first. Later they returned to the villages to fetch their wives and children, or to get married. But there are also those who marry urban girls working in the same place with them, but this tendency is not widespread yet.

The newly-weds set up their own homes far away from their relatives and villages. They form small nuclear families. In the towns, their families form part of the urban community, usually much bigger than their former village. Their neighbours are strangers, not relatives or long-standing friends, and their relationships with neighbours are often not very warm, although there is usually closer affinity and solidarity among ordinary working class families than among the more affluent families, whose affluent homes are often surrounded by high and strong walls. Life in the town can sometimes be lonely and so occasionally many of them return to their families in the village, especially during illness, before childbirth or during holidays to celebrate such festivals as the Eid or *Hari Raya*. But those who return to the villages are seldom the wealthy who make up the upper class. More often than not they go for holidays in other parts of the country or overseas.

Clearly the link with the village is still strong, especially among the lower and middle classes, even after living many years in the town. A young man or woman looking for a job in the town will often contact his relatives or friends in town, where he can expect free board and lodging while waiting to find employment. Sometimes, even after securing employment, they still try to rent or build a house near the relative's or friend's house. Because this happens quite often, we find that in certain towns, particularly in the slum areas, there exist communities where the people are related or at least come from the same state, if not the same village. In this way the atmosphere of their village of origin can be maintained. Such a continuation of the village social environment is also found in many of the Malay enclaves established in some of the towns. Besides that, the family and the village elements also have their influence on the upper class. Although not very common, we still find the practice of taking relatives or people from the same village or district for certain jobs. This practice is more widespread in political compared to administrative appointments. Even in the choice of Cabinet and Executive Council members, family relationship and place of origin continue to show some influence, sometimes leading to open nepotism.

The position of women has also changed. In the village a married woman usually helps her husband in the field. But in the town the wife, unless she is working, usually remains at home while the husband goes to work. A large proportion of women, especially from the lower and middle classes, do domestic work. They cook, wash, look after the children and serve their husbands when they return home. So they have become more tied to the drudgery of the kitchen. The upper class wives, because their husbands have high positions and salaries, can afford to have servants and maids, and thus they do not have to do domestic work themselves, although sometimes they render some help or supervision. They have plenty of free time which they utilise by involving themselves in voluntary organisations, doing welfare work and so forth.

Although some wives remain at home, there are also those who go to work, usually in places different from their husbands. The working husbands and wives meet at home only for brief periods, particularly when their working hours are different. This happens especially among workers in the lower class. Besides going out to work the women still have to look after the home. So the burden is much heavier on them than on the husbands.

At the same time women continue to be the objects and symbols of entertainment, though in a different form and style. Their physical beauty is often exploited like an ordinary commodity. They are often shown half-exposed in advertisements. There are also many women who fall prey to prostitution. The chauvinistic males within society look down rather contemptuously upon women as a whole. The degradation of women is also manifested in the practice of providing lower wages and less facilities to those who work. There are some industries, like electronics, which prefer to take women because they are hardworking and loyal, and because they do not involve themselves very much in trade union activities. They are badly paid.

On the other hand, there are also many women who have gone for higher education and can compete with men for high positions in administration and business. Nowadays there are more women in the universities than men and generally they achieve better results. Although their work and responsibilities are the same as those of men, in fact, sometimes they play better roles and perform better than men, yet the opportunities open to them for promotion and lucrative positions are limited. So generally speaking, the changes that have taken place continue to keep the status of women lower than that of men.

As for social problems, many have reared their ugly heads. In Chapter 2 it was pointed out that in the villages, poverty is still rampant, and the gap between the village and town folk, or the rich and the poor, is ever-increasing. Today, even though the incidence of poverty has been reduced significantly, yet there is still hardcore poverty in existence and relative poverty – the gap between the rich and the poor or the haves and have-nots – getting worse. The pace of migration from village to town is growing, due to growth of industries, administration and education.

Not all those who go to town possess adequate qualifications or manage to get good positions and high salaries, which will enable them to live comfortably. Many of the poor in the village come to try their luck in the town. They do not possess sufficient or sometimes any education at all. So, at best they become labourers, office boys, gardeners, drivers, guards, policemen, soldiers and the like. Because of their low incomes they cannot afford to rent or build a decent place to live in. That is why many of them land in slum areas which are found in abundance on the fringes of bigger towns.

Especially after the May Thirteen Incident the opening of many new slum areas in Kuala Lumpur and Selangor was encouraged by the local UMNO chieftains. As the flow of migration to urban areas increased, the slum dwellings became bigger and more numerous. For example, in the Federal Territory in 1973, the total number of squatter families reached about 36,000 with a total of about 200,000 people. This was more than 30 per cent of the total population of the territory. An estimate shows that more than about 20 per cent of the slum dwellers were Malays. By 1994 there were nearly 215,500 slum dwellers in Selangor and more than 184,000 in the Federal Territory. Now, despite forceful evictions of slum dwellers and others being transferred to new housing schemes, there has not been much decrease in their number. Many slum areas are still found in several towns, especially Kuala Lumpur, Johor Bahru, Ipoh and Georgetown.

Slum squatters continue to form the majority of the urban poor. The big majority are from the lower class with small incomes and little prestige, and although they live in the towns they lack modern facilities. In the slums there are often no proper roads and drains, the surrounding areas are full of rubbish, filth and dirty water. Life is miserable. The situation becomes worse because many of the young squatters are unemployed. They do not have much education. Employment is hard to find. In the village an unemployed person can still help in the field, but in the town unemployment means no job and no income. Unemployment gives rise to various social problems. One of the most serious is robbery, but there are other related criminal activities.

Unemployed youths have no income, but they have many needs. So they always feel oppressed. It is not difficult for them to gang up and indulge in drugs and crime. At first it may be done on a small scale, but later it can develop into something big and serious. Their parents cannot control them. It is true that the family can serve as a social control, but in the urban areas the traditional values that teach respect for the old have been much eroded. The sanctions in society which restrain a person from acting wildly have been weakened. The education system does not provide to help the young with strong ethical and moral values. So, once a social disease has set in, it easily becomes chronic and society itself feels incapable of curing it. Over and above these problems, the slum communities are not stable. On many occasions squatter homes have been demolished by the authorities. Some of these unfortunate squatters have been given small flats which are also lacking in facilities, or have shifted to other areas which are further away. Who are the poor who have to face the problems? Are they the victims of the policy of encouraging Malay urbanisation without planning for employment opportunities?

Among the young women and girls who have left their villages to work in factories, the problems are quite different. Usually, because of the small incomes that they earn, they have to share a house or room with their fellow workers. Life in the town, away from parental control, gives them a sense of false freedom. They readily imitate others to get some joy out of life, buying expensive dresses and going out with newly-acquired male friends. Unfortunately not all these men have noble intentions. Many a woman worker has fallen victim to some irresponsible young man and has been left stranded and pregnant, out of wedlock. There are quite a few men who act as pimps to drag the girls into prostitution.

Weak religious or moral principles, the sense of false freedom and the desire to "ensnare" a man in the wrong way, can lead these young women to all sorts of misfortunes. Many of them are sexually exploited by irresponsible pleasure-seekers, because in the town there is no protection at all for the young woman who has just left her village in search of her fortune. Of late, there has been an increase in cases of abandoned babies, a large number of them Malays.

Turning now to new groups that have emerged, we can discuss them within the framework of the system of social stratification existing now. Within this system three classes can be found, namely the upper, middle and lower classes. In traditional society the upper class consisted only of royalty and the chiefs, but at present there are other categories too, such as senior government politicians, administrators and entrepreneurs. The sultans still exist as symbols of sovereignty in the Malay states, while the governors head the former Straits Settlements of Penang and Melaka. The sultans and their families continue to enjoy a privileged position, but the influence of the chiefs can be said to have almost diminished.

Politicians have emerged as a significant phenomenon after independence, the most senior among them serving at national level as cabinet ministers and as executive councillors. Some of them have family ties with members of the traditional upper class. At present most of the leading politicians have plebeian backgrounds and have attained their position more through achievement than ascription. Some of them, who have reached the top, have their own cronies who have been helped or sponsored to be involved in big corporate enterprises, and they have succeeded to become prominent corporate figures. But a number of them have failed.

Administrators had already emerged and played a significant role during British rule. At the beginning, status or recruitment into the civil service was through ascription, but after independence higher education has become the most important factor determining the level of achievement. Following Malayanisation, many senior positions in the civil service, judiciary, military and police have been occupied by Malaysians, the majority of them Malays. Secretaries of ministries and their deputies, state secretaries, generals and senior police officers all make up the upper crust of the bureaucracy. As for the entrepreneurs, they are the most successful in business and industries; some of them are owners or directors of various companies. After independence their number has increased, many of them coming from the ranks of active government politicians or those who have retired from politics and administration. Nowadays they are closely associated with the powerful in government as well-known cronies.

The middle class which did not exist in traditional society has emerged now as a result of economic, politico-administrative and educational developments which took place during British rule and since independence. The middle class fills fewer political and social positions than the upper class but more than the lower class. Many of the Malays belonging to this class are government servants. This is because the Malays were always given preference in recruitment to the civil service, and after independence the Constitution fixed a quota of three Malays to one non-Malay in the service.

Although most officials in administration are Malays, in the professional fields their numbers are few, for example in 1973 only 13 per cent of the executives, 13.5 per cent of the engineers, 17.9 per cent of the accountants, 11.6 per cent of the scientists and 7.6 per cent of the doctors, are Malays (*see Table 10.1*). In 1997, the percentage of Bumiputera in various professional fields increased as shown in the following: engineers 37.0 per cent, accountants 15.7 per cent and doctors 31.3 per cent. By 2005 there was a further increase of the same professions to the following: engineers to 46.0 per cent, accountants to 20.8 per cent and doctors to 36.7 per cent. The increase was very much due to government policies of encouraging or sponsoring them (*see Table 10.2*). Many of these professionals work in the private sector, and they constitute an important category in the middle class of any society. In fact some of them can be categorised as being in the upper class. Other categories of people included in the middle class are those who are active in business and industries, serving as managers and executives. The Malays also form a small minority in this category, as observed in the same table.

Within the lower class, the biggest group is Malay. The two most important categories included in this class are the peasants and workers. The working class has emerged from the growth of towns and industries. The present-day peasants are the continuation of their traditional counterparts. They formed the largest economic category in the Malaysian society and until now their proportion is still big (59.7 prcent in 2000). A large number still concentrate on traditional paddy cultivation, but now nearly half of the Malay peasants are involved in cash crops like rubber and oil palm. They still live in the villages, but an increasing number have gone into new land settlements where community life is both more planned and organised.

The workers consist of two categories, namely, those working with the government and those in the private sector. Those in government service occupy lower positions as labourers or office boys in various departments, or as rank and file in the uniformed and armed services. As for those in the private sector, they work as labourers in estates and in factories. This group is increasing in size in Malay society, especially with the growth of industries in the urban areas. But to a certain extent their number has perhaps been diminished proportionately with the increase in the number of foreign migrant workers from Indonesia, Bangladesh and others. It is estimated that migrant workers in this country number more than two million. Some of them have entered without legal documents. Many of them have also opened up illegal settlements and housing.

The differences between one class and another within the stratification system, viewed from their political influence, type of work, amount of income and social prestige, distinguish them clearly as classes. This will be discussed further. For the time being it is sufficient to note that differences can also be seen between individuals and groups within the same class. For example, socio-economic differences can be seen clearly among the villagers, the majority of whom are peasants.

There are peasants who own land and those who do not. There are those who rent out part of their land or work on their own land, and those who work on land belonging to others. Their incomes, types of houses and lifestyles are quite different. In fact even the evaluation of members of the society according to their social positions is different; in other words, there are some who are more respected than others. Thus even among the peasants, people can be divided into the rich, middle or poor peasants. There are social scientists who further divide the upper class into the upper-upper and lower-upper categories, and also subdivide the middle and lower classes into the same type of two-layer category.

The existence of categories within each of the three classes does not reduce the significance or importance of each class as a social reality within the social stratification system existing in contemporary Malay society. The social distances between various classes are distinct, especially between the upper and lower classes. Just as in the days before British rule, the present upper class is also the focus of political, economic and social influence and power. Only two differences between that time and now can be perceived. First, although the sultans had real power previously, nowadays that power remains only as a symbol, because real power has been transferred to a new group. Second, if in the past power and influence tended to concentrate on the same person or group, nowadays there is specialisation; there are certain people or groups having only certain powers or influence in certain fields, for instance, the politicians in politics, the administrators in administration, and the capitalists in economics.

But between these groups there are overlapping areas which link them together. There are some politicians, although their number is decreasing, who have a traditional upper class background. There are senior politicians and administrators who involve themselves in economic activities, and as capitalists or entrepreneurs they try or hope to get the help of other politicians, for example for getting large bank loans, to enable their business or industry to succeed. As for the politicians, some of them look for aid or contributions from the capitalists when they want to improve their party's or their own financial standing. There are many ties of common interest which strongly bind members of the upper class. More and more now we find those with powerful political positions use these positions to acquire contracts and huge bank loans to strengthen their own or their nominees' economic positions.

Nowadays people are willing to use their wealth in order to obtain or improve their political position in the governing parties, through such well-known practice as money politics, because with important or strong political positions acquired they can easily amass more wealth. It is not surprising therefore that large scale corruption occurs between and among politicians and businessmen at the top. But corruption is not confined only to these groups; it is in fact widespread all the way down the line among all types of officers, especially those in the police, immigration and the administrative service, who form the middle and lower classes.

It is not surprising therefore that in recent years Malaysia's position has been sliding down according to annual studies carried out by Transparency International on perception of corruption in a number of countries, including Malaysia. One of the reasons why corruption is increasing has often been attributed to the failure of the Prime Minister to fulfill his 2004 election pledge to wage war against it.

Those in the upper class live in luxurious style. They have high incomes – from their honest earnings as well as from corruption that is rampant among them – which enable them to live in a more opulent style than other classes. In Kuala Lumpur and Selangor, they live in exclusive areas like Kenny Hill, Damansara Heights, Country Heights and other exclusive areas in Kuala Lumpur or Petaling Jaya. So too in the other towns, they also have posh areas for their residence. Their houses are big, complete with all kinds of modern equipment and sometimes decorated with expensive antiques. They become members of clubs which used to be exclusively for people with similar status, but slightly opened up to others now, such as the Lake Club and Royal Golf Club in Kuala Lumpur, for instance. Through these clubs they are also able to further strengthen their social relationships, occasionally drinking and golfing together, and sometimes discussing or even concluding political and business deals.

The middle class, as has already been mentioned, emerged only recently and is more prominent in the urban than the rural areas. There might be some similar characteristics between the lower-upper and upper-middle categories, or between the lower-middle and the upper-lower categories. In the rural areas the school teachers and moderate land owners may be categorised in the lower middle class. But in the urban areas, the professionals, civil servants and business executives are seen to be in the upper middle category. On the whole it can be said that the middle class stands out quite distinctly from the upper and lower classes.

Politically and administratively they do not have as much power as the ruling elite, most of whom are from the upper class. But they tend to be closely linked with the elite because they often provide services to this group. They sometimes serve as middlemen or even as leaders at the state or district level. Only a few of them, especially those from the professional group, have managed to achieve positions of national leadership. Economically their position is midway, their incomes being neither too high nor too low. In their daily life they are influenced by Western ways, probably as a result of the education that they received. But at the same time they are also attracted to some traditional ways. Some of them appear to have dual personalities because the opposite pulls of traditional and modern life, or between rural and urban values, often put them in a great dilemma. The middle class are often considered to easily "bend with the wind".

In contrast with the other two classes, the lower class has little or no power and influence at all in important economic and political spheres. They are only approached and persuaded to give their votes once in every four or five years during general elections or whenever there is a by-election. That is the only recognised influence that they have. Although this influence has powerful potential, yet the Malaysian voters have not used it for more than half a century to institute change of government. After the elections they are never asked about or consulted on any problem; everything is determined by the ruling elite from the upper class, who wield the real power and influence. The common factor among members of the lower class is their low position on the economic and social scale. Their living conditions are depressed and in sharp contrast to those of the upper class.

In the villages the peasants live in small houses or huts usually without piped water and electricity. There is little furniture or other equipment; very often they sit on the floor, sometimes using mats only when there are special guests or on special occasions. In the towns the workers live in small flats and barracks, or more often, in over-crowded slum areas. In terms of health, the slum environment is always miserable and oppressive. Development that has taken place has not only resulted in new class formations, but has caused the socio-economic gap of inequity between the rich and poor to be much wider. Further, the conditions of especially the poor in the lower and middle classes have worsened because they, their families and their children do not enjoy easy access to good schools and well-equipped hospitals, which are either far away or expensive.

Even though their life is difficult and their status low, most members of the lower class, especially the peasants and workers, do not yet have many common social ties or shared sentiments. First, they constitute a much bigger segment of society than the upper and middle classes and most of them are widely scattered, not concentrated in the towns. In fact, the poor are segmented. Second, although many of the workers who have drifted to the towns still have relatives and friends in the villages, they actually live in two different worlds. They work in places distant from one another and in different occupations; in the paddy fields or rubber smallholdings, and in factories or offices. Their social environments are no longer the same and thereby their attitudes and values become divergent. Politics among the two subgroups tends to emphasise their common ethnic identity, but seldom stresses their common fate and destiny as members of the lower class, as victims of exploitation and suffering.

The stratification system in Malay society is not static. In fact members of the same class are not always from the same family generation after generation. Generally the most important factors that influence social mobility today are education and politics. But they do not guarantee fully because there is large pool of graduate unemployment and politics do not always guarantee success. Mobility can occur within one generation or inter-generationally. There is a possibility for change to occur; some climb upwards, others slide downwards.

There is social mobility. For example, a few from the peasant background may succeed in higher education and get into jobs which elevate them to the middle class; they may be teachers or administrative officers, for example, who succeed in politics, eventually becoming even ministers (as in some rare cases), and thus moving into the upper class. On the other hand, there may be some members of the royalty who will slide downwards and end up having nothing except their royal titles, which in themselves are insignificant. Then there may be businessmen who become bankrupt and end up as manual workers. But on the other hand, there have been cases of a few prominent corporate figures who have lost their position and whose corporations have gone bankrupt, but they themselves remain personally wealthy and so have been able to maintain their lifestyle.

Although social mobility exists and there is opportuniy for those in the lower class to climb upwards, this opportunity is limited. Within the same generation the opportunities for those in the upper class to strengthen their own positions are better than the opportunities of their counterparts in the other classes to move upward. For example, an ex-minister or retired senior civil servant can easily sit on the board of foreign or local companies or in statutory bodies. In this way he merely changes role without affecting his class position.

In Malay society today, a handful of retired officers and politicians almost monopolise most company directorships. A study of the Registry of Companies shows that out of 1,526 Malays who have become directors 45 persons (or 3 per cent) own shares valued at $7,480,000 or 50 per cent of the shares of all registered Malay directors, and many of these were in politics or administration before. Of course the number now is more and the shares that they own are much bigger. Members of the middle class, who do not have influence or political ties, cannot hope to have such opportunities. As for those in the lower class, barring very exceptional cases, they have no chance whatsoever to become a company director.

Where individual families are concerned one can assert that a large number of children inherit their parents' jobs. Children of businessmen often become businessmen and many children of doctors often become doctors, just as there are a number of children of senior politicians in government now who are children of prominent politicians too. On the other hand, there are considerable numbers of children of policemen who become policemen, while paddy cultivators tend to follow in their parents' footsteps, although nowadays there is a large number of young people who have abandoned work in the paddy fields in search of better opportunities elsewhere.

Much depends on whether a father can afford to give his children the facilities for improvement. A businessman can train his son and provide capital for him to become a businessman. But can a policeman provide the same opportunities for his son? A doctor can afford to send his children to a well-established school and good tuition centres, in fact, they often can supervise the children's study at home. But a peasant must be satisfied with an inadequately equipped and poorly staffed rural school for his children. Being himself uneducated, he is unable to supervise the children at home. In a competition between the doctor's and the peasant's children, under normal circumstances, the former will easily win. Granted that there are also peasant children who have succeeded in becoming doctors while children of doctors have failed, but such occurrences are relatively rare and the safe guess is that the percentage involved may not be very significant.

The opportunity for upward mobility among Malays, through education and business in particular, is much wider now than ever before, owing to the availability of scholarships for higher education and loans of capital as well as sponsorship and other kinds of support to help them succeed in business. Since much depends on aid and sponsorship, perhaps that is why mobility among Malays now is often referred to as "sponsored mobility". This is made possible by the provision of Malay privileges as enshrined in the constitution.

However, the number and amount of aid available is still limited. Scholarships and bursaries can be given to those entering colleges and universities, but the majority of children of peasants have problems even entering good secondary schools. Loans of capital cannot be given just to anybody requesting them. In the last analysis those who have influence or property that can be used as security are the ones who get aid. It is not easy for a peasant or a worker to get bank loan to buy a low cost house, even if he is a Bumiputera.

Sponsored mobility, made possible by various types of aid and loans, can be defended only as a short-term policy. It can increase the number of people in the upper and middle classes slightly. But it does not change the structure of Malay society; the stratification into upper, middle and lower classes continues, with the lower class still forming the majority. The lower class does not want special privileges which exist only in theory, which they are denied due to the monopoly of the upper and middle classes. What they really need is more equality of rights and opportunities which will place them on par with members of the middle and upper classes, especially in the realms of politics, economics, education, health and so forth. The discrimination against these people which exists simply because they are the lower class must end.

Thus we see clearly that in the existing social system, special privilege is enjoyed mainly by a small minority from the upper class. Many of them enjoy these rights and opportunities not because they merit these privileges, but because of their class position in the society. There are many from the lower and middle classes who show greater ability and merit, but they are unable to manifest them owing to the inherent obstruction of the class system.

It is clear that there is need for this class barrier to be torn down so that all the potentialities of the lower class can be liberated and manifested in full. The likelihood of this happening is greater when government plans and policies for development focus more on the lower class, to help the poor and the disadvantaged. Obviously such plans and policies could benefit the ordinary Malays more, because they form the majority of the lower class, but at the same time they would not exclude non-Malays from the same class to benefit too. ❈

6
WEALTH, EXPLOITATION AND THE ECONOMY

In the preceding chapters we have touched on some facets of the economy. Some of them will be referred to again here in greater detail. It has been explained that at the early stage of the development of Malay society, during the Neolithic period, its social system was simple. There were two stages of economic development then. First came the hunting and collecting stage, when much of the life in society was determined by the environment. After this came the second stage of crop cultivation and animal domestication. During this stage there were many who were already able to control or adapt the environment to serve their own purposes. In both these stages the objective of production – whether hunting, collecting, cultivating or domesticating – was to meet the requirements of life in the society itself.

Production was for consumption and the unit of production was also the unit of consumption; these units were in the form of families, smaller during the first stage, but bigger during the second. There was close cooperation among members of society, and society's produce was shared and enjoyed by all of them. Usually production was just enough to meet the basic needs of society, and if there was a surplus it was kept for their own use. There was no effort to produce surplus for exchange simply because the situation did not demand exchange; society was self-sufficient and channels for such exchange just did not exist.

But gradually the situation changed. Surpluses began to be produced as agricultural production developed and social groups became bigger with chiefs or rulers as their leaders. Part of these surpluses was submitted to the leader in the form of taxes or gifts and part of it was bartered or traded. At the beginning the exchange was on a small scale, usually between neighbouring groups. It was not centralised. But later, particularly during the time of the Melaka kingdom, trading activities were carried out on a large scale.

Melaka was the trading centre for neighbouring areas as well as the focal point where the faraway countries from East and West met. Among the main commodities of trade were spices, tin and textiles. The traders recognised the sovereignty of the ruler and paid taxes of up to 10 per cent to him to enable them to participate in the trade economy. The foreign traders were provided with special areas from which they organised their business, and the sultan appointed an officer called the *Syahbandar* to oversee them.

The economic position of the rulers and chiefs of Melaka became stronger with the increase in trade. But their strength had other bases as well. In Melaka and its territories, most of the common people carried out agricultural activities, and they could be mobilised to pay taxes or send tribute to the rulers and chiefs. But usually the rulers or chiefs had their own entourage consisting of slaves or indentured servants who worked on the royal lands. The wealth accumulated by the rulers and chiefs was often used to beautify their palaces and glorify their way of life, in keeping with their rank and position. Part of their riches was kept in the form of gold, silver, jewellery and other valuables; and among other things these riches could be used for "financing" war, but never as a source of capital investment for any major economic undertaking.

However, both the political and economic situation disintegrated after the fall of Melaka to the Portuguese. Various minor rulers or chiefs set up their own little kingdoms, usually at a river mouth, where they could control traffic, and collect tributes and taxes from people in agriculture or trade. These rulers and chiefs continued to maintain their entourage, some of whom worked on the land. In addition to this, the Chinese worked in tin mines in some parts of Perak and Selangor. Some rulers or chiefs owned a few mines and earned quite substantial incomes from them. But there were also other mines which were leased out and only provided revenue to the rulers and chiefs in the form of taxes. What was clear was that, after the fall of Melaka and right up to the British intervention, the Malay economy was dependent mainly on agriculture and trade, while the rulers and chiefs continued as the elite group controlling the economy as well as politics.

What happened after the British came? By the time the British decided to intervene in the Malay states, they had already reached their peak as an imperial power, controlling a huge empire overseas. With the industrial revolution, a new capitalist class had emerged in England and they had widespread influence throughout the government. The British capitalists and banks had financial surpluses, which they could invest in the colonies to develop primary industries in order to produce the raw materials required by the British factories. Companies owned and controlled by the British were launched in the Peninsula during the early decades of the last century to run tin mines, rubber estates and agency houses.

British capital here increased quickly and by the 1920s it amounted to about $1,680 million, nearly half of which was invested in rubber estates.[12] Most of the estates were big, over 2,000 acres, with some over 5,000 acres, and they were in the most fertile areas. The mines were in the richest zones, using machines and technology that had never been seen here before. It was interesting to notice that the structure of the organisations was such that many of them had interlocking directorships, i.e. over the banks, plantations, and agency houses. The British had very tight control over the entire structure.

The development of mines, estates and commerce strengthened the capitalistic enterprises of this country. The system expanded slowly but steadily and enormous profits accrued from the investments. Until the outbreak of the Pacific War, the British were very prosperous. Tin and rubber were and still in great demand in the world market, although in Malaysia tin production has declined in importance now. These industries also attracted Chinese and Indian entrepreneurs, but their participation was limited as they could not mobilise the large amount of capital needed, as the British had.

With a few exceptions most of the rubber estates they owned were of medium size, rather large smallholdings actually, while the mines were relatively small, without modern machinery or technology, such as the dredge. In commerce, especially in the rapidly growing urban

---

12. Callis, 1942.

centres, shops carried out the business of selling commodities required by the community. Most of these shops and small companies were owned by Chinese and Indians. Besides that other traders had also moved into the rural areas to start businesses there. These traders later became middlemen who bought rural produce to sell in towns, and bought imported goods to sell in the rural and town areas. These traders, as middlemen, constituted a vital link in the long chain connecting the village economy with that of the local town and the countries beyond.

At the beginning Malay involvement in estates and commerce was virtually non-existent, even on a small scale. Most Malays lived in rural areas, and were involved with traditional agriculture. They not only lacked capital but also the skill to do business. Life in the village fulfilled most of their needs. On the other hand, the Chinese and Indians had left their homes as pioneers in search of a better life, and many of them were willing to try anything that could bring them quick wealth. In addition, some of the Chinese who wanted to start business easily obtained aid from their clan organisation in the form of loaned capital. Such facilities did not exist for the Malays.

It would not be true to say that the Malays do not have any business tradition. Since long ago Malay traders had sailed the seas. They were prominent during the heyday of Melaka. But most of the trade they undertook was in the form of barter, and often under the patronage of the upper class. With the coming of the Europeans the economic position of the rulers and chiefs was weakened considerably, and under the British administration they had to depend mostly on their pensions.

The British had introduced a money economy, in which money became the main form of capital. In the past, surplus income was used by members of the upper class to add greater opulence to their way of life, not for investment; in fact, forms of economic activity requiring financial investment hardly existed then. When the British introduced new economic activities the ruling class had already lost much of its financial strength.

If there was any change for the rural Malays as a result of the new economic system brought by the British, it was in their participation in cash crop agriculture. Rubber clearly could produce more income than *paddy*. In many newly opened areas rubber was encouraged, and even in some established *paddy* areas, rubber was planted as a supplement. Rubber, unlike *paddy*, cannot be consumed and has to be sold; the financial proceeds from the sales in turn are used to purchase food and other commodities needed. This further extended the money economy, and the role of middlemen in the rural areas thus became more important. The significant participation of rural Malays in estates and mines was as labourers, but their number was small compared to the Indians and Chinese. But before the British came into the Peninsula, there were some traditional chiefs in Perak who owned tin mines.

The British had encouraged Indians to migrate from southern India to become workers on their estates, and Chinese from southern China to work in the mines. They did not employ the Malays, in line with the policy that Malays should continue doing traditional agriculture – for otherwise who would produce the rice? They also believed that the Malays made neither hardworking nor stable labourers since their family links to their villages were strong, allowing them to quit or return home whenever they wished. It was difficult for the Chinese and Indians to do so because their homes were far across the sea. At the same time, it could be said that such division of labour could have been deliberately done by the British because it would facilitate them to carry out the divide and rule policy. Finally, the Malays also showed some preference for such jobs and more preference later for those as office workers and policemen, for example.

The spread of a money economy into the rural areas had some adverse effects on the people who engaged in traditional occupations like *paddy* planting, fishing and rubber tapping. In the *paddy* areas particularly, there was quite an acute shortage of land. The opening of new land could not keep up with the increase in population because many areas traditionally under *paddy* had been exhausted. Land had not been a problem previously, but after World War II the situation worsened. There were many villagers who had to sell their land owing to financial difficulties. The transfer of land through sales was quite common not only among the *paddy* farmers but also among the rubber cultivators. But now there is a lot of idle land because many among the young have migrated to the towns to get more lucrative jobs.

Among those who had the means to purchase land were the middlemen, who often acted as creditors as well. They often bound the villagers with debts, and this often led to the villagers being forced to sell or mortgage their land. There were also other groups of creditors. At the same time there were also small groups of well-to-do villagers who were in the position to save money and buy land for the purpose of accumulation. Most rubber producers had to sell their rubber, and even some *paddy* cultivators had to sell part of their produce. The prices offered to them were determined outside the agricultural communities themselves, and by middlemen who were deeply rooted in the villages. When the villagers were bound by heavy debts to the middlemen then the prices of their produce could easily be fixed by the latter.

As a result of the land shortage and of financial exploitation, the life of the poor villagers became more depressed. The differences between villages and towns, and between the poor and the rich became more marked. These contrasts could be seen not only in their incomes and lifestyles, but also in the facilities available to them such as schools, hospitals roads and electricity. Even within the rural areas the gap became wider, especially between the "haves" – such as middlemen and landlords – and the "have-nots", mostly those who owned little or no land, and as a result had to work on other people's land as sharecroppers, rentiers or wage earners.

For a long time the socio-economic inequity between the haves and have-nots largely cut along ethnic lines between the Chinese and the Malays. But nowadays there is growing tendency for such inequity to also develop intra-ethnically within the Malay community. For example, the Gini coefficient (which shows economic gap) among Malay/Bumiputera was quite high in 1970 (0.466) and went down significantly in 1990 (0.429), but went up again in 2004 (0.452).

After independence several political and administrative changes took place following the transfer of power from the British. But the economy changed very little, for the economic system established by the British continued. Estates, mines and commerce that were owned by the British continued to be controlled by them. So too were many of the big companies and agency houses. For instance, at one time Harrisons and Crossfield controlled about 200,000 acres of rubber estates, Guthrie Corporation about 180,000 acres and Sime Darby Group about 160,000 acres. Guthrie was later taken over from the British in what was known as a "Dawn Raid".

Sime Darby, Guthrie and Golden Hope recently merged to become the biggest plantation entity in the country, under the name of Sime Darby. The total area controlled by these three companies was equivalent to about 860 square miles, bigger than the area of Perlis, Penang and Province Wellesley, which covers only 800 square miles. Besides estates, they also owned or controlled some big mines and commercial houses and served as agency houses. Their profits were large; for instance, Sime Darby made $15 million in 1970, and this increased to $60 million 1973 and $184 million in 1978, while Guthrie made $40 million in 1970 and about $45 million in 1978.

In 1970 figures showed that the total share capital amounted to $5,329 million, divided as follows: foreign capitalists $3,377 million (63.3 per cent); Chinese ownership $1,450 million (27.2 per cent) and Malay interests $125 million (2.4 per cent). In the same year the proportion of Malay ownership in agriculture (i.e. estates), mining and commerce was less than 1 per cent; in manufacturing, banking and insurance between 1 per cent and 3.5 per cent, and in transport a sizeable 13.3 per cent.

In all sectors except transport, foreign ownership ranged from 50 per cent to 75 per cent. According to Raja Mohar Raja Badiozzaman, the government economic adviser under the premiership of Razak Hussein and Hussein Onn, some foreign investors earned profits as high as four times the amount they invest. In April 1976 the Deputy Finance Minister told Parliament that profits and dividends earned by foreign investors were $435 million in 1966, $555 million in 1969, $1,342 million in 1974 and $1,017 million in 1975. In 1995 the share capital in limited companies as estimated for the Peninsula amounted to RM179,792.2 million. The estimated amount owned by foreign capitalists was roughly RM49,792.7 million (or 27.7 per cent) compared to the Malay interests if RM36,981.2 million (or 20.6 per cent), Chinese RM73,552.7 million (or 40.9 per cent) and Indians RM2,723.1 (or 1.5 per cent). By 2004, the estimated totals of share capital at par value was RM529.8 billion, made up of 18 per cent owned by Malays, 40.6 per cent by non-Malays and 32.5 per cent by foreigners. Recent figures show that the pattern of foreign ownership has changed due to the changing pattern of foreign investment in the country.

In 2002 the five biggest sources of foreign investments were Germany, USA, Singapore, Netherlands and Japan, amounting to US$1,330 million, US$702 million, US$268 million, US$160 million and US$155 million respectively. But by 2005 the situation changed as follows: USA (US$1,357 million), Japan (US$966 million), Singapore (US$768 million), Netherlands (US$441 million) and Korea (US$177 million). According to the American Chamber of Commerce survey in 2005 the total US interests in Malaysia was US$30.0 billion, mainly "in the oil and gas sector, manufacturing, and financial services".

At present, a large proportion of the Malays still concentrate on small-scale agriculture in the rural areas. Of course the proportion is much smaller than in the past. Most of the planting, mining and commercial activities began and developed in the Federated States, especially Perak and Selangor; however, substantial amounts of trading were undertaken throughout Penang and much rubber was planted in Johor, besides the Federated States.

But in the Unfederated States agriculture still predominated, mainly *paddy* planting in Kelantan, Kedah and Perlis, although some was undertaken in Perak and Melaka too. These planting, mining and commercial activities did not take place in the villages, and so did not bring direct benefit to the villagers. As such, the rural Malays continued to be concentrated in states and areas that were relatively undeveloped and considerably backward. They spent most of their time in traditional agricultural activities such as rice cultivation, which has low productivity.

In the four states which received little development, more than 70 per cent of the population are Malays: in Terengganu 93.9 per cent, in Kelantan 92.8 per cent, in Perlis 79.4 per cent and in Kedah 70.7 per cent (*see Table 2.1 and 2.2*). In terms of distribution of population more Malays live in the rural areas than other races; i.e. 85.1 per cent of Malays live in these areas, while the remaining 14.9 per cent are in the urban areas, which are gazetted as those having a population of more than 10,000 (*see Table 3.1 and 3.2*). Most of the villagers engaged in agriculture, and normally the size of land they worked was very small.

According to the Agricultural Census of 1961, out of 454,000 farms registered in the Peninsula, 48 per cent were less than 3 acres, 20 per cent from 3 to 5 acres, 20 per cent between 5 and 10 acres, and 12 per cent between 10 and 99 acres. No up-to-date figures are available, but presumably the pattern has not changed very much. This is the distribution according to the size of farms and not according to ownership of land (*see Chart 1*). There was an estimate which indicated that about 25 per cent of the cultivators do not own land and so have to work on land belonging to others. As in the past, a large proportion of the rural people work on their own land of three to six acres, their main activities being rubber tapping and *paddy* planting. Compared with the other ethnic groups involved in agriculture the percentage of Malays is much higher in *paddy* than in rubber.

It has been admitted that poverty is a major problem facing this country. Based on the government's own studies, in 1970, 791,800 out of 1,606,000 households in the Peninsula or 49.3 per cent were poor. The incidence of poverty was 58.6 per cent in rural areas and 24.6 in the urban. By ethnicity the poverty incidence was highest among the Malays (64.8 per cent), followed by Indians (39.2 per cent) and Chinese (26.0 per cent) (*see Table 6.1*).

Five years later it was found that the incidence of poverty in the Peninsula had gone down to 43.9 per cent although the total number of poor household had gone up to 835,100. Out of this the proportion of the poor in the rural areas was about 54.1 per cent. The percentage of those in the rural areas carrying out agriculture was 63 per cent. The proportion was higher among *paddy* cultivators (77 per cent), followed by fishermen (63 per cent) and rubber small-holders (59 per cent). The states which had poverty percentages higher than the national figure of 43.9 per cent were: Kelantan 65 per cent, Perlis 59 per cent, Terengganu 55 per cent, and Kedah 48.9 per cent.[13]

The figures in 1999 show a greatly different picture. The total number of Malaysian households was about 4,800,000, out of which 409,300 (or 8.5 per cent) were poor. In the rural areas there were 323,200 households (14.8 per cent) that were poor. By 2004, out of all 5,459,400 households, 311,300 (or 5.7 per cent) were poor. The percentage of the poor in the rural areas was 11.9 per cent and in the urban area 2.5 per cent. Poverty is still a serious problem in the villages, but the worst conditions are in the hinterland Kelantan, Kedah, Terengganu, Sabah and Sarawak. (*see Table 5*)

---

13. Anand, S., 1973:52

In 1999 the overall incidence of poverty for Malay/Bumiputera, Chinese and Indian was 12.4 per cent, 1.2 per cent and 3.5 per cent; whereas in 2004 it was 8.3 per cent, 0.6 per cent and 2.9 per cent. Comparing rural-urban categories by ethnicity, we find that in 1999 the poverty incidence for the Malay/Bumiputera, Chinese and Indians was 17.5 per cent, 2.7 per cent and 5.8 per cent, while for 2004 it was 13.4 per cent, 2.3 per cent and 5.4 per cent respectively (*see Table 6.2*). When we talk about rural poverty we really mean Malay/Bumiputera poverty, since large majority of the rural people are Malays and Bumiputera or *Orang Asal* (indigenous people) in the hinterland of Sabah and Sarawak. But this does not deny the fact that there are also non-Malays in the rural areas and new villages and many of them are poor too. However, their number is comparatively much smaller.

Poverty also exists in the towns, but according to the 1975 estimates the number was only 105,200 households or 12.6 per cent of the total number of poor in the country. The percentage of poverty amongst the town population that year was about 19 per cent. Figures in 1999 showed that the number (and percentage) of the urban poor went down to 86,100 households (3.3 per cent). By 2004 the percentage went down further to 2.5, although the absolute number was bigger, i.e. 91,600 households (*see Table 5*). Most of them lived in the urban squatter (slum) areas. Clearly, the incidence of poverty in the towns is comparatively much smaller than in the villages, and in the towns the Malays form a minority.

The criterion used by the government to measure poverty is income. At present a household of five is considered to be poor if its monthly income averages around RM500. (In 1997 it was RM460 for Peninsular Malaysia, RM633 for Sabah and RM543 for Sarawak, based on the household size of 4.6, 4.9 and 4.8 respectively). Let us now examine the distribution of incomes in the country, bearing in mind the poverty line of RM500 per household per month. We will look at the earlier figures for the purpose of comparison.

In 1970 the average household income in the Peninsula was $264, but the urban average was $428, while the rural one only $200. Out of all households in the Peninsula 27 per cent earned less than $100 and 31 per cent earned between $100 and $200; in other words 58 per cent of all households earned less than $200 per month. About 90 per cent of those earning less than $100 and 76.2 per cent of those earning between

$100-$200 came from the rural areas. In the rural areas, 82.6 per cent of the households earned less than $200 while those earning less than $100 accounted for 34 per cent. Since most of the rural households are Malay, it is not surprising that the average income of the Malays was low – $172 per month per household – compared to the figures for the Indians and Chinese which were $304 and $394 respectively.

By the year 1997 the gross average income for the whole of Malaysia was RM2,607, whereas the amount were RM2,038 for Malay/Bumiputera, RM3,737 for Chinese and RM2,896 for Indians. In the urban areas the average monthly incomes for the whole country was RM3,406, with the averages for Malays, Chinese and Indians being RM2,769, RM4,071 and RM3,291 respectively. As for the rural areas the average income for the whole country was RM1,669, while the averages for the various ethic groups were RM1,498, RM2,668 and RM2,019 for the Malay/Bumiputera, Chinese and Indians respectively.

The latest figures for 2004 showed that the average monthly income for each household for the country as a whole (at current price) was RM3,249, with households in the town averaging RM3,956 and those in the rural areas much lower at RM1,875. The average household income distribution according to ethnicity was as follows: Malay/Bumiputera (RM2,711), Chinese (RM4,437) and Indians (RM3,456). All these figures show that the Malays have the lowest incomes compared to the other ethnic groups (*see Table 7.2*).

It is well-known that average incomes do not reveal the reality of income differences existing in society. Whether in the rural or urban areas, among the Malays or non-Malays, there exist large income disparities due to such factors as occupation and ownership of property or capital. The seriousness of the problem can be seen from the following figures. In 1957 the 20 per cent of the households who earned the highest incomes, accounted for nearly 50 per cent of the total income in the country, while the 60 per cent who earned lower incomes, accounted for only 30 per cent of all income.

The situation deteriorated in 1970, when the incomes controlled by the top 20 per cent had risen to 55.7 per cent, while incomes of the middle 40 per cent and the bottom 40 per cent were 32.9 per cent and 11.5 per cent. In 1990 the distribution was 50.4 per cent for the top 20 per cent, 35.3 per cent for the middle 40 per cent and 14.3 per cent for the bottom 40 per cent. By the year 2002 it had further worsened. The incomes controlled by the top 20 rose slightly to 51.3 per cent of the total income, the 40 per cent in the middle range accounted for 35.2 per cent and the lowest 40 per cent accounting for only 13.5 per cent of the total. The Gini coefficient rose from 0.429 in 1990 to 0.452 in 2004, showing that the economic gap had increased.

Furthermore, between 1957 and 1970 the average income for the top 10 per cent rose from $776 to $1,130, while that of the lowest 10 per cent had fallen from $48 to $38. Then between 1990 to 1995 the mean incomes for the top 20 per cent rose from RM5,202 to RM6,268. The mean incomes for the lowest 40 per cent dropped from RM867 in 1997 to RM865 in 1999. Who forms the group with the lowest incomes at the bottom category? Which group's income declined during those periods? The answer is simple: the majority of them were Malays. Actually, even the mean incomes do not tell the truth because they hide the fact that a large amount of wealth and capital are concentrated in the hands of only a handful of multi-millionaires and billionaires made up of different ethnic groups, the majority of whom happen to be Chinese. The question now is, when the national per capita incomes rise from year to year, do the incomes of those in the lower strata, whether they are Malays, Chinese, Indians, Ibans and Kadazandusuns, also increase?

The clear, incontrovertible fact is that the reverse happens. The poor become poorer. Those who really benefit from the rising national incomes are those in the upper strata of society. Thus, the gap between the upper and lower classes, between the rich and the poor, becomes ever wider. So, whereas absolute poverty has improved over the years, relative poverty has worsened. With this kind of adverse development, it looks like the group of hardcore poor will remain for a long time.

There is yet another factor that tends to worsen the poverty situation of the people. This is the ever increasing inflationary trend that is manifested in the rising prices of commodities, particularly the daily needs. Of late inflation has resulted from increase in the prices of petrol and diesel as well as charges for highway tolls. Of course it may be argued that these increases affect all categories of the population. But certainly the burden is much heavier on the poor than the rich.

The real incomes of the former will drop much faster than the increase of their incomes. On other hand companies and businesses, which are synonymous with the capitalists who control them inevitably manage to reap huge profits from the increases of the different prices and rates. So, besides making life more difficult for the poor, inflation can have the effect of widening further the socio-economic gap.

Poverty and increasing economic disparity are actually the result of the present economic system based largely on the *laissez faire* philosophy, which has been since from the colonial days. This philosophy was widespread in the West, particularly in Britain in the nineteenth century, when its economy was growing and its empire expanding. The main feature of this philosophy is that economic activities and those undertaking them should be free from government control or interference. The economy is supposed to be free, with free market competition being encouraged, for the purpose of producing high quality goods, as well as for controlling the market.

The criteria for success is the amount of profits made; the bigger the profits the greater the success. In this competition the success of one group in defeating another can lead to monopoly. Monopolists can have absolute power to do anything necessary to ensure maximum profits, thus proving their success. Monopoly-capitalists can fix high prices for their produce and low incomes for their workers. As a result there will be concentration of wealth on one hand, widespread and acute exploitation and poverty on the other.

It is to be expected that the *laissez faire* system is preferred by those already in strong economic or political positions, because in any competition they can always emerge the victor. We have seen how the British colonialists, with political power in their hands, could easily control the rich economic resources in the country: the estates, mines and commerce. They made huge profits, the bulk of which was taken back to their own country and very little used for the development of the colonies.

Economic power in the hands of the British monopoly-capitalists continued even after independence. The *laissez faire* system which became well-rooted during British rule has remained. Consistent with this economic system, the private sector plays a big role, and large investments are needed in this sector from local as well as foreign investors. Foreign investment is most welcome, and encouraged with all kinds of incentives such as pioneer status. But as we have seen earlier in this chapter, although in the past British investment here exceeded any other, the Americans, Japanese and Australians are also making headway now.

Admittedly, the system practised in this country is not totally *laissez faire* in nature, because there is also some amount of state intervention in certain sectors, the most dominant being in petroleum industry. Be that as it may, does this system benefit the Malays, or for that matter any of the poorer people in this country? Before answering the question we need to summarise the main concepts of the system: (a) the government guarantees full freedom in economic activities; (b) the private sector is expected to play a major part in the economic development of the country; and (c) competition is encouraged in order to achieve efficiency and maximise profits.

In this country there are economic activities involving land, housing and transport which are partly organised by the government or by quasi-government bodies, but in terms of capital invested they are rather small compared to the private sector. Since the government considers the role of foreign investment to be so important, it is making an effort to attract them. In the 1970s a cabinet committee was formed, the appropriate laws were amended and many delegations sent overseas, all for the purpose of convincing foreign investors that this country was stable and promised large profit for their capital.

The government realised that in spite of all the money it spent and the projects it carried out, it could never achieve its development targets entirely on its own effort. Should its performance fall short of expectations, its political position would be threatened. This is why until now the role of private investors becomes important, not only for economic but also political reasons.

One of the main arguments put forward by ministers and government officials in defense of foreign investment is economic, namely that it creates jobs and so helps to overcome the unemployment problem. They argue that many Malays will benefit from it, because a large proportion of the new employment is reserved for them. Perhaps the other reason, which always remains unexpressed, is that foreign investment also provides opportunities for ex-politicians and ex-civil servants to become directors or even shareholders. There is some truth in all these arguments. Keeping these groups happy is one of the ways to maintain their political support. But the question is, are industrial growth and employment opportunities made possible only through foreign investment?

Surely there are other alternatives, for instance, the government itself can provide more capital, or mobilise it through cooperatives. What needs to be brought in from outside is only the expertise not available locally, and this should be used to advise and train local personnel. As an example, through the Employees' Provident Fund (EPF), billions of dollars have been saved. Why is it these savings are not fully used as capital for undertaking some viable projects which can preferably be run on a cooperative basis? Unfortunately, recently much of the workers' money in EPF has been used, or more appropriately abused, to save many a crony company from their ailments.

In 1996, when Eric Chia was entrusted by Prime Minister Dr. Mahathir to save the ailing Perwaja Steel, EPF gave the company a loan of RM500 million, with no record showing whether this loan was repaid or not. In 2001, EPF together with Danaharta and the Pension Trust Fund tried to help Time.com which involved a well-known crony of Mahathir, Abdul Halim Saad. EPF subscribed RM269.28 million for 81.6 million shares at RM3.30 each. This effort proved to be a failure. Much earlier, following the disastrous project that was undertaken under Mahathir's direction to salvage the tin stockpile, apparently EPF suffered a loss of RM600 million in what was known as the EPF-Mahakuwasa Scandal. These were the known ones. There were unknown amounts from EPF whch have been purportedly used for investments on bond, equity and instruments of the share market. Until now there has been no explanation of what really happened to so much of the worker' contributions that were committed to various known and unknown projects.

As mentioned earlier, right to the present, foreign investors are given a number of privileges, and are not restricted from transferring home the profits that they make. Most of the factories that they built under pioneer status were in towns and very few in the rural areas, despite the fact that under the location-incentive programme more factories were expected to go into rural areas. The development of industries in the towns also had the effect of further widening rural-urban economic disparities. Usually factories with pioneer status worked three shifts in a 24-hour day, which had adverse effects on the workers' health. The majority of workers in these factories have always been women. Salaries paid to them were low – most of the female workers in the electronic factories seldom take home more than RM300-400 clean income a month.

Many ministers and officials are known to have justified these low salaries by saying that if they were raised, then fewer workers could be employed. They rationalise that it is better to have more employed, though with less pay, than have fewer employed in order to pay them well. But why think only in terms of reducing the workers' incomes? What about reducing the enormous profits made by the capitalists? The monopoly-capitalists indeed bleed this country of its wealth and exploit the workers. Is it not true that Matsushita Electronics, for instance, managed to recoup its capital after only five years in operation, and after that have reaped only profits?[14]

Why not lay down conditions that part of those huge profits should be used to raise salaries and improve the terms of service for the workers, without reducing their number? The answers to these questions are quite simple: if too many conditions are laid down then they would go against the *laissez faire* principles, and if the profits of the foreign investors are reduced then they would not wish to invest here. Minimising the wages of workers is a much simpler thing to do. After all, workers in pioneer industries face many obstacles from many employers who often get government backing to form their own trade unions. Who gains and who loses in this process?

Another adverse effect of this type of economic system can be seen from the difficulties faced by Malay businesses. It is now the declared policy of the government to encourage Malays to participate in commerce and industry, which at present are still dominated by non-Malays and foreigners. Before independence the Malays were mostly occupied in rural agriculture, lacking in capital and ability and not encouraged by the colonial rulers to participate in the new economic activities. Even after independence the Malays were still very much in the agricultural sector. In 1957 out of about 1,023,000 Malays

---

14. Husin Ali, 1978: p. 83

employed, around 749,000 (or 73.3 per cent) were in agriculture, and only 58,000 (or 5.7 per cent) in manufacturing and commerce, compared to the Chinese who had 40.2 per cent and 29 per cent of their population in these same sectors respectively.

By 1970 the number of employed Malays increased to about 1,432,000; those in agriculture were about 925,000 (or 64.6 per cent) while those in manufacturing and commerce were about 154,000 (or 10.8 per cent). Among the Chinese the percentage was 28.5 in agriculture and 37.4 in manufacturing and commerce at this time. The latest distribution of the labour force in 2005 was as follows: agriculture 1,405,700 (12.9 per cent); manufacturing 3,132,100 (28.7 per cent); retail and wholesale trade 1,927,200 (17.7 per cent) and government services 1,052,800 (9.7 per cent). No figures are available on the ethnic distribution according to sectors for that year. But for 2000, for the Bumiputera, they were as follows: in agriculture 61.5 per cent, in mining 62.6 per cent, in manufacturing 54.7 per cent, in construction 42.1 per cent, in transport and communication, wholesale and retail business 40.0 per cent, finance and insurance 50.5 per cent, and services 65.8 per cent.

Actually the percentages of people in the manufacturing and commercial sectors also include the entrepreneurs or executives. Non-Malay entrepreneurs have had much experience, have invested a lot of capital and were established earlier in these new economic activities. Their position is much stronger than that of the Malays, who are still struggling to participate in these activities. The free enterprise system expects them to compete. Logically, the strong can easily defeat the weak. Many Malay entrepreneurs have been forced to wind up their business as a result of stiff competition, their inexperience as well as lack of network to support them for capital, loans as well as supplies. It is just well-nigh impossible for anybody without sufficient capital, experience or network, be they Malay or non-Malay, to compete against the monopoly-capitalists who are already well-entrenched in the business.

An important development has taken place recently which will further strengthen the free market system in the country. In pursuant of its globalisation policy, the United States has been promoting agreements to set up free trade areas all over the world. In this region there is the

AFTA (Asian Free Trade Agreement). There is some resistance to this from some political parties in the opposition and a number of NGOs. A small group within the ruling UMNO is also opposed to it for fear that certain conditionality in the agreement would weaken the NEP. Nevertheless, owing to the strong US lobby, it looks like Malaysia will finally sign the AFTA after all.

It has been argued that in this predominantly globalised world where the free enterprise system strongly prevails, it is almost impossible for Malaysia to remain outside AFTA. Unfortunately, the process of globalisation brings with it elements of what may be viewed as new forms of imperialism or colonialism which would work against the interests of developing countries that have weak bargaining power. AFTA, being part of this process is feared to be harmful to the interests of the peasants, the majority of whom happen to be Malays, and the workers which have substantial non-Malay component. Thus, with the strengthening of the predominantly free market system by the AFTA, the majority who will suffer from their ill effects will ultimately be the poorer section of the people of all ethnic groups, including the Malays who are in the majority.

Let us now see what has happened at the village level. As already mentioned, at that level there have already emerged landlords, middlemen and moneylenders, many living in the villages while the remainder outside. Some of them have become powerful enough so that they can themselves determine the levels of rent, profit and interest that they want to extract from the villagers. In this way they affect adversely the villagers, particularly the poor peasants. They are capable of taking several exploitive measures and can make the life of the poor peasants miserable. There are laws to regulate rents and interest, but they are not effective.

Middlemen are also usually landlords and moneylenders in the villages, and so it is easy for them to exploit the peasants, especially when they have monopolistic power. Can they be controlled effectively? Actually it is not possible as long as the *laissez faire* system prevails, because under this system they are regarded as functional and must be given the freedom to perform their roles. So, the landlords will continue to be free to fix high rents, the middlemen to buy low from and sell high to the peasants, and the moneylenders to determine the interest rates for their advances and loans. They will be free to exploit; so, they will also be free to inflict poverty and misery among the poor who form the majority of the people.

As for the lower level workers, the Malays form the minority in estates, mines and industries. But they are a significant majority in the government administrative and uniformed services. A large number of them are not organised into union (for after all only abut 10 per cent of the workers in the country have been unionised) and in several sectors their emoluments are rather low. In fact a good number of them still have low salaries and poor housing. The urban workers may appear to have higher incomes than the peasants, but the cost of living is much higher in the towns and furthermore the villagers can still get some supplies of their own needs from the environment. The trade union organisations have been asking for minimum wages to be fixed but their demand have fallen on deaf ears.

In the long run the *laissez faire* system can only be the root of many problems and an obstacle to progress for the Malays. If this view is taken, then there is a great need for an overhaul to reform the economy. Such a strongly-felt need by the Malays was manifested in the May Thirteenth Incident. Superficially, it appeared to be a communal conflict, but the basic cause was discontent over economic and political issues. The government seemed to realise this and that is why it tried to redress the situation by introducing economic changes after the incident. The New Economic Policy (NEP) was introduced with the aim of (a) eradicating poverty without regard to race, and (b) restructuring society so that there would be greater participation by Malays in industry and commerce. This will be discussed at greater length in Chapter 6.

Actually the NEP, which provides the guidelines for the Second and Third Malaysia Plans, are not as radical as has been claimed. It is true that the government expenditure allocated for development under these plans increased greatly, when compared to those of earlier plans. Since then the amount has been going up steadily and there was a substantial jump from the seventh to the eighth Plan. This can be seen from the following:

First Five Year Plan (1956 - 60)	RM 973 (million)
Second Five Year Plan (1961 - 65)	2,150

First Malaysia Plan (1966 - 70)	4, 242
Second Malaysia Plan (1971 - 75)	10,398
Third Malaysia Plan (1976 - 80)	18,039
Fourth Malaysia Plan (1981 - 85)	33,454
Fifth Malaysia Plan (1986 - 1990)	53,017
Sixth Malaysia Plan (1991 - 1995)	58,165
Seventh Malaysia Plan (1996 - 2000)	67,500
Eighth Malaysia Plan (2001 - 2005)	110,000
Ninth Malaysia Plan	195,256

Up to the Fifth Malaysia Plan the expenditures have been roughly nearly doubled with each successive plan. But the increase was small from the Fifth to the Seventh Plan, and it jumped only for the Eighth Plan. Under the Second and Third Malaysia Plans about a fourth of the allocations were for agriculture, particularly for drainage and irrigation, land settlement and replanting projects. These were not new projects but the continuation of previous ones on a bigger scale. Strictly speaking, all these plans are actually no more than summaries issued every five years of expenditures allocated by the government for development.

But expenditure on new industries and mega construction projects increased under the premiership of Dr Mahathir, and these have continued under his successor Abdullah Badawi. Although at the beginning the latter said he was not going to do so, he was soon launching huge multi-billion dollar regional corridors in the southern, northern and eastern parts of the country, mostly with the financial support of PETRONAS.

As expected, these development plans have shown no indication at all of changing the *laissez faire* system as introduced by the British colonialists, simply because they are not meant to do so. Although some reforms have been introduced in the NEP – such as encouraging government statutory bodies to participate in economic activities like commerce, industries and construction, encouraging and assisting Malays in business, and concentrating on development in the less-developed states like Kelantan, Terengganu, Kedah and Perlis –the old colonial economic structures have basically remained unchanged. Much money has been spent on rural areas for agricultural development, yet this same economic system, which gives a free hand to the exploiting groups, is retained.

The landlords, middlemen and moneylenders are still operating on a wide scale although the threat that they pose to the poor peasants is being exposed; this is even admitted by the government. At the same time the control of the country's economy by foreign monopoly-capitalists is still firm. In fact their position will grow even stronger with the government moving so fervently towards attracting foreign investment into the country and also with the growing globalisation process. The prospect of peasants and workers' conditions improving is not very bright.

In its attempt to restructure Malaysian society, the government is determined to achieve the target of 30 per cent Bumiputera control of share capital by 1990, which was actually not met by that year. In fact, the government claims that by 2006 the Malay equity had reached only about 18 per cent. This claim has been challenged by a think-tank, Asian Strategy and Leadership Institute (ASLI), which claimed that according to its research, the said equity has gone beyond the target. In keeping with the restructuring objective the Malays are encouraged to participate in commerce and industry, and the government has formed various government-linked companies (GLC) to participate actively in these fields. ASLI opined that capital in the GLCs should have been included in the Malay equity, but because they are not, the equity is lower than it should be.

It must be stressed that the 30 per cent is not the percentage of Malays who will be involved, but the amount of capital that they, as a group, will hopefully control. To be sure, they will mostly come from a small group of already privileged Malays in the upper class. So, what will happen is not to change the structure of the economy, but merely to provide more opportunities for a small group of already privileged Malays to participate and reap greater profits. Malay capitalists sometimes do not have sufficient capital and experience to compete with the already established local and foreign capitalists and so, in the final analysis, they may end up merely as "sleeping partners" for the big capitalists. To what extent this will help the economy of the Malays, especially the poor in the rural area, remains a big question, despite arguments on the trickle down effect .

In 1970 the amount of Malay shares was a mere $126 million, and by 1975 it had increased to only RM768 million, showing an annual increase of RM128 million. As of 1975 there was still more than RM23,000 million needed to reach the target, and this amount must be accumulated within 15 years, which meant about RM1,533 million per year. According to the government figures of 2000, the total amount of share capital in the country was about RM332,417.6 million, but the Malay equity achieved was only 18.9 per cent or RM62,976 million. There was shortage of 11.1 per cent or RM36,898,000. By 2004 the total share capital was RM529,768,700, but the Malay equity was still at 18.9 per cent. In other words, the absolute amount of shortage had grown much bigger (*see Table 9.1*).

When 1990 passed, the target of 30 per cent Malay equity had not been met. Obviously, there is a big and increasing amount of Malay capital that needs to be mobilised in order to achieve the target. How could such an amount be obtained? Would it be possible for the percentage of Malay shares to increase if foreign investors are sought after perhaps more fervently than mobilising Malay capital?

There are several steps by which it may be possible to achieve the projected 30 per cent. One way is to mobilise all Malay savings and turn them into capital. But this amount would still not be enough. Alternatively, compulsory savings may be suggested. But this is easier said than done. As has been repeatedly said, most Malays are poor and their incomes unstable. It is difficult for them to save, and if they are forced to save, then life will be more difficult for them and their families. Furthermore, the act of compulsory saving, even for what may be considered a noble end, would be viewed by many as an infringement of their freedom, which is supposed to be guaranteed under the present political system and by the constitution.

A second way is to have the government issue more loans, on its own, or through certain banks and statutory bodies. However, since loans require securities, then clearly the number of people who can take them is limited. Furthermore, political, personal and family ties will ensure that only those who are in established positions will gain access to the loans. Naturally, those who will gain are only a handful. The government can also increase the number of statutory bodies like PERNAS, Urban

Development Authority (UDA) and SEDC, and give them bigger capital outlays in order to manage their affairs more effectively.

Under the present circumstances the number of bodies that can be established and the amount of capital that can be allocated is rather limited. The national income is not that big. For instance, in 1976 it was only RM5,655 million, while in 2006 it had risen to RM106,304 million. The national expenditure for 1976 was $8,000 million: $5,600 million for recurrent and $2,400 million for capital expenditures. In 2006 it rose to RM128,015 million with RM97,744 million for recurrent and RM30,571 million for development expenditure.

The expenditure for development under the Third Malaysia Plan was estimated at $18,555 million, with about 65 per cent to be allocated to the rural areas, because not only were they the ones that required development, but also because they were also the most important source of votes. Under the Ninth Malaysia Plan, the total expenditure is about RM200,000 million; although the aggregate allocation for economic development constitutes 44.9 per cent, only 5.7 per cent is for agricultural development.

For a number of years the government has been resorting to deficit financing and consequently has incurred large amounts of public debt every year. Therefore it is difficult to increase substantially the allocations to statutory bodies. Any allocation made by the government to them will be viewed as direct government participation in the private sector. This would be viewed as going against the *laissez faire* philosophy that the government upholds. So long as the government continues to believe in this system, its participation in the private sector will ultimately serve no more than just as a token of its concern. In fact, over the past few years government involvement in and expenditure on statutory bodies have been decreasing.

A third way to increase the percentage of Malay capital is to curtail the rate of non-Malay and foreign investments. But such a move could kill the country's economy. At present, contributions from all groups are needed to sustain the system so that the capital to be invested for development will continuously increase, for only in this way can national income and subsequently per capita income be increased. The government's strategy is to increase Malay capital in an expanding economy. Any restriction in the accumulation and investment of capital of other groups, merely for the purpose of increasing the percentage of the Malay share, goes against the grain, because it would stunt the growth of the economy as a whole, or at least it would limit the contribution of the private sector towards development. Worse still, such a restriction would be interpreted in racial terms as an attempt to strangle the growth of the non-Malay economy. This would endanger not only the economy, but also the politics of the country.

Finally, we could consider the policy of nationalisation. This will be discussed at greater length in the following chapter. But what needs to be mentioned here is that this policy is in direct opposition to the *laissez faire* system being upheld now. To carry out this policy, drastic changes are needed economically and politically. Is this possible under the present situation and leadership? If it is possible, then not only the pattern of capital ownership in industry and commerce will change in this country, but also the nature of the overall plans and strategy for fighting poverty will be transformed. If these changes are not possible, then we have to prepare ourselves for the possibility of failure, i.e. failure to achieve the two prime targets of the NEP: the eradication of poverty (which is now more the relative rather than the absolute poverty) and the restructuring of society. This is what seems to be happening now.

7

DEVELOPMENT POLICIES: SUCCESS OR FAILURE?

This chapter attempts to critically discuss the government's development plans, evaluating them in the context of the various problems elaborated in the earlier chapters. These development plans were spelt out clearly in several of the previous five-year plans. Since 1956 eleven such plans have been drawn up. From these plans there appear to be two important phases in the development policies and strategies adopted in this country.

The first one was promoted by Abdul Razak Hussein as Director of the National Operations Council (NOC) following the suspension of Parliament in 1970. The plan was summed up in the New Economic Policy (NEP) and provided with details in the Second and Third Malaysia Plans. The second phase is found in a number of policies expounded by Dr Mahathir Mohamad, especially during the earlier terms of his premiership. Detailed plans in pursuant of his policies were presented clearly in the Fourth and Fifth Malaysia Plans published during the earlier part of his tenure and the Second Long-Term Draft Plan of 1991-2000.

The ensuing discussion will focus mainly on the broad policies and strategies of these plans. Only slight attention will be paid to the details of the plans and the financial allocations under various headings. Since the various Malaysia Plans give quite complete statements on what they intended to do and achieved, it is not necessary to repeat them here. Those who want to know about the intentions and details of the plans can go directly to the source. Here the plans will be explained solely with the purpose of evaluating and criticising them where appropriate. An attempt will be made towards the end to suggest broad alternative policies, strategies and plans.

The Second and Third Malaysia Plans were largely continuation of the three preceding five year plans. Since the first Five Year Plan which was introduced in 1956, it had been stated that the intention of the government was to alleviate rural poverty, reduce unemployment, provide social facilities particularly in education and health, and strengthen the defence of the country. Under Razak, what was known as the Red Book was introduced to provide overall details and guides for all development plans and projects.

However, only since the Second Malaysia Plan have the overall objectives of the government been clearly spelt out. This plan was formulated after the May Thirteenth Incident, which threatened the country's very basis of unity. As stated earlier, although the incident appeared to be a racial conflict, it was recognised that the root causes were some basic economic problems. Such admission was made by prime minister Razak, in his speech introducing the NEP when Parliament reconvened in 1971.

Through the mass media it was explained that the main strategy of the NEP was to promote National Unity. To achieve this the government intended to carry out a policy with a two-prong objectives, namely: (a) eradicating poverty and providing more employment opportunities for the people irrespective of their ethnic origin; and (b) accelerating the process of restructuring society in order to correct the existing economic imbalance, so that the identification of certain economic roles by race could be reduced and then finally abolished.

These two objectives of the NEP formed the basis of the Second Malaysia Plan. But before the Third Malaysia Plan was launched the security of the country came under serious threat, especially from local communist party elements who stepped up their activities following the fall of Indochina. The question of security was included as another important objective under this plan. As the then Prime Minister, Hussein Onn explained in its Preface, "A major assault on poverty, a vigorous and continuing effort in the task of restructuring society as well as the strengthening of our national security, are the triple thrusts of the Third Malaysia Plan".[15] It has been emphasised that the two original objectives of the NEP could not be achieved unless there was security. What was previously a two-pronged strategy had become three-pronged.

In the following paragraphs, we shall discuss only the two original objectives, because it is beyond our means to discuss the third.

Let us begin with the first objective, the eradication of poverty. Three questions that arise here are: (a) what are the groups considered to be poor?, (b) what are the roots of their poverty?, and (c) what are the steps to be taken to eradicate poverty? The answers to these three questions are found largely in the Third Malaysia Plan.

According to this plan the poor are found in the rural as well as the urban areas. They were spelt out as "*paddy* growers; rubber smallholders; coconut smallholders; fishermen; estate workers; residents of New Villages; agricultural labourers; the Orang Asli".[16] In 1970, 49.3 per cent of the total number of households in the country lived in poverty. "Of all poor households, about 74 per cent were Malays, 17 per cent Chinese and 8 per cent Indians." Furthermore, "Of all Malay households 65 per cent were in poverty compared to 26 per cent for Chinese households and Indians 39 per cent".[17] It is clear that the problem of poverty then was very much the problem of the Malays, the majority living in the rural areas.

As for the roots of poverty, a paragraph in the Third Malaysia Plan reads, "The lack of productive employment opportunities is the major cause of poverty. Open unemployment and under-development of human resources resulting from the lack of complementary inputs such as land, capital and entrepreneurship underlie poverty in every sector of the economy".[18] Prior to this, the Mid-Term Review of the Second Malaysia Plan (MRSMP) stated that the low incomes of the poor people in the villages were caused by the uneconomic sizes of farms, by the farms' infertility or unsuitability for cultivation, and by the use of outdated technology and by the lack of modern methods. From both these documents it is clear that the roots of poverty as emphasised

---

15. TMP, 1976: v
16. *Ibid*: 45
17. *Ibid*: 5
18. *Ibid*: 27

by the government are low productivity owing to lack of productive employment and the use of outdated methods.

In connection with the steps that have been taken, the Third Malaysia Plan stressed that "the rapid economic growth attained during the Second Malaysia Plan period enabled the alleviation of the poverty problem".[19] In the long run the government strategy to reduce poverty contained four elements:

(i) "The opening up of over four million acres of land for settlement by the landless and those with uneconomic holdings; the irrigation of an additional 300,000 acres for double cropping ... to about 700,000 acres in 1990; the replanting, rehabilitation and redevelopment of 1.8 million acres during the 20-year period of high-yielding rubber, coconut and pineapple production;[20]

(ii) "... relieve current population pressure in the most congested sectors of agriculture[21] by encouraging poor farmers and fishermen to be active in more productive agricultural and non-agricultural sectors, widen opportunities for rural youths to get expertise that are expanded in the agricultural and modern industrial sectors;

(iii) "... the provision of better and more efficient services in the fields of housing, transportation, water supply, electricity, education, health, nutrition and family planning;

(iv) "... the accelerated creation of productive employment opportunities in the secondary and tertiary sectors of the economy ... the promotion and dispersal of industrial development will emphasise the need to channel more capital to small-scale and labour intensive industries."[22]

Actually the fourth element was also for the purpose of eradicating poverty in the urban areas. Besides this, steps were taken to raise real incomes by providing low-cost housing and other public services.

Turning to the second objective of the NEP, i.e. the restructuring of society, there were two aspects that needed to be emphasised. First, in the prevailing circumstances ethnic imbalance existed in

---

19. *Ibid*: 27
20. *Ibid*: 74
21. *Ibid*: 87
22. *Ibid:* 74-75

various sectors and at all levels of employment. For instance, as already noted earlier, most of the Malays were in the rural-agricultural sector, while the majority of the Chinese were in the manufacturing and mining sectors, and the Indians in the estates. As a result, the association or identity of race with employment in certain sectors arose: Malays as peasants, Chinese and Indians mostly as labourers, but in different fields.

In fact, when the same sector was examined, such as government services, there were also some types of jobs that were monopolised mainly by Malays, for instance, as administrators, policemen and soldiers; and there were those where Chinese dominated, such as in the professions, as doctors, engineers, accountants and so forth. Sometimes it was found that in certain types of occupations, the lower levels were made up mainly of one ethnic group, while the upper levels are made up largely of another.

Second, in the ownership of productive assets there also existed an imbalance. In the Peninsula there were about seven million acres of land used for agriculture. Out of this, 4.2 million acres (or 60 per cent) was under rubber cultivation. Out of all the land under rubber, about 37 per cent was owned by Malays, 42 per cent by non-Malays and 21 per cent by foreigners. Considering the rubber estates alone, three-quarters of those which exceeded 2,000 acres were owned by foreigners. Chinese and Indians also owned some big estates, but most of them smaller than 2,000 acres. No Malays owned big estates, but in Kelantan there were some small estates of more than 100 acres which were Malay-owned.

The total *paddy* land area was about 1.1 million acres. There were no figures available regarding ownership of *paddy* land, but there were not many holdings of over twenty acres. Normally *paddy* cultivators worked on their own uneconomic holdings or work on others' land as tenants when they had none of their own. Now there have been more areas opened for oil palm in resettlement schemes and also in the villages.

Regarding share capital the picture was as follows:

	1975		2004	
	$ (*million*)	%	RM (*million*)	%
Malay and Malay interests	768.1	7.8	199,037.2	18.9
Malay individuals	227.1	2.3	79,449.2	15.0
Malay interests	541.0	5.5	20,587.3	3.9
Other Malaysians	3,687.3	37.3	214,972.8	40.6
Chinese			206,682.9	39.0
Indians			6,392.6	1.2
Others			1,897.3	0.4
Nominee Companies			42,479.1	8.0
Foreigners	5,434.7	54.9	172,279.6	32.5
Total	9,890.1	100.0	529,768.7	100.0

Source: TMP, 1976: Table 4-16, p. 86 and RM-9 Table 16-6, p. 356

In order to reduce the imbalance explained and achieve the objective of restructuring society, some of the steps taken were:

(i) "Increase the share of the Malays and other indigenous people in employment in mining, manufacturing and construction and the share of other Malaysians in agriculture and services so that by 1990 employment in the various sectors of the economy will reflect the racial composition of the country;

(ii) "Raise the share of the Malays and other indigenous people in the ownership of productive wealth including land, fixed assets and equity capital. The target is that by 1990 they will own at least 30 per cent of equity capital with 40 per cent being owned by other Malaysians;

(iii) "Foster the development of entrepreneurship among the Malays and other indigenous people so as to effectively contribute towards the creation by 1990 of a strong and viable commercial and industrial community among them;

(iv) "encourage and support private investment both domestic and foreign".[23]

---

23. *Ibid*: 49.

Viewed superficially, both the objectives of the Third Malaysia Plan as formulated in the NEP appeared to be attractive. But when examined closely, the weaknesses became more obvious. Let us take the first objective, the eradication of poverty. The Third Malaysia Plan as well as the Second Malaysia Plan recognised the existence of poverty and were able to identify the groups which were considered poor. But its analysis of the roots of poverty was not satisfactory. A clear analysis of these roots is important because they will largely determine the strategies and programmes to be undertaken for the eradication of poverty, in the same manner that a suitable cure for an illness can be given only after it is correctly diagnosed. In a manner of speaking, it would be disastrous to diagnose tuberculosis as just a common cough to be treated with an ordinary mixture.

The Second Malaysia Plan did not examine and analyse the roots of poverty. The Review of the Second Plan and the Third Malaysia Plan mentioned it in but a few sentences. As shown earlier, the most important factor that was emphasised was low productivity. Undoubtedly, there was a lack of productive employment and a rather widespread use of old methods. But there was no mention at all about the system that allowed for a portion of the poor people's labour to be taken away either directly or indirectly. For example, among the peasantry the share-cropping system being practised widely resulted in their having to give up a large part of their produce to the landlords; and in marketing there often existed a system of monopoly which resulted in the peasants getting low prices for their produce and being charged high prices for the commodities that they required daily.

We have already stated in an earlier chapter that the poor peasants were victims of various kinds of exploitation at various levels, by the big businessmen and capitalists at the national level, and also by monopoly-capitalists at the international level. The ones who had to bear the brunt of all these levels of exploitation were the peasants. The exploitation as well as the system that perpetrated this exploitation is not mentioned at all in official publications or policies issued by the government dealing with poverty. Naturally the reason was that this system is directly connected with the *laissez faire* philosophy strongly upheld by those in authority and benefited many party leaders and activists.

As repeatedly mentioned, poverty was rampant in the rural areas. So it was appropriate that a large portion of development expenditures be allocated to this sector. Out of $18,555 million estimated for total development expenditure under the Third Malaysia Plan, about $4,730 million (or 25.5 per cent) was for agricultural and rural development. Out of the latter amount, about $3,306 million was concentrated on three projects, namely $2,010 million for the opening of new land schemes, $675 million for replanting of rubber, $621 million for drainage and irrigation.

The opening of new land is indeed necessary to overcome the problem of "land hunger". But as already examined elsewhere[24] these land schemes were still far from adequate even to meet the needs of the annual increase of the peasant population. There is still no provision regarding the ownership of the land following the death of the original settler; whether to be inherited to one of the children or subdivided according to the Muslim law of inheritance *(fara'id)*. Furthermore the development is relatively expensive, and the debt burden on the settlers was rather heavy.

Rubber replanting is certainly beneficial, for ultimately it could increase the productivity of the holding. But it is easier for replanting to be done on estates than on the small farms which sustained poor families. As for the landless peasants they could not possibly get any financial aid for replanting because they do not have any land to replant, although they contribute to the replanting funds collected from tax or cess on the rubber they produce.

Nobody denies the benefit that *paddy* cultivators could derive from drainage and irrigation. But in the irrigation schemes like Muda in Kedah, for instance, there were many problems related to "ownership of land, land tenure and rising production cost as well as marketing and credit system which are not satisfactory".[25] About a third of the *paddy* cultivators had insufficient or no land at all. In *paddy* areas there was little land left for cultivation. But the number and size of families were still increasing. In the long run this would give rise to a serious land problem, unless there are other employment opportunities provided that could attract the peasants from overpopulated areas.

---

24. Husin Ali, 1976: 37-46.
25. Shamsul Amri, 1976: 74.

At that time, production costs of manufactured goods were increasing, and this affected the prices of commodities consumed by peasants. The structure of marketing for agricultural produce is basically unchanged. The middlemen are still powerful in the villages and in many cases they are also the owners of land and rice mills. Although the National Padi Board (LPN) had taken over the role of purchasing most of the *paddy*, it did not provide the peasants with the same extra services that were often given by the middlemen and so the middlemen could undercut the Board. As a result, some serious conflicts occurred between the two parties.

Unfortunately the Board operated almost like the middlemen themselves, merely as individual purchasers and not on a cooperative basis. The middlemen continued to be important sources of credit for the peasants, binding them with high interest rates. It was true, for instance, that the Agricultural Bank provided credit facilities to farmers, but often those who managed to get loans or credit were the ones who had security, and more often than not they came from the more well-to-do and influential groups of society.

The amount of expenditure for agriculture and rural development was indeed sizeable, and those responsible could justifiably feel proud of it. But the question was, did the poor peasants gain much from it? In the new land schemes we heard of settlers being burdened with debts incurred from the cost of developing the schemes. In the Rubber Industry Smallholders' Development Authority (RISDA), serious corrupt practices had been exposed at that time, involving millions of dollars which by right should have gone to the smallholders for replanting rubber. In the drainage and irrigation schemes, substantial profits were made by capitalists who supplied expensive machinery and tools. In all these schemes those making the pile were often the big contractors.

Under the free enterprise system there is always serious competition for facilities, aids, loans and profits. In such stiff competition the strong are often the winners. As already noted, the estate owners can replant more easily than the smallholders, and the smallholders are more fortunate than the landless peasants who do not qualify to get replanting aid. In the same manner as the capitalists, contractors and middlemen do not face such difficulty in benefiting from the big outlays on various projects. The competitive *laissez faire* system, when practised in a society with socio-economic disparities, will only result in widening the gap further. Those who are on the losing end are mostly the weak who form the majority, although it cannot be denied that a few of them do derive some benefit. This serious problem is not addressed by the government.

The objective of restructuring society had a number of weaknesses. Generally, the idea was to encourage Malays to enter the modern sector which was dominated by non-Malays. By implication it was also supposed to encourage greater non-Malay participation in economic activities and types of occupation that were primarily filled by Malays, which actually did not happen. But, the underlying motive was actually to increase the number of Malay businessmen and industrialists and to enlarge their share in the ownership of important factors of production. In other words the objective was to provide opportunities to some Malays to become businessmen, industrialists or capitalists and benefit from the present economic system.

This objective manifested the dreams of a few Malays in the upper and middle classes, who hoped to benefit even more than before from the processes of socio-economic development taking place under the successive five year plans. No doubt it was good to have more Malays in business and industries, in fact, it would be much better if they did not stop short, simply taking over from their non-Malay counterparts, but instead go beyond to replace the foreign monopoly-capitalists who still have a strong grip on the country's economy. What was unfortunate was that all developments taking place under this objective were to be carried out within the framework of the *laissez faire* system. The implication for the poor and the weak peasants, who formed the majority in this country, was certainly not favourable.

It was clear that the goal of the restructuring process was horizontal and not vertical parity. The objective aimed at a more balanced distribution of Malays and non-Malays in similar types of occupation within the same strata. In the lower strata of society, for example, if there were fewer Malays than Chinese as industrial workers, then the proportion of Malays should be increased; so too, if there were fewer Chinese than Malays in land schemes, then the number of Chinese in turn should be increased in the same sector. Similarly, if the number of Malays who were businessmen and executives within the middle strata was small, compared to the Chinese, they should be increased in number, while on the other hand, if non-Malays demanded that they should be given more opportunities in the government services, then the government had to respond positively to them. The same process applied to the upper strata. But this process did not happen in practice. Many non-Malays felt threatened by what they considered to be mainly a one way process of Malay encroachments into their traditional economic fields.

It need not be emphasised that it was difficult to achieve this horizontal parity which, it was hoped, would reduce the identification of race with certain types of employment or economic activities. This difficulty was probably the reason why only the question of Malay participation in business and industry was concentrated on. There was a greater possibility of limited success in achieving this goal, especially with the help of government and quasi-government bodies, and also because of the strong political pressure from the Malays on this matter. Such pressure would always remind the government of the May Thirteenth Incident, which actually gave birth to the NEP.

In comparison, vertical parity was seldom emphasised. The most serious manifestation of vertical disparity in society was the widening gap between the rich and the poor. The policy of restructuring society within the framework of the *laissez faire* system could and in fact did create a small group of Malay *nouveaux riche* who have much bigger incomes than the peasants. It is possible for the new Malay rich to cooperate with non-Malay capitalists, both domestic and foreign, to exploit the wealth of the country and the low-income peasants and workers in order to maximise their profits.

Of course the standard of living of a handful of Malays rose, and a few among them became millionaires; but the problem of poverty among the peasants still remained unsolved. True, the incidence of poverty decreased, but the gap of socio-economic inequities became wider between the rich and poor, both inter- and intra-ethnically. It is not the intention here to say that the Malays should be discouraged from business and industries, but it must be noted that the encouragement given and the efforts carried out within the free enterprise system would only perpetuate greater socio-economic inequality, exploitation and poverty among the people. It becomes clearer that the NEP benefited mainly a handful few already in privileged position.

During the period of the Third Malaysia Plan, the total amount of investment needed for implementing all projects was estimated at about RM44,200 million, out of which the estimated investment in the private sector was about RM26,800 million (or 60.6 per cent). This showed to what extent the government placed its hopes on the private sector to achieve its development programmes. Investments in the private sector depended heavily on foreign investment, and that was why the government appeared to be greatly worried when the amount of foreign investment in this country fell short of expectation. What would happen if the target for foreign capital was not reached?

The aim of foreign capitalists was inevitably to reap as much profit as possible under given conditions. In fact the investors would not accept government interference or control. There was no guarantee that they would cooperate fully to implement the objectives of the NEP, particularly if by doing so their interests were undermined. Under the existing system there is very little that could be done to control or influence foreign investment. These investors would surely be more concerned about their profits than the success of the Malaysia Plan. A greater amount of foreign investment would result in its further entrenchment in the country's economy. This would stimulate the continuation of the present economic structure and system. Consequently, poverty among the people and a widening gap between the poor and the rich would continue and intensify.

It appeared that there were already many shortcomings and problems that had arisen from the NEP and its implementation under the Third Malaysia Plan. What were the other steps which could serve as complements or alternatives to the existing programmes in order to achieve the main objectives of the NEP? As mentioned earlier, an effective medicine must be administered according to the diagnosis of the disease. It was acknowledged that the most serious single "illness" suffered by the majority of the people was poverty. Poverty was not entirely a Malay problem because there were others from different ethnic groups who were also poor, but of course the majority was Malay. Poverty is a social and economic ailment, resulting not only from socio-economic, but also from political factors.

Certain political ideologies stimulate certain economic systems to perpetuate themselves. Capitalism or the free enterprise system, for example, is an ideology that encourages and gives full freedom to big foreign and domestic capitalists to control the economy and allows for the socio-economic exploitation of the majority of people. Therefore, in order to eradicate poverty it is important not only to take economic measures to reduce poverty, but also to change the political orientation from that which favours foreign and upper class interests to one which favours the national and lower class interests, from that which perpetuates the politico-economic systems and structures of exploitation to one which seeks to dismantle them.

It has been repeatedly noted that as a result of the *laissez faire* system introduced during the days of colonialism, foreign monopoly-capitalists have been free to control various sources of wealth in this country and to send home profits and dividends year after year. The biggest rubber estates and the richest tin mines in the world found in this country were owned and controlled by foreign monopoly-capitalists. On 15 April 1976, Parliament was informed that the amount of profits and dividends taken out of the country was in the region of $435 million in 1966, $555 million in 1969, $1,342 million in 1974 and $1,017 million in 1975.

Assuming that, during the five-year period of the Second Malaysia Plan, the amount taken away averaged $800 million annually, it meant that the total amount is $4,000 million, or 55.1 per cent of the total public expenditure under the Second Malaysia Plan. This money was therefore unavailable for use in the country's development. At the same time the national debt had increased from RM5,016 million to RM11,178 million during the same period under the Second Malaysia Plan, an increase of $6,162 million.

Viewed logically, can a political and economic system which allowed the wealth of the country to be drained away to such an extent that it must borrow for development be called a good system? If the answer is "no", what then should be done? One way of overcoming the problem, as done by some Third World countries, would be to carry out nationalisation programmes. But such programmes are often considered to be too radical, probably because they go against the principles of the *laissez faire* system. The countries which carry out nationalisation often have two objectives.

The first is to eradicate all vestiges of colonialism; this is a political objective. Many countries have succeeded in gaining political independence, but their economies remained under the domination of their ex-colonial masters, and it is through this economic domination that the former colonialists were able to bring about new political pressures for their own benefit. This kind of situation is often referred to as neo-colonialism. Therefore, through nationalisation an ex-colonial country strives to secure a genuine politico-economic independence. The second objective is more economic in nature. By nationalisation it is hoped that the wealth of the country would not be drained out of it to enrich a handful of wealthy people, mostly foreign capitalists living thousands of miles away, but instead to be used fully for the development of the country and welfare of the people.

It is hard to deny that benefits can be derived from a nationalisation policy, whereby the state controls the main sources of wealth. The country's wealth can be used for various types of development for the benefit and welfare of the people. Take the example of $1,017 million that was taken away as profits and dividends by the foreign monopoly-capitalists in 1975, as mentioned above. Just imagine how many schools could be built with that amount of money. If the cost of each school was two million ringgit – an amount of money that could build a big well-equipped school – then during that year alone 500 schools could be built. What about the other years? Certainly more than just schools could be built – hospitals, low-cost houses and so forth for the poor people.

This country is rich, but since so much of its wealth had been drained away since colonialism began, we are still short of good and well-equipped schools, hospitals and cheap homes, especially for the needy poor. Genuine nationalisation policies aim at using the wealth of the country for the benefit of the people and not for a handful of wealthy monopoly-capitalists. So there should be no reason for it to be opposed by the government and the leaders who claim to be really concerned about the plight of their own poor people.

But many arguments have been put forward against this policy. The opponents often gave examples of failures in other countries. They said that, under the Labour government, Britain nationalised some of her industries, like coal and steel, and, as a result, many of these industries faced all sorts of difficulties leading to heavy losses, although before nationalisation they were able to make huge profits. But these people failed to explain why this happened. What happened was that some of the former owners and directors continued to serve, even after the industries were nationalised. Naturally, they were unhappy with the change that had taken place, and so, by using the positions they held, they tried to cause damage or failure that could discredit the nationalisation policy. However, they did not succeed to such an extent as to turn the clock back to the previous system of private ownership, not until very much later.

Indonesia has often been cited as another negative example. In Indonesia, following its nationalisation policy, those industries that were once owned or controlled by the Dutch were suddenly transferred into the hands of local politicians, generals and capitalists, to be administered by them. Most of these people were opportunists who were more concerned with their own interests than with those of the country and the people. The failures in these countries should certainly serve as good lessons and guidance to those who intend to carry out nationalisation. To guarantee its success, the whole country, government, directors and operators should be committed not to personal profit but to the welfare of the people first, and should not tolerate corruption and mismanagement.

What is interesting is that the vociferous opponents of this policy gave examples only from countries which have failed in their nationalisation programmes. Why not present some examples from countries that have succeeded? In the Arab states almost all of their rich oil wells were formerly controlled by western monopoly-capitalists. During that time these states were poor and often looked down upon with contempt. But what happened after Libya, Iraq and Arabia nationalised their oil? They became wealthy and consequently looked up to with reverence both in the East and West, though sometimes reluctantly.

With rising national incomes they have been able to develop much faster now than ever before. Many countries have been paying visits to these Arab states with the hope of getting loans and aid. Since the nationalisation programmes in those countries have proven successful, local opponents to the same policy tried to offer new explanations. They said that the case of oil was different because of its high demand on the world market. Be that as it may, it should be admitted that many Middle Eastern rulers who nationalised their petroleum have amassed wealth for themselves and their families more than they have spent for the welfare of the people. Most of them were feudal and authoritarian in nature.

It must be admitted that in Malaysia all is not based entirely on the *laissez faire* system. To be fair, a number of enterprises and services have been state-owned. Hitherto, the petroleum industry is run by the state under PETRONAS. Besides, there were also several businesses, industries or services that were managed by government or by quasi-government bodies, such as electricity, postal service, water, railways, shipping, aviation, airports, hospitals, schools and universities. Some of them, like the railways, were running at a loss. It appeared that many of the public corporations and businesses that have been taken over by such public corporations have failed because they had to face stiff competition from the private sector or were badly managed.

Malaysian railways, for instance, found difficulty in competing with private transport and haulage, partly because of their own inefficiency. But on the other hand electricity and postal service were running well and recording huge profits. There were also public corporations that were established under the direct or indirect auspices of the government mainly for the purpose of implementing the NEP, like MARA, UDA, PERNAS and SEDC. Some of them did well while others faced difficulties because they had to compete with private ones that were already firmly established and had great experience in operating under the present free enterprise system.

But what about those public bodies which did not have to face competition from the private sector? Electricity and postal service are good examples. The National Electricity Board (LLN) was a great success and made huge profits. So too with Pos Malaysia. The rates imposed by them on the public had not increased significantly over the years. If it were run by the private sector, perhaps patrons would even have to pay for street lights. The rates would always be on the increase, just as the prices of consumer commodities are now increasing.

It might be argued that if the nationalisation policy was fully carried out in major industries and protected from competition of the private sector, their chances of success would be greater. But still there would be some people in the government who would sigh and say, "We do not have enough expertise, we lack know-how. It is not easy to manage all the industries." The same kinds of sighs were heard from those who opposed independence before, when they said that the country lacked administrators, soldiers and so forth. If they felt so strongly about this, why didn't they launch a crash programme to train and produce the needed expertise? The Third Malaysia Plan did not seem to give priority to this question.

Let us now turn to the second phase of the policies and plans for development in Malaysia, which were initiated by Dr Mahathir Mohamad. Many have argued that his policies and plans were essentially based on the NEP. Basically I agree, but it must be noted that Mahathir injected new elements that made his brand of policies and plans for development different from those found during the first phase. Among these elements were policies relating to: (a) Look East, (b) Malaysia Incorporated, (c) Privatisation, (d) Industrialisation, (e) Agriculture, (f) Allowing UMNO in business, and (g) New Development Policy. It will be evident later that these new elements in the policies and plans were basically aimed at achieving much faster and to a bigger scale the second objective of the NEP, namely, creating more and bigger Malay capitalists and entrepreneurs in industry and commerce. To certain extent his desire to improve the lot of the Malays whom he saw as being backward, partly because – as he saw it – certain Malay characteristics caused by genetic factors which he had propounded in his book *The Malay Dilemma*. But it appears that the policies and plans he initiated have not been much guided by the ideas expressed in the book.

Right from the time he became Prime Minister, Dr Mahathir was demonstrating that he wanted to bring about changes in different fields. At first he moved forward the Malaysian time by half an hour, because he said he wanted people to start work earlier. Then he declared he wanted improvement in the administration; for this reason he promoted a slogan for a clean, efficient and trustworthy government. The time change caused a little bit of disruption at the beginning, but soon everything settled down very well. As for the slogan of clean, efficient and trustworthy government, it was initially welcomed with much enthusiasm. But as time went by, the government and the administration did not improve, but instead corruption and inefficiency became more widespread, and now the slogan is hardly heard anymore.

But without question, Dr Mahathir has left a strong mark especially in economic development. Dr Mahathir wanted Malaysia and the Malays in particular to become modern within the shortest time possible. The policies and plans that he had begun to publicly enunciate showed his underlying conviction that the modernisation of the Malays could be achieved best by following the capitalist path for development. About two years after he came to office on 28 June 1983, Mahathir circulated a memorandum entitled "New Government Policies" to government officials "to avoid misunderstanding and misinterpretation". Four aspects of the new policies explained in the memorandum covered Look East, Malaysia Incorporated, Privatisation and Leadership by Example. In short and precise way he clearly explained what each meant.

On the Look East policy, Mahathir stated it meant "emulating the rapidly developing countries of the East in the effort to develop Malaysia".[26] He stressed matters that deserved attention should be such values like diligence and discipline in work and loyalty to the nation, and not giving priority to buying goods from or granting all contracts to companies from the East. But what really happened was that these values did not seem to be imbibed, but on the other hand capitalists from Korea and Japan were able to make use of the environment created by this policy to increase their investment of capital and export of their goods (particularly when Mahathir declared "buy British last", following some controversy with Britain in the early 1980s), and to obtain major contracts for a number of big projects that were undertaken by the Malaysian government.

Perhaps the unstated objective of the Look East Policy was to emulate the capitalist development that had taken place in Japan, Korea and Taiwan, which enabled them to move very far ahead of Malaysia, although they started almost on the same point about four decades ago. There has been no sign that this had been achieved. Perhaps due to all these reasons, the Look East policy as such seems to have been quietly dropped.

As for Malaysia Incorporated, the Prime Minister explained the concept meant that "Malaysia should be viewed as a company where

---

26. Mahathir, in Jomo, ed.: 1.

the government and the private sector are both owners and workers together in the company".[27] He defined the concept as "cooperation between the government and the private sector for the latter to succeed, thus make greater contribution to national development".[28]

In pursuit of this we find that in a number of subsequent five year plans, the proportions of private capital contribution for development increased and, in fact, exceeded that of state capital. A large number of Malays, mostly cronies of Dr Mahathir or other senior politicians, were encouraged in business and they were provided easily with facilities for huge bank loans, sometimes without any collateral except the support and verbal guarantee of some very powerful politicians. On one hand, this move was thought necessary to encourage the growth and development of Malay capitalists in business and industries. On the other, apparently there was not sufficient trust between the politicians and administrators who were majority Malays with the local or foreign businessmen who were mostly non-Malays, mainly Chinese. During the financial crisis in the last decade of the previous millennium, many Malay businessmen faced great difficulties and were unable to honour their loans. Most of the loans, particularly to cronies, were written off and the government had to come to the rescue through Danaharta.[29] Although the Malaysia Incorporated policy is not much talked about now, the idea of welcoming and encouraging the private sector to play an important role in development is still very much alive.

As regards Privatisation, Dr Mahathir simply said "it means the opposite of nationalisation ......the transfer of government services and enterprises to the private sector". Linked with privatisation is the concept of corporatisation, which means transforming public enterprises into companies that are registered with the Registrar of Companies. Although there are bases to consider them distinct of one another, yet it is often found that corporatisation is just a stage towards privatisation. It was assumed that public run enterprises usually ran at a loss because they were inefficient, wasteful and not competitive. When the policy

---

27. *Ibid*: 1.

28. *Ibid*: 2.

29. This body was instituted by Parliament in 1998, with the aim of buying over non-performing loans of banks. It appeared to have been used especially to rescue ailing companies and capitalists who were clearly associated with the government and/or some top government leaders.

of privatisation was first introduced and implemented, it was thought that only services and enterprises that ran at a loss or made lower than expected profits would be privatised. But what happened was that even such big services that were running well and making good profits, like electricity, postal and telecommunication were also corporatised or privatised. Ironically, they did not run much better after that.

Privatisation has given wide opportunities for awarding directorship, business, contract and so forth to cronies, who after all seldom became genuine and successful Malay capitalists or entrepreneurs. An example is the case of electricity; part of its supply was privatised to the Independent Power Producers (IPP), which supplied to Tenaga Nasional (formerly LLN) at high prices that were fixed. Ironically, although a number of Malays obtained the IPP, the owner of the biggest IPP is a Chinese capitalist, obviously a well known crony.

It is true that profits of some enterprises, like Tenaga Nasional and Telekom Malaysia, increased after privatisation or corporatisation. For example, in 1994 Tenaga Nasional recorded an increase of profit from RM1.14 billion to RM1.74 billion. But in 1996 it decreased substantially because the IPPs took away something like RM800 million. As for Telekom Malaysia, their profit rose from RM1.08 billion in 1991 to RM1.57 in 1995.

But the tragedy of it all was that the burden of payment on consumers became heavier. Charges for phone calls increased from 13 sen per call to 9 sen for the first three minutes and 3 sen for each additional minute. Beginning 1996 the charges for electricity rose from 19.68 sen/kWh to 20.7 sen/kWh. In the same manner, despite the large profits reaped by privatised highways, tolls have been repeatedly increased, in some cases by 100 per cent, like the Karak highway increase at one time.

During the premierships of Razak and Hussein, much attention was comparatively focused on the improvement of agriculture and the socio-economic plight of the peasantry. But during Dr Mahathir's tenure, less importance was given to these to the point that there appeared to be neglected. Nevertheless, a National Agricultural Policy (NAP) was produced in 1983, much of the content believed to be crafted by Dr Mahathir. The main aim of NAP was to improve peasant incomes by increasing productivity, among others by regrouping various small farms into mini estates.

There was no plan to have complete self sufficiency in rice, instead around 20 per cent of the local requirement would still be imported. Malaysia spent over RM10 billion annually on imports of food products, and there was the intention to reduce this amount by encouraging domestic production. During the 1980s, the agricultural sector's performance dropped seriously. The NAP remained very much just on paper. Indeed agriculture was neglected.

Dr Mahathir wanted to concentrate more on industrialisation – especially heavy industries. In 1986, Malaysia published its first Industrial Master Plan (IMP). Malaysia was a late-comer to industrialisation. Whatever that had been carried out lagged behind so-called "normal pattern" and showed many imbalances. The IMP wanted to correct these as well as identify the right type of heavy industries to develop. To promote the steel industry, Dr Mahathir entrusted one of his well-known cronies, Eric Chia, to salvage what was regarded as an ailing company, Perwaja.

Instead of saving it, Chia drove Perwaja to almost bankruptcy, incurring losses to the tune of around RM3 billion and bank debts amounting to over RM8 billion. An auditor's report that was tabled by the then Deputy Prime Minister and Finance Minister Anwar Ibrahim showed that there were corrupt practices and other hanky panky. Although Chia was brought to court much later, it was actually on a minor charge, for which he was acquitted on technical ground. Perhaps his strong links as a crony of a Prime Minister then saved the day for him. Apparently he is still financially strong, although Perwaja never recovered and was sold to a private company.

Another major heavy industry project was the 'manufacture' of what was touted as a national car, Proton. When it was started, this project was criticised by a few prominent academics as being uneconomic and bound to failure. But they were either ridiculed or threatened by the Prime Minister. Actually, this car project depended on two subsidiaries related to Japan's Mitsubishi; Proton used Mitsubishi engine and about 60 per cent of the parts and so the Japanese car company was ensured of very handsome profits. Of course some Malay businessmen managed to gain as vendors, distributing the cars or supplying parts, but their gains were nothing comparable to the huge profits reaped by the Japanese monopolists.

Although some training was given, there was no significant transfer of technology, although the industry opened some avenue for some Malays to become technicians or specialised workers in the car industry. Whatever benefits the majority of ordinary Malays managed to obtain from this project, they were not comparable with those cornered by the minority of foreign together with local capitalists. It appeared that the Malaysian cars of different types have not been competitive in the international market, unlike their Japanese and Korean counterparts. But Proton cars have been able to capture the local market mainly because they are relatively cheaper than imported cars, owing to the protection policy by imposing heavy taxes on imported cars.

Even before the industrialisation plans were able to show signs of success, Dr Mahathir had jumped into the next advanced stage of announcing the Multimedia Super Corridor (MSC). This corridor, stretching from Kuala Lumpur to Putrajaya, was to be developed for multimedia usage and also investment. There were a lot of efforts to attract foreign and local investments, but they have not been as successful as expected. Of course, a Multimedia University was successfully set up, but the other MSC projects have not been able to create, promote or stimulate an impressive growth of a local core of multimedia expertise and enterprises.

An indirect effect of the MSC was that it tended to develop sophisticated multimedia technology mainly in the area of the corridor, especially among government departments, educational institutions, private companies and individuals. The rest of the country, particularly the rural areas and the hinterlands, remained behind. As such, the technological gap between the corridor and the outlying areas as well as the people living in them have become wider, thus worsening further the condition of socio-economic inequity in the country. Obviously this affected the Malays more than the other communities, as they formed the majority in the outlying areas.

As already indicated in an earlier chapter, Dr Mahathir encouraged his party and leaders or members of the party to be involved in business. Perhaps he believed this as one of the most effective ways to produce more Malays participating actively in business and industries. UMNO leaders at various levels began to vie for important positions because these could easily open the door for getting contracts, business licenses and shares that would enable them to become rich quickly. After becoming wealthy, a number of them could easily indulge in money politics to achieve higher positions and more political power. So, wealth and power could always reinforce each other mutually.

It is quite normal that, unlike those occupying the lower and middle rung positions, the top leaders in UMNO often avoided entering into business or getting licenses and contracts directly for themselves. They often resorted to having nominees from among very close relatives and cronies, who were often not involved in active party politics, though close to the centre of power. In this way a lot of Malay capitalists, corporate figures and entrepreneurs were created through sponsorship. At the same time they also resulted in corrupt practices. As usual, the common Malays who were supposed to be guaranteed special positions and privileges hardly benefited at all from these policies and practices.

Finally, under Dr Mahathir, what was called the New Development Policy (NDP) was introduced in 1990. The NDP did not depart very much from the NEP, in fact, it was essentially based on the latter's two-prong objectives, namely poverty eradication and restructuring of society to promote national unity. Among the critical aspects of the NDP are the following:

- create optimum balance between economic growth and equitable distribution;
- ensure balanced growth of primary economic sectors to achieve optimum growth;
- reduce and finally eradicate economic and social imbalance that will benefit all people;
- promote and strengthen national unity by reducing economic inequity among various states and between rural and urban areas;
- establish a progressive society where all people enjoy high quality of life, possess positive social and spiritual values as well as national pride and patriotism;
- develop human resources, including disciplined and productive work force, and improve expertise to face the challenge of industrialisation;

- establish science and technology as important basis for socio-economic planning and development, especially of modern industrial economy; and
- while concentrating on economic development, pay equal attention on environmental and ecological protection and ensure sustained growth.[30]

The above intentions appear to be very attractive indeed, but unfortunately more on paper than in implementation. Resulting from the implementation of various pet plans, policies and projects of Dr Mahathir, as elaborated earlier, economic distribution became more imbalanced and only a small group of people, not all people, have really benefited from economic growth. Because of growing concentration of wealth in the hands of a few and the adoption of divisive ethnic politics, the national unity agenda has really gone nowhere despite fifty years of Merdeka. Among others, the educational institutions and the media have failed to create a sense of pride and patriotism in society, even among the young. Spiritual values seemed to slide down together with the increase of immoral and criminal activities, which included corruption, rape, robbery, drug abuse, abandonment of babies and so forth.

The efforts to industrialise have failed to succeed more because of mismanagement, inefficiency and corruption at the top rather than lack of discipline and productivity at the bottom. Although science and technology were applied more for development, yet they were still not enough; for instance, the allocations for R&D in Malaysia are small compared to South Korea. Finally, the concern shown for environment was admittedly more prominent following the NDP compared to the past. But the government has failed to control such environmental hazards as excessive air and water pollutions resulting from factory and motor vehicle emissions, regular flooding and landslides, resulting from development projects that were not well-planned as well as poor drainage, deforestation that have resulted from both legal and illegal logging, and so forth.

Despite all the noble intentions of the NDP, under Dr Mahahir the Malays at large did not benefit much from it, although it was supposedly aimed at helping to improve the economic lot of the ordinary Malays. No doubt the incidence of poverty among them declined over the years,

---

30. Malaysia, 1991.

but hardcore poverty still existed and relative poverty had worsened with the widening gap of socio-economic inequity. A small coterie of Malays at or close to the centre of power were able accumulate wealth for themselves. Improvements in incomes of the broad mass of people at the lower levels have often been negated by inflation and rising prices of daily needs.

Although the socio-economic positions of rural Malays improved, they were relatively slight and should have been much better in view of the wealth of the country and the availability of quite abundant natural resources. The implementation of the restructuring objective under the NEP, which was continued by the NDP, favoured a small number of Malays although some non-Malays also gained from it. Many of the measures carried out in pursuant of the first objective of alleviating poverty, which was supposed to be irrespective of race, nevertheless appeared to exclude the majority of poor non-Malays. The Indians in the estates felt it most.

After Dr Mahathir retired as Prime Minister, he was succeeded by Abdullah Ahmad Badawi, his deputy. Abdullah was a contrast to Dr Mahathir – apparently more humble, religious and presented by the UMNO-owned, -controlled or -influenced media as "Mr Clean". But he appeared to have neither vision nor direction. Abdullah repeatedly promised better governance, transparency and to wage war against corruption.

But soon he was breaking all of these promises. If indeed there was real intention to be transparent, the media could have played an important role to expose all types of mismanagement and corruption in government, especially among those linked with high profile government figures or institutions that had become even more rampant than ever. But they were tightly controlled; not only they did not cover stories on corruption implicating government leaders, they were also not allowed to publish news on certain opposition leaders and parties, except for the purpose of distortion or disinformation.

At the beginning Abdullah declared that the government would not waste public money on mega projects, but later he appeared to have been in a hurry to announce and implement, may be in anticipation of the impending the 12th general elections in 2008, a number of mega projects. These included constructing a second Penang bridge linking the island to the mainland, costing around RM3 billion, and three corridors for economic development in the southern, northern and eastern parts of Peninsular Malaysia, which altogether would fetch an estimated combined cost of over RM25 billion. A smaller part of the expenses would be met by the government through PETRONAS while the bigger part would come from the private sector through local and foreign investments.

Although the government claimed that these projects would be of great benefit to the country, cynics have expressed that those who would profit most would likely be capitalists or corporate figures, most of them relatives and cronies of the government and party leaders. Much doubt has been expressed if these projects could ever improve the socio-economic conditions of the poor, lower income and middle income groups, a large section of them Malays. Instead, contractors, developers – not necessarily just Malay – and capitalist-cronies, would profit most.

In terms of policy, two aspects where Abdullah tried to show he departed from Dr Mahathir was to give greater emphasis to agriculture and biotechnology. Quite correctly Abdullah explained that agriculture formed the most important basis of the Malay economy and an important way to uplift the economy of this community was by improving agriculture. Abdullah declared he wanted to strengthen agriculture and to treat this as an important aspect of his economic policy. To demonstrate that he was serious about it, he appointed a senior member of his party and cabinet to be in charge. But it is disappointing that the financial allocations for agriculture, as in the budgets tabled by the PM who is also the Finance Minister, and in the Ninth Malaysia Plan, were not impressive and did not reflect its declared importance. Out of the estimated RM2,000 billion total expenditure, only 5.7 per cent were committed to agriculture, whereas the proportion of people involved is much higher than that.

No plans have been announced to give more land to peasants, to review the land tenure and tenancy systems, to improve methods of increasing productivity, to stabilise prices and to correct the market structure so that the agricultural producers could get more returns from the sale of their produce. What has been constantly emphasised is the slogan "agriculture is business". This certainly would be easier for those with capital to undertake, but not for peasants and rural people who do not even earn enough for decent living. Actually, there is nothing basically wrong with the policy of producing small and medium agricultural capitalists or businessmen, so long as they do not exploit or take advantage of the peasants and greater efforts are concentrated on uplifting the general socio-economic status of the peasantry at large. This has not happened.

The second aspect is biotechnology, which Abdullah sees as an important industry for generating new sources of wealth. The focus of biotechnology is to be in the fields of "agriculture, healthcare, industrial activities and bio-informatics". Together with this there were also plans to increase the rate of R&D, which is still low compared to some developing countries like South Korea, and also to increase the number of skilled workers and researchers. But only about RM2 billion is allocated under the Ninth Malaysia Plan for this new area of biotechnology, despite Abdullah's great enthusiasm on it.

Under Abdullah, there has been concerted effort by the youth leaders, especially his son-in-law to restore and strengthen what they call "the spirit of the NEP", claiming that this is the only way to help the Malays progress. But as it was during the time of Dr Mahathir, now under Abdullah the interests of a few leaders and cronies are being promoted and defended in the name of the Malays as a whole. Those who questioned the need to extend the NEP or called for its replacement were quickly branded as anti-Malay and unpatriotic. Anwar Ibrahim, the former deputy prime minister and leader of the People's Justice Party (PKR) has been branded as such. In fact, he had also been accused of being pro-Amercian and pro-Jew, and of currying favour with the Chinese in order to get political and electoral support.

Anwar argued that the time had come for the NEP to be replaced by what he outlined as a Malaysian Economic Agenda. The reasons he gave were: (a) after 37 years since the NEP was introduced, the economic situation of the country and people have changed and this called for the NEP itself to be reviewed, (b) the NEP has been used or abused by a small group of people at the top to grab the wealth of the country for themselves but all in the name of the Malays, a large segment of whom have still remained in disadvantaged positions, and (c) even in the treatment of the poor, the NEP has often been implemented to favour the Malays to the exclusion of non-Malays; so Anwar has been insisting that justice must be given to all irrespective of ethnic or religious backgrounds. The fact remains that despite fifty years of Merdeka, the constitutional guarantees for special position of the Malays and the NEP, UMNO leaders have failed to uplift the majority of Malays to the level of non-Malays, particularly the Chinese who do not enjoy the benefit of the NEP, especially in the economic and educational fields.

What is to be done? What alternative policies for development should be adopted to help the majority of Malays who really need help?

First of all there is need for the NEP to be reviewed and replaced by a new economic plan that would ensure the wealth and resources of the country are not monopolised by only a small coterie of people who have already enjoyed power. Instead they should be distributed fairly and evenly to the majority of people comprising different ethnic groups. In other words more public expenditure must be concentrated on these groups so that they would have a greater share of the country's wealth. There has been tendency for the UMNO-BN government to implement policies and plans that in the ultimate analysis have not helped the poor and disadvantaged Malays as much as they should.

Let us take as an example the state of Terengganu, which is rich in petroleum. For about 20 years until 1999, when UMNO ruled Terengganu, the state government received petroleum royalty totaling about RM7 billion. This royalty had helped the state to achieve the second highest income per-capita in the whole country. But at the same time it was the state with the second highest incidence of poverty (about 17 per cent), the first being Sabah. There has been impressive physical development in the state capital, adorned with many imposing government departments, commercial centres and hotels. But some of the rural scenes have not transformed much since Merdeka. Not only poverty is widespread, the socio-economic gaps between the rich and the poor, the towns and the rural areas, have widened. The revenue from petroleum had not been wisely spent for uplifting the poor people and developing the rural and other backward areas.

Taking the country as a whole, the gross revenue earned by PETRONAS in the past couple of years has been in the region of RM70 billion per annum. It has been estimated that up to 2004 the total net savings of PETRONAS from export of oil and gas since the beginning totaled around RM300 billion. But hitherto, there is only around RM50 billion left. There has never been any public accounts disclosed; in fact, there has been no account submitted even to Parliament. PETRONAS is completely under the jurisdiction of the Prime Minister. Apparently, during Dr Mahathir's tenure of office, about RM150 billion of the PETRONAS money had been spent on mega projects, which many believe to be wasteful and uneconomic. Abdullah is now following Mahathir again, this time in the use of its revenue for mega projects. It would have been more meaningful had it been used also for providing cheaper and better schools and education, hospitals, health services and housing for the poor from all ethnic groups.

Some UMNO leaders create the fear among ordinary Malays that if the NEP is replaced then their future would be jeopardised. Actually, by concentrating more of the country's wealth for uplifting the lives of the poor and developing the rural areas, the biggest benefactors will be the Malays because they form the majority – about 70 per cent of the poor and in the rural areas. Besides, this could reduce not only the existing socio-economic gaps but would also remove a serious source of dissatisfaction among the non-Malays if assured by words and actions that being poor like the Malays they also have equal stake in the country.

Secondly, the economic system in the country should never be based entirely on the free enterprise system. But this does not mean that all factors of production should be totally nationalised or state-owned. As we have seen, Dr Mahathir was completely against nationalisation and in favour of privatisation. In fact he branded nationalisation as 'communistic' and those in favour of it as "willing to cooperate with the communists and become their front".[31]

This is rather an extreme view of someone seemingly lacking in rational arguments. Are all those who oppose poverty and who wish to redress it by nationalising the country's wealth and utilising it for the poor and marginalised necessarily cooperating with the communists? Are the Arab states which have nationalised their oil part of the communist front? Unfortunately, many of the Arab states that own or control petroleum are so feudalistic and authoritarian that they do not

---

31. Mahathir, 1976: 106.

pay much attention to the majority poor. Instead they have been more interested in personal and family gains and personal aggrandisement. Those people opposing nationalisation also say that it is a policy of 'grabbing' other people's property, arguing that it is against Islam.

Who have really been grabbing and even plundering? Is it not the imperialists and colonialists who came with their boats, guns and cannons, who murdered and subjugated the local people, who colonised the country and then took over the best lands and the richest mines? Were they not the real plunderers? Unfortunately, nowadays there are also some of the richest and most powerful leaders in the country who with their cronies and relatives have been plundering the wealth of the lands and neglecting their own peoples. Is it not true that by having power to dominate the economy they could easily perpetrate exploitation and injustice? Are not these very same things opposed to Islam?

The basic question here is not just about private ownership, but the injustices resulting from private ownership and control of the country's wealth. By condemning it as communist policy and anti-Islamic, was Dr Mahathir also damning the late Prime Minister Razak and several other ministers because they signed the declarations in Algiers (1971), Lahore (1974) and Dakar (1975), which upheld nationalisation as a means of achieving social justice? The first was a meeting of non-aligned states, the second a meeting of Muslim states and the third of developing nations.

The nationalisation policy could never be easily accepted by any government or leader upholding the *laissez faire* system and depending on foreign investments in the private sector for the country's development. But it must be stressed that, as long as foreign investors and the free enterprise system remain strong, the eradication of poverty and the restructuring of society would be difficult to succeed. How would it be possible to control or plan development within the private sector which guarantees full freedom to make maximum profits? But with a nationalisation policy it would presumably be much easier to plan so that profits from nationalised industries could be used to finance development projects and encourage greater Malay participation in business and industries that are socially controlled.

It is not the intention here to argue for the full adoption of the nationalisation policy although it needs to be stressed that a completely *laissez faire* system is not desirable. What is required is actually nationalisation or state ownership of only certain important enterprises and services that are really essential. The petroleum industry is already state-owned in this country, but the unfortunate thing is that the revenues from petroleum have not been properly managed and distributed for the benefit of the majority of people who need assistance. On the other hand, it has almost been, and continues to be, squandered on monumental and mega projects which in the long run have benefited only a small number of people by way of obtaining contracts, businesses and commissions from them.

Such services like water and electricity should have continued being state-owned and never privatised. It would be most unfortunate if privatisation predominates over health and education, which appear to be taking place now. Anyhow, for state control or nationalisation to operate best, the projects must be supervised and manned by people who are incorruptible, dedicated and efficient. Otherwise they would fail too.

Thirdly, there is need to strengthen the cooperative movement. Nationalisation is one important aspect within the policy of liberating the people and the country's economy from the grip of a minority of wealthy people, both local and foreign. In the developing countries, especially those which have experienced colonialism, nationalisation will first of all affect the foreign monopoly-capitalists who own and control the big estates, mines and commercial houses. In addition, there are also some local landlords and capitalists who dominate the economy. A large number of them are very close cronies of the powers that be and also cooperate closely with the foreign monopoly-capitalists.

They control production and marketing at the national and state levels, and also on a smaller scale at the village level. The *laissez faire* system provides the fullest means and opportunities to the capitalists and landlords to carry out all kinds of manipulation and exploitation in order to maximise their profits. Many studies have been undertaken and have shown that the worst victims of exploitation by landlords and capitalists (who often act as middlemen and moneylenders too) are the poor peasants in the rural areas.

One way of reducing the adverse effects of the middlemen and moneylenders is to encourage the development of a strong cooperative movement. But this movement must operate and be effective at all levels. Take the fishing industry as an example. At the first stage – catching the fish – boats and nets are required. At the next stage – when the catch is to be sold – there are other requirements, such as transport, ice storage and market demands. If cooperatives are set up only for buying boats and nets, there is the possibility for sabotage or obstruction in the form of high rates imposed for transport or storage by capitalists who do not wish to see the cooperatives succeed. Only if the cooperatives control all the boats, nets, transport, storage and markets, will the movement be guaranteed success.

A highly successful cooperative movement can certainly raise the fishermen's standard of living, because profits that are normally made by owners of boats, storage and transport operators as well as markets under the free enterprise system, can be earned by the cooperatives instead. Thus, the fishermen can benefit through better wages and prices. In the same way the standard of living of *paddy* cultivators can be improved if all the work of ploughing land, supplying fertilisers, providing credit, milling and marketing are undertaken by cooperatives. In the past cooperatives in the country have failed because of inefficiency, financial mismanagement and dishonesty of the operators. These problems have to be overcome.

In a way, the cooperative system is quite directly opposed to the free enterprise system. In both fishing and *paddy* cultivation, for instance, the cooperative system should be concerned with the welfare of the fishermen and cultivators, while the *laissez faire* system is more concerned with the profits that can be made by such groups as landlords, middlemen and moneylenders. When the cooperative movement is not strong or is encouraged only as a token, then it can easily be undermined by companies or individuals competing against it. Therefore, in order to guarantee the success of the cooperatives, suitable conditions must be provided which can restrict or completely remove all forms of private competition which may threaten them. But of course this would affect the delicate constitutional matter guaranteeing the legitimate rights and interests of business, which would require to be amended first.

The best move would be to give cooperative movement full powers to operate initially within a particular industry, sector or area. But it is much more effective if the movement extends to all sectors in the country which affect the lives of the peasantry. In other words, the cooperative philosophy and system must replace the *laissez faire* system and philosophy. Only in this way can poverty be effectively eradicated and the standard of living of the rural people improved. The success of the cooperative movement in certain countries like Denmark need to be studied in the course of any attempt to improve our own.

Another important way to achieve this objective is by introducing a comprehensive land reform programme. Efforts to open up land settlements, provide facilities for drainage and irrigation, fertilisers, credit and so forth, as already carried out under the various development plans, actually form only part of land reform. They are important but inadequate because they do not alter the structure of land ownership and the tenancy system that currently exists. There is no limit to the amount of land that can be monopolised by rich landlords and capitalists, although admittedly there are not very many of them who own more than 25 acres of land, for instance. Sometimes they resort to extortionist methods whereby the poor peasants become victims, the sharing system giving them only a small portion of the product of their labour or their meagre holdings confiscated due to their inability to repay loans at exorbitant rates of interest.

In a situation where most of the land is controlled by a few landlords, then the tenancy system would benefit the owners more than the operators. In some countries land ownership is limited to only 25 acres and the rest redistributed among the landless peasants. In some others all lands in certain areas are controlled and worked collectively by the people in those areas. What is earned is then redistributed among the people and used for carrying out local development projects. There is need to study, devise and implement an appropriate and comprehensive land reform policy which could change the systems of ownership, production and tenure necessary for the development of this country and the progress of the people. That having said, foreign experiences cannot be replicated in toto without first evaluating them.

To conclude, it has been argued in this chapter that there is great need for change in plans and policies regarding the economy so that there can be greater emphasis on general socio-economic improvement of the poor and lower income groups than the creation of a small number of the new rich. This would ensure more equitable balance, which has become ever more skewed now owing to past policies and plans. The three alternatives presented towards the end of the chapter cover only a major part of the wider context of development that should and could promote greater equity and justice. The wider scenario covers the following aspects:

- balance between growth and distribution;
- balance between centre and periphery; urban and rural, ethnicity and gender;
- balance between economic development and environmental protection;
- balance between physical development with social and moral development;
- balance between the needs of the individual with the needs of society;
- balance between economic and human development as well as material and spiritual values;
- balance between culture and tradition with science and technology; and
- balance between rights of the rich and powerful, with justice for the poor and weak.
- These aspects cover a very wide area and show how complex the process of promoting and achieving development can be. It is difficult and complex in all countries, perhaps more so in a multi-ethnic society like Malaysia.

8
MULTI-ETHNIC SOCIETY

We have discussed Malay society and its problems in the preceding chapters. It is well-known that the population of the country is multi-ethnic. In the 1970 census, the population of the Peninsula was 8,810,348, made up of 4,685,838 Malays (53.2 per cent), 3,122,350 Chinese (35.4 per cent), 932,629 Indians (10.6 per cent) and 69,531 Others (0.8 per cent). By 2007 the total population (including Sabah and Sarawak) had grown to 27.173 million, with the Malay constituting 50.68 per cent, Chinese 23 per cent, Indian 9.6 per cent, Non-Malay Bumiputera 11.0 per cent and Others 1.2 per cent. The Malay majority over the rest combined is quite significant in size.

It is necessary for us to view and examine the position of the Malays in connection with the other ethnic groups. The Malays form only part of the bigger whole. When we focus our attention solely on them, we see only part of the picture. The Malays and their problems have to be viewed in relation to the other groups and within the context of the whole country.

The Malays in the Peninsula have long had relations with other ethnic groups, not only those from this region but also from other areas. Geographically, the Peninsula is strategically situated; the Malacca Straits is an important waterway connecting the East and the West. For centuries traders have stopped in these parts, seeking shelter and victuals, as well as trade. Perhaps these factors attracted the early traders to settle here. By the 15th century Melaka had emerged as an important and busy centre for government and trade. Travellers and traders converged on Melaka, coming from Java and other islands in the Archipelago and all the way from Arabia, India, China and later Europe.

These foreigners did not come for trade alone. Some of them eventually settled here, married to local women and raised families. There were also religious functionaries who stayed back to spread their beliefs, first Hinduism and later Islam. In Melaka, besides the traders and religious functionaries, quite a few foreigners were accepted into the upper class. *Sejarah Melayu (The Malay Annals)* mentions some officials of Indian origin (the most prominent being Mandaliar) serving the Court of Melaka, and the marriage of one believed to be a Chinese princess (Hang Li Po) to an early Melaka ruler.

So, even then there were already socio-economic relations through trade, involvement in government and mixed marriages in both the lower and upper strata of society. But we must remember that at that time the position of the Malays (or the government) was strong. Probably this was because the foreigners were few and some of them came only for a short time, although some others stayed behind. Those who settled here were easily assimilated into Malay society.

Migration, particularly of Chinese and Indians who were searching for a livelihood or for a place to settle, took place with the encouragement of the British after the introduction of their rule in the Malay states. There were two major categories of immigrants. First were those who came from the outlying islands within the Archipelago, who shared a similar history and culture with the Malays in the Peninsula. They were the Javanese, Sundanese, Acehnese, Banjarese, Bugis, Minangkabau and so forth. Most of them came on their own, but quite a large number were brought in as contract labourers, especially the Javanese. Some of them opened up new settlements or worked in existing villages, while others became workers on estates or in various government departments. Because of their cultural affinities with the Malays and the absence of religious obstacles, they could easily inter-marry with and be assimilated into the local community. Eventually they regarded themselves, and were regarded by others, as Malays.

The second category consisted of those originating from India and China, who were brought in as contract labourers to work in the estates and mines and in government departments, e.g. railways and the postal services. Others came on their own initiative, trying their luck in trade, beginning with small sundry shops in towns and villages. A few Indians and Ceylonese filled vacancies in the professions, as lawyers, doctors and engineers. The Indians, Ceylonese and Chinese are all of different stock, and have different cultures and religions from the Malays, although owing to history there are some cultural affinities between the Malays and Indians. Furthermore, they worked and settled in areas quite far away from the Malay villages. There existed social distances between the Chinese and Indians, as well as between these two groups and the Malays. They carried on with their own lives within their own environments.

A society with multi-ethnic groups living separately but under the same political system, resulting from the history of colonialism, is often referred to as a plural society. This concept was used by a Western writer, John Sydenham Furnivall, who studied the situation in the East Indies, now Indonesia, and Burma when they were under the Dutch and British rules respectively. According to him, in the plural society ". . . different sections of the community (live) side by side but separately, within the same political unit". He further adds, "Each group holds its own religion, its own culture and language, its own ideas and ways . . . Even in the economic sphere there is division of labour along racial lines".[32] Furnivall's plural society concept is often used to analyse society in this country. Although Furnivall uses the term 'race' for each of the separate groups, perhaps it is more appropriate here to use the term 'ethnic group'.

Shibutani and Kwan put forward the interpretation that ". . . an ethnic group consists of those who conceive of themselves as being alike by virtue of their common ancestry, real or fictitious, and who are so regarded by others".[33] They further say that each ethnic group often is ". . . united by emotional bonds and concerned with the preservation of their type . . . they speak in the same language . . . share common cultural heritage".[34] Based on these views, the Malays, Chinese and Indians may be regarded as the main ethnic groups in the Peninsula. They manifest all the elements mentioned by Shibutani and Kwan.

---

32. Furnivall, J.S., 1948: 304-305.
33. Shibutani, T., Kwan, E.M., 1965: 47
34. *Ibid*: 40.

Multi-Ethnic Society 161

Although there are sub-groups within the Malay society, namely Javanese, Minangkabau, Bugis and others which also have their own languages and customs, very often they are categorised as Malays because they regard themselves and are regarded by others as Malays. The bases for these, as explained in Chapter 1, are both legal-constitutional as well as socio-cultural. So too, even though there are different clans among the Chinese, each with its own dialect and often involved in varying economic activities, generally they regard themselves and are regarded by others as just Chinese.

As it is, it is not so difficult to identify different ethnic groups by their outward appearance. Besides that, they each also manifest characteristics and cultural norms that are different and easily distinguishable. The Malays are Muslims, who are required by their religion to pray, fast, pay religious tithes and perform the Hajj to Mecca; but not all Malays fulfill these five pillars of Islam. Their attire and food are generally influenced by their religious beliefs and cultural values.

As for the Chinese, although they are often associated with Buddhism and Taoism, they do not adhere strictly to these beliefs. Their religious faiths do not seem to permeate their everyday life as Islam does among the Malays, especially those in the villages. The Indians are quite devout Hindus and often perform their religious rituals. Each ethnic group has its own language and cultural heritage, and is proud of them. Quite a big number of Indians and Chinese are Christians. There is also a large number of Indian Muslims.

The factors which distinguish and separate different ethnic groups are not limited to hereditary characteristics. There are other factors related to the process of development and achievement among the various ethnic groups. In 1970 figures about 2,530,433 or 28.7 per cent of the people in the Peninsula lived in urban areas, which are those gazetted as having more than 10,000 people. About 14.9 per cent were Malays, 47.4 per cent of the Chinese and 34.7 per cent of the Indians in the country lived in the towns (*see Table 3.1*). The non-Malays were concentrated in the towns, mostly in the states which from the beginning provided the most opportunities for development from rubber estates, tin mines and commerce, namely Penang, Selangor, Perak and Negeri Sembilan. By 1995 the urban population had gone up to 54.7 per cent. No ethnic distribution is available, but the impression is that the process of urbanisation during this period has been faster among the Malays than the others.

The distribution of population is also connected with types of occupation and levels of incomes. In the rural areas Malays are involved with agriculture, especially in *paddy,* rubber and more recently oil palm; Chinese are mostly involved with rubber tapping, vegetable gardening, mining and petty trading; the Indians with tapping in rubber estates. In urban areas various types of urban occupations, for instance, labour and management in manufacturing, construction and business, are mostly undertaken by the Chinese. But in the government services and the lower ranks of the uniformed services, the Malays form the majority.

The ethnic distribution according to occupation or economic activity can be seen clearly in (*see Table 8.1*). Following these tables, in 1970 more than two-thirds (67.6 per cent) of the labour force in agriculture were Malays, 24.8 per cent in mining, 28.9 in manufacturing, 21.7 in construction and 23.5 in commerce. On the other hand, the Chinese formed 21.4 per cent in agriculture, 66 per cent in mining, 65.4 per cent manufacturing, 72.1 per cent in construction and 65.3 per cent in commerce. The figures in 2000 showed that the percentage of Malays in agriculture (including forestry and fishing) was 78.5; whereas in mining, manufacturing, construction and commerce the percentages were 50.1 (*see Table 8.2*), 55.2, 42.2 and 42.4 respectively. As for the Chinese 16.9 per cent were in agriculture, 38.5 in mining, 30.7 in manufacturing , 47.8 in construction and 50.2 in commerce.[35]

In terms of income, the average rural income in 1970 was about RM200, while the urban average was slightly more than double at RM418. The urban to rural ratio then was 1:2.14 but by 2004 it slightly declined to 1:2.11. In 1997 the average rural income was RM1,669, while the urban average was RM3,406. As already noted in the previous chapter, in 1970, out of 1.6 million households 49.3 per cent were below the poverty line, which was estimated at $25 per capita per household, or about $150 per household with six members. Among those regarded as being poor 89.2 per cent were in the rural areas. Most of the Malays are in the villages, and so it is not surprising that compared to the other groups they had the lowest average household income with $172, compared to the Chinese and Indians who had $394

---

35. Malaysia, 1991.

and $304 respectively. From 1999 - 2004 the average incomes for the Malay/Bumiputera, Chinese and Indians were RM2,038, RM3,737 and RM2,896. In the rural areas the averages were RM1,498, RM2,668 and RM1,488, while in the urban areas they were RM2,769, RM4,071 and RM3,289 respectively (*see Table 7.2*).

There is also some racial pattern in the distribution of educational and political affiliations. In 1970 and 1975 the distribution of the student population of all levels can be observed from (*see Table 11.1 and 12.1*). Generally the percentage of Malays at different levels of education increased between 1970-1975 from 53.4 to 55.2 per cent at primary level; from 51 to 54.4 per cent at lower secondary; from 48.8 to 60.7 per cent at upper secondary; from 43.4 to 54 per cent at post-secondary; from 49.7 to 65.1 per cent at pre-university; from 82.9 to 85.4 per cent in diploma courses; and from 39.7 to 57.2 per cent in degree courses.

Although the school should be a good place for students of all ethnic groups to mix, it seems that certain ethnic groups concentrate in certain schools. According to the Household Survey of 1967-68, 87 per cent of the Malay children went to Malay schools, 85 per cent of the Chinese to Chinese schools and 67 per cent of the Indians to Tamil schools. Only in the English schools did there appear a rather mixed combination of the various ethnic groups.[36] Unfortunately the situation has gone worse. According to the Strategic Plan for Education 2007, announced by the Ministry of Education, about 93 per cent of Chinese are in vernacular National-type Chinese School, while the same percentage of Malay students are in the National Schools, which use the Malay language as medium of instruction.

1970 was the first year that government and government-aided schools changed to Malay medium; this change occurred gradually, so that by 1980 all classes at primary and secondary levels were conducted in Malay. But this did not change anything much in the educational structure because it still left schools in different mediums with only one ethnic group predominating.

As indicated above, schools which were originally in Malay medium continue to be predominated by Malays, while national-type schools in the urban centres continue to be predominantly non-Malay. There are

---

36. Chander, R, 1970.

no more government English schools now. At the post-secondary level, in most of the well-known schools in the urban areas the majority of students are non-Malays, while most of the science schools established by MARA continue to admit only Malays until very recently when some of them admitted a few non-Malay students.

In the teachers' training colleges there is some inter-ethnic congregation, but the Universiti Teknologi Mara (UiTM), despite being raised to the status of a university, is still exclusively for Malays just as the Tunku Abdul Rahman University is almost exclusively for Chinese. Among the various universities, the University of Malaya seems best to reflect the population composition, although there is ethnic polarisation in some faculties. The National University (UKM), the University of Agriculture (UPM, later renamed Universiti Putra Malaysia), and University of Technology (UTM) have a high percentage of Malays, but slowly more non-Malays have been admitted to achieve ethnic balance.

More universities have been established now, but the majority of students in the state universities that teach mainly in the Malay medium are Malays, while those in the private universities, most of which use English as the medium of instruction, are non-Malays. As for those who are studying overseas, about three quarters are non-Malays (mainly Chinese) who finance their own studies and the rest are Malays, almost all of whom have the advantage of getting government scholarships.

In politics it can be said that most of the political parties are comprised solely or predominantly of one ethnic group as members. The policies and structural organisations of these parties are communal; each has membership that is exclusively from one ethnic group. Among the Malays there are two big parties: UMNO, which is based on rather liberal Malay nationalism; and PAS, which claims to champion Islam, whose members are entirely Malay. The People's Justice Party (PKR), which is much younger than the other two but growing in importance, is largely social-democratic in orientation; its membership is open to all ethnic groups, but the majority is Malay although the Chinese and Indian components are growing.

The People's Party (PRM) and the Socialist Party (PSM) whose memberships and programmes are also multi-ethnic to fight for the interests of the depressed and less privileged groups, irrespective of ethnic origins, have Malays and Indians as their majority members respectively. The Chinese are concentrated mainly in the Malaysian Chinese Association (MCA), Gerakan and the Democratic Action Party. The membership of MCA is open only to Chinese, but DAP and Gerakan, although claiming to be multiracial, have only a sprinkling of Malay and Indian members. The Malaysian Indian Congress (MIC) is strictly an Indian party.

From before independence UMNO, MCA and MIC cooperated within the Alliance, but following the May Thirteenth Incident, PAS, Gerakan and several other opposition parties joined hands with the Alliance to form Barisan Nasional and later the Government. Their cooperation was purely organisational and confined to the leadership level. Although the BN coalition claims to be multi-ethnic, each component party continues with its own communal policy aimed at attracting support from its own community. PAS left the BN after about four years.

There are clearly marked differences in language, religion, culture, areas of residence, economic activities, political orientation and educational affiliation among the Malays, Chinese and Indians, but nonetheless they are not compartmentalised completely from one another. There is certainly a great social distance between the majority of them, but at the same time there exist inter-ethnic relations, albeit limited. There are villages, townships or towns where different ethnic groups live side by side; there are many estates, factories and other places where they work together; there are political parties in which they are all active; and there are various levels of educational institutions that children of different ethnic groups can attend.

Interaction occurs at various levels. At the level of friendship there are close relationships among individuals every day, or occasional visits during festivals. In institutions such as schools, market places, clubs and cinemas for instance, men, women and children of various ethnic groups are able to interact and strengthen their social ties. At the organisational level there are many political and non-governmental organisations which serve as means for promoting common activities and interactions that strengthen inter-ethnic relations.

The process of inter-ethnic integration continues to occur especially at the three levels mentioned above. This process can be seen more clearly in different strata of society. We have seen that Malay society is divided into the upper, middle and lower classes. The same division also prevails among the Chinese and Indians, and so the whole country can be analysed within the framework of the same stratification system based on their socio-economic structure. The one significant thing is that within each stratum the roles played by the three ethnic groups are different, thus depicting specialisation of roles among them.

As we have discussed earlier, the Malay upper class consists of the rulers, senior government politicians and administrators, and a handful of capitalists. The picture is different among the non-Malays. Of course there has never been a ruler among them, although, since independence, there have been some ministers, but most of the Chinese concentrate on economic activities, as proprietors and directors of commercial companies, plantation estates and also mines. Their number is bigger than that of the Malays. As already noted, in 1970, out of the total amount of $5,329 million of share capital of limited companies, only 2.4 per cent belonged to the Malays, or 27.2 per cent belonged to the Chinese, while foreign ownership 63.3 per cent. By the year 2004 the pattern had changed. Out of the total RM529,768.7 million share capital, Malays owned 18.9 per cent, Chinese 39 per cent, Indians only 1.2 per cent and foreigners 32.5 per cent (*see Table 9.1 and 9.2*).

Among members of the upper class there are some strong links. There is a kind of joint venture, where each ethnic group tries to integrate members of another ethnic group into its own sphere of influence. For instance, the Chinese capitalists try to get ex-civil servants or ex-ministers to participate in their economic enterprises, usually as directors (although this is often in name only, because most of them are only glorified PROs). At the same time many big Chinese *towkays* or successful professionals are accepted into the traditional Malay system, and awarded decorations and titles such as *Tun*, *Tan Sri*, *Datuk* and so forth. Many of them are leaders of the ruling parties, at the national or state level. Besides that they are also members of exclusive clubs like the Royal Golf Club and the Lake Club. So it is not only economic and political interests that link members of the upper class, but also common social activities.

Within the middle class there is also some occupational specialisation. As mentioned earlier, a large number of Malays have been absorbed into the administration; at present the 3:1 quota for admitting Malays into the civil services is still maintained. Many graduates enter these and other services, such as teaching, the military and the police, where the Malays also form the majority. On the other hand, middle class Chinese are mainly in the professions and in business. As evident in (*see Table 10.1*), in 1973 more than 60 per cent of the architects, town planners, engineers, medical doctors, dentists, managers and salesmen are Chinese.

By 2005, out of a total of 42,414 registered professionals the percentage of Malay had risen to 38.8 per cent, with the Chinese at 48.7 per cent and Indians 10.6 per cent. The percentages of Malays in some of the professions are as follows: Accountants 20.8, architects 45.3, medical doctors 36.7, dentists 44.4, engineers 46.0, surveyors 47.2 and lawyers 38.0. Chinese still form the majority in all, except as surveyors (*see Table 10.2*). The percentages of Indians in most of the professions are much higher than their composition of the population.

The Chinese are the majority as professionals in the private as well as the public sector. But their number is small in the civil and military services, just as the Malays are in small proportion in business and industry. Quite a good number of Indians are also found in the economic fields where the Chinese predominate. The concentration of Chinese and Indians in the professions and business may be perpetuated in as much as their opportunities to enter the civil service continue to be restricted.

Among the various groups in the middle class there is a similar style of life. Their educational achievement, especially at the secondary and post-secondary levels, used to be mainly through the English medium although now it is more in the Malay and Chinese mediums, with hardly any in the Tamil medium. In their daily life they tend to be modern or westernised. This facilitates social relationships among some of them.

At the state or town levels, there are sometimes understandings and relationships worked out between Malay administrators and non-Malay professionals and businessmen who have similar interests. They become members of the same clubs and spend a lot of their time playing billiards, tennis and golf or just boozing together. In fact in big cities like Kuala Lumpur they gather in places like the Royal Golf Club, the Selangor Golf Club and the Selangor Club. There are also members of the upper class, some of them ministers, who join these clubs, but their number is small. Although there are bases of integration among members of the middle class, there can also be acute conflicts among them which may spread to the upper class. This will be discussed later.

Within the lower class too there are elements of ethnic specialisation in particular occupations. A large majority of the Malays are peasants in the rural areas. There are some Malays who work as estate labourers or used to work as mining workers too, but their number is few. In the towns most of them are in the lower ranks of government services, working as office boys, gardeners, policemen and soldiers, but there are also an increasing number now, both men and women, who have become factory workers.

Compared to the Malays, there are not many Chinese who are peasants, and compared to the Indians there are not as many Malays who are estate labourers. But in the mines (when they were at their height), building construction and factories, the proportion of Chinese workers exceeds all the other groups until now. The Indians form the majority of estate labourers, and there are also many of them who serve as workers in the government departments, such as public works and railways. Nowadays, migrant workers have become more dominant, replacing or overcoming local workers in some sectors, such as construction work and in factories.

The process of inter-ethnic integration among groups in the lower class seems to be slower than that in the upper and middle classes, although quite often strong working class solidarity is displayed in some trade union disputes. The influence of religion and culture among them is stronger. Between the Malay peasants and Chinese workers there are wide social gaps and the ties or feelings of solidarity among them are limited. The gap becomes wider and in fact sometimes creates suspicion and animosity when some employers use religion and culture (as have happened in some factories) to separate workers ethnically in order to weaken them when they try to unite to form unions. But in areas or states where they form the minority, for instance in Kelantan, most of the Chinese in the lower class have assimilated into the Malay way of life, eating Kelantanese cooking, putting on the local sarong or headgear and speaking in the dialect of that state.

The discussions up to this point show two important things. First, although there are strong bases for group division according to ethnic origins, that is not the only division existing in society. Within each of the ethnic groups there are also quite clear-cut class categories. If the ethnic divisions are vertical in nature, the class divisions are horizontal. Vertical divisions according to ethnic groups are determined by factors that are hereditary or ascribed, while the horizontal divisions according to class are determined by new differentiating factors, such as economics and politics, and connected with achievement of groups or individuals in society. Along with these two categories based on ethnicity and class there are also two forces at work on members of the society: the force that tends to pull them closer according to ethnic group and that which tends to pull them closer according to class. And so, in their social behaviour and actions they may be more influenced by ethnic or class interests.

Second, there does not exist an ethnic stratification system. In other words there is no system whereby each stratum or class in society is made up of only one ethnic group and ranked higher or lower than another. In other words not all Malays are in the upper class or all Chinese in the lower class, or vice versa. This is quite different from the situation in South Africa, or to a limited extent, even in the United States. In South Africa, especially when Apartheid was practised, skin colour could determine social position: the blacks are always regarded as lower than the whites economically, politically and socially, and they always remained and were regarded as belonging to the lower class. There existed a colour line there which does not exist here now, although during British rule there was a situation which put the British in the upper layer high above the local people within the social stratification system existing then.

As we have discussed earlier there is strong evidence to show that class categories cut across ethnic lines. Within each of the classes there are Malays, Chinese and Indians. However, the percentage of Chinese earning more than $3,000 a month and owning property is higher than the percentage of Malays, while there are more Malays than Chinese among those who earn less then $150 and live in poverty in the lower class. At the same time a lot of Indians perceive that the majority of them are in the worst socio-economic category, although their condition is better than those of the indigenous population in the hinterland of the Peninsula, Sabah and Sarawak.

Third, the common view generally held is that economic and political power is divided ethnically. The Malays are supposed to hold political power while the Chinese hold economic power. This view is prevalent across the Straits of Johor and finds enthusiastic support amongst a section of the people in Malaysia too. In fact this view is rather misleading. It is true that there are more Malay ministers and administrators than Chinese, but there are also Chinese who share political power with the Malays and have quite strong political positions. In the same way there are more Chinese than Malays who are businessmen or entrepreneurs, although there is an increasing number of Malays who share economic power with their Chinese partners. What is important is that not all Malays have political influence and power, and not all Chinese are economically influential or powerful.

The Malays who really hold political power are only a small group from the upper class and to some extent middle class. So too the Chinese who monopolise the economy are mainly from the upper class. The Malays in the lower class and a large section of them in the middle class do not have much political power; they only have the opportunity to vote once every five years. So too, the majority of Chinese, most of whom are in the lower class, do not have any economic power. In fact, irrespective of whether they are Malays, Chinese or Indians, the majority of the people in this country do not hold any political or economic power. Power is in the hands of the powerful, and in the political and economic spheres in this country, it is in the hands of a tiny group of people made up of the various ethnic groups who usually can cooperate with and help one another rather closely.

The most important thing, which is often forgotten, is that a great deal of real power is in the hands of foreigners, especially the former colonial and present neo-colonial powers. Sometimes they have much greater power and influence than the Malaysians. In the economy, for example, as was already mentioned, in 1970, foreign interests controlled about 63 per cent of all the share capital of limited companies which totalled $5,329 million; or in greater detail 75.3 per cent in estates, 72.4 per cent in mining, 63.5 per cent in commerce, 59.6 per cent in manufacturing and 52.2 per cent in insurance. This foreign ownership was about two and half times larger than Chinese ownership and twenty-five times larger than the Malay ownership (*see Table 9.2*).

But by 1998 the picture changed quite significantly. It showed that although the share capital had increased substantially to RM93,667 million it constituted only 31.8 per cent for the whole country. The proportion of British interest in this country was still substantial but the proportion of US, Singaporean and Australian interests are getting larger. As indicated earlier, a survey in 2005 indicated that the US assets in Malaysia was more than US$30 billion. Through this economic control, which until recently was given teeth by the presence of their military might, these foreigners are able to wield considerable influence in this country. But the real test will come when there is political tension or crisis in the country.

Now we can turn to something else. Why is it that communal feelings are still strong although there have been attempts by various groups to reduce them? After the Second World War several communal clashes occurred in various places, such as Batu Pahat (1945/6), Batu Malim, Raub (1946), Batu Kikir (1946), Penang (January 1958), Pangkor (May 1959), Bukit Mertajam (1967) and the biggest, Kuala Lumpur (May 1969), followed twenty years later by comparatively minor ones in Kampung Rawa, Penang (1998) and Kampung Medan, Selangor (2001).

Recently inter-ethnic sentiments have run quite high, causing tensions. There is always fear that they could erupt at any time into serious conflicts or even violent clashes. What are the reasons? Below I try to summarise and discuss the patterns and causes of such conflicts.

Generally, communal clashes arise from differences and subsequent conflicts of values or interests, or both together. There are differences in the values of the Malays and the Chinese, owing to their different religious and cultural backgrounds. Furthermore, there is a social distance between them, and so most Malays do not know Chinese values very well and most Chinese are quite ignorant of Malay values, despite the fact that they have been living side by side for so long. The education system and mass communication have not been used by the powers that be to promote greater understanding of each other's values and cultures.

Of course sometimes the people as well as the government just ignore these value differences although they may know about them. This situation may give rise to unnecessary misunderstanding. First, it is possible for one ethnic group, out of ignorance and not deliberate intention, to hurt the feelings or arouse the anger of another group. For example, if a Chinese peasant living upstream rears pigs, and the river is used by Malays far downstream for bathing and taking ablution, then a major and violent clash could easily happen.

Second, since they are mutually ignorant of one another's religious and cultural backgrounds, they tend to have misconceptions of one another, taking the form of what social scientists call stereotypes. Certain characteristics which are often looked down upon are attributed to certain ethnic groups as a whole. For instance, there are Malays who regard the Chinese as dirty, as cheats and always obsessed with money-making. In the same way there are Chinese who picture the Malays as being lazy, spendthrift and prone to amusement. Probably, these attributes are true of some Malays and some Chinese, but not true of all of them. As a result of these stereotypes, prejudices grow. When each group is prejudiced against the other, tensions can easily develop, and explode into communal clashes. Unfortunately, both the Malays and Chinese have many negative stereotypes of the Indians, so that they are often looked down by both.

Third, differences or conflicts of interests often occur in the economic and political spheres. During the colonial days opportunities were limited for the local people, but after independence the door was opened wide to them for upward mobility. From one five-year plan to another, a good number of development projects were planned and there was much more money to be spent. All of these opened new opportunities for workers, businessmen and contractors. Because some Chinese had more capital, experience and know-how, they were able to gain much more from business and contracts than Malays or Indians.

Most of the Chinese businessmen and contractors were members of MCA, a component of the BN. The MCA indirectly became a channel for them to gain the businesses and contracts. Because of their association with the government they were also able to participate in the process of government. On the other hand, with the development of crony capitalism especially under Dr Mahathir's rule, Malay cronies have also been able to get big contracts and projects. Quite often, because of lack of capital and expertise they farm out these to Chinese capitalists or contractors, following the Malay-Chinese economic collaboration often referred to as the 'Ali Baba' system and collect commissions without doing much work. Of course there have also been some enterprising Malays who have struggled to build up themselves very much on their own.

In politics many Malays have succeeded to reach top posts. The system of parliamentary democracy has enabled some common people to move upwards and become leading members of the government, as federal ministers, state executive councilors (Exco) and so forth. As UMNO is the backbone of the BN, many of its leaders were appointed to various government posts after their election victory in 1974. Hitherto, the Malays still dominate over the other ethnic groups in the BN in terms of the top political positions held. Many Chinese, Indians and others often feel sidelined, but they are easily silenced by UMNO's powerful position and after being given cabinet or state Exco jobs.

From these political positions, some of them, Malays and non-Malays as well, have successfully shifted to economic activities and entrench themselves there. Actually speaking, only a small number from the upper class have been the main beneficiaries of political and economic privileges after the achievement of independence. They form a limited circle. At the state and national levels few could enter that circle. Some politicians, businessmen and professionals, like lawyers, accountants and so forth, tried to break into that circle, but seldom succeeded to be admitted into it. The majority of them were from the middle class. A large number of non-Malays and also some Malays from this category became very frustrated. Tension often ran high.

In addition, the Malays feel that they ought to have a greater share in the business and industrial activities, while the Chinese feel they ought to be given more opportunities in politics and administration. The Malays feel restless with what they believe to be excessive economic power in the hands of the Chinese, while on the other hand the Chinese are dissatisfied because they feel left out in politics and administration which are monopolised largely by Malays as a result of the quota system. The Indians get very dissatisfied because many of them feel they have been marginalised and that their community remains lagging behind in the economy as well as education, and their share equity is very low compared to their population.

At the same time there is acute competition to get contracts, licenses, jobs, promotions, places in the universities and scholarships. Under the special provision in the Constitution, Malays are often given special favour and treatment. So, particularly among most non-Malay members of the middle class who compete for these and often fail to get them, success or failure is often interpreted as being caused by the ethnic factor. But not all Malays are happy because only a small minority among them who are already in privileged position have easy access to these special privileges or positions.

Anyhow, feelings of dissatisfaction have been easily expressed in ethnic terms by some political parties and also other organisations. The BN has many component parties, but almost every party is made up of one ethnic group and tries to get support from the same group, especially during general election campaigns. UMNO presents itself as champions of the Malays. The pro-Malay issues that they constantly voice tend to give rise to uncertainty and even dissatisfaction among the MCA and Gerakan, which are the Chinese wings of the BN. In the same manner when MCA and Gerakan take up issues to attract Chinese support, members of UMNO become apprehensive. Although their interests sometimes seem to be in conflict, yet the leadership of the various component parties in the BN has been able to maintain organisational unity. As for the MIC, it is weak and its leadership is not effective in fighting for the interests of their own community which is made up very largely of the deprived from the lower classes.

From outside the BN there are also communal pressures. The PKR, which is a new party, tries to promote a multi-ethnic appeal but faces difficulty in the system that is dominated by ethnic politics; nevertheless, it is gaining popularity. Before PAS joined the BN, they regarded the Chinese as a threat to the future of the Malays and felt that the UMNO had sold out to the Chinese. After it joined hands with UMNO it was difficult for PAS to continue with this line of propaganda. But there was a large following of the party that did not agree with PAS leaders for joining the BN. They did not change their views, and continued to voice their dissatisfaction loudly.

On the other hand, among some chauvinists within the ranks of the DAP, for example, it has always been asserted that the Malays, or more correctly the government, wants to abolish Chinese language and education and force the Chinese and Indians to remain as second and third class citizens. In fact, religious and cultural issues have been increasingly made use of by both chauvinist Malays and Chinese to gain wider support.

During 2006 we saw many religious issues, like conversion, apostasy, burial location, destruction of temples being raised especially by the Hindus, which worsened ethnic tensions with Muslims.

The communal nature of politics in this country today is determined to a great extent by the middle class, and its influence has seeped downwards to the lower class. The peasantry, most of whom are Malays, and the workers who are majority Chinese and Indians, are in the most depressed socio-economic positions. Although much has been said about Malay privileges, the Malay peasants have gained almost nothing, especially when compared to the immense profits made by the upper class and foreign monopoly-capitalists. Opportunities for good jobs and facilities for education and medical services, particularly the private ones are more easily available to Malays and non-Malays from mainly the upper class and the middle class to some extent.

Although several development programmes have been in existence for some time they have not made much headway towards solving the basic problems of poverty, landlessness, unemployment and inflation; in fact the latter two have worsened. Generally, as the most exploited groups, Malay peasants and non-Malay workers suffer most and in this sense they share almost the same interests. But their dissatisfaction and disappointment are often expressed in ethnic terms.

Claims and accusations of a communal nature made by the top leadership of various political parties easily arouse the emotions of their members at the lower levels. The Malay peasants not only see themselves as being poor, but when comparing their sad condition with others, they see that the rich, especially those around them in the towns, are mostly Chinese. Most of them perceive the Chinese middlemen in the villages as not only manipulating the prices of the commodities they buy and sell, but also as controlling the livelihood of the villagers. Although there are those among them who can see and feel the effects of socio-economic injustices and often get angry about them, they are unable to understand, and more often than not are unable to interpret the basic causes of these injustices. There are some who attempt to interpret but they usually end up blaming the non-Malays as a whole.

To the Malays, the most common stereotype of the Chinese is that they are rich businessmen, and the most common stereotype of the Indians – particularly the Chettiars and the Sikhs – is that they are moneylenders. Owing to these stereotypes, Malays tend to lose sight of the fact that the businessmen and moneylenders consist of only a small number from those communities in the country. Of course there are also peasants and workers among the Chinese and Indians, and their plights do not differ very much from Malay peasants and workers.

Among the urban non-Malays there is still a widespread claim that Malays control the government, and that they use their power to suppress the non-Malays. When Chinese and Indian workers or hawkers have to deal with government officers they often have to face Malays. Sometimes language difficulties occur which easily give rise to misunderstandings. Furthermore, if hawkers, for instance, hawk without a license in some restricted areas, it is usually Malay policemen who take action against them. It is difficult to convince those already burning with anti-Malay sentiments that the governing elite consists only of a handful from the upper and middle classes, from various ethnic groups, and that some non-Malays also make up a large segment of those in government services serving as doctors, engineers, high school teachers and so forth.

Finally, we find that because of the prevailing divide and rule policy of the government, certain issues and actions are often twisted and manipulated by them and their controlled media for the purpose of mobilising public support for them. Recently two issues and actions have come to the fore, which manifested certain genuine grievances of the disadvantaged or marginalised categories of people. Unfortunately, they have been turned into narrow ethnic politics to serve the political interests of primarily the governing parties. The first is the NEP issue while the second is the demonstration by HINDRAF.

As indicated earlier, the NEP issue was sparked when Anwar Ibrahim declared that the NEP should be ended and replaced by a 'Malaysian Economic Agenda'. As explained earlier, Anwar argued that after more than 35 years, we find that: (a) development is slower and per-capita income is much lower in Malaysia than South Korea, Taiwan and Singapore, although they were almost on par forty years ago, (b) government figures show that the average incomes of Malays, especially at the lower and middle levels, are smaller than average incomes of non-Malays in the same categories, (c) in the name of helping the Malays, the ruling Malay elite has used the NEP in order to enrich themselves and their cronies that include Malays and non-Malays, thus causing socio-economic inequity to widen, and (d) in an attempt to please the Malays, the NEP has been used to help the Malay poor but unfortunately excluding the poor from other ethnic groups, thus causing ethnic discrimination and dissatisfaction.

Anwar has explained that his Malaysian Economic Agenda aspires to fight leakages and promote faster development so that Malaysia can catch up with the three countries mentioned above; to bridge the income gaps between the Malays and non-Malays; to stop the plunder of the wealth of the country by a small coterie of those in power together with their cronies; to close the growing gap between the very rich and the poor; and to give equal opportunities and treatment to all especially the poor and lower income groups, irrespective of their ethnic origins.

In their reaction, UMNO leaders, especially some among the youths who have used the NEP and their relationship with the top government leaders to enrich themselves, accuse Anwar of selling out to the non-Malays, especially Chinese, in order to gain their political support. By distorting Anwar's agenda and arousing fear and anger among the Malays about their future, these UMNO leaders and the media that they own or control play blatant racial politics in order to discredit Anwar and the party he leads, and instead try to muster Malay support for themselves and their party by lies and distortions.

As for the HINDRAF demonstration in Kuala Lumpur at the end of 2007, the estimated 30,000 who participated were of course moved by different types of motivation. But it cannot be denied that a large number of them were dissatisfied with their own socio-economic plight, the neglect of their education system, the destruction of some old established temples, and reports that many Indians died while in police custody or were killed in Kampung Medan by some trigger-free policemen or unknown perpetrators in 2001.

There appeared to be two mistakes committed by a few leaders of HINDRAF. Firstly, the indirect suggestion that there was ethnic cleansing of Indians, and secondly, the allegation that the poor plights of Indians have been due largely to the constitutional provision that gives special position to the Malays and denying the Indians the same. This provided some racialist UMNO leaders with the support of the

UMNO-BN controlled media to distort the facts and give a racial spin to the whole demonstration. HINDRAF as a whole was accused of being anti-Malay; although some of their leaders had emphasised that they were not against the Malays as a community but against UMNO which dominate the government. Worse still, some of their leaders were alleged to be closely linked with the Tamil Tigers in Sri Lanka.

The MIC leader equated UMNO with Malay and claimed that being anti-UMNO is similar to being anti-Malay. Little did he remember that Malay support for the opposition parties, especially PAS and PKR, during the last two elections have almost been as sizeable as that of UMNO. The UMNO leaders and their media kept on harping that HINDRAF was against Article 154 of the Constitution in order to arouse Malay anger. At the same time they tried to spin the story that Anwar was also in total support of HINDRAF, because Anwar went to the court when the HINDRAF leaders were brought there from police custody.

The truth is that even before the demonstration itself, Anwar had come out with two statements, disagreeing with the HINDRAF stand on Malay special position. He categorically stated that the UMNO-BN government and not the Malays should be blamed for the Indian plight, and that similar plights of the poor and marginalised Indians are also shared by Malays, Chinese, Ibans and Kadazandusuns who are equally marginalised. His appearance in court was merely to emphasise the right of HINDRAF or any other organisation to hold peaceful assemblies, consistent with the provision of the Constitution.

It is clear that economic, social and cultural differences that have been inherited from the past are still strong even today and often act as factors causing separation and conflict between the ethnic groups. These differences become exacerbated and turn into dangerous clashes when there are groups and parties which make use of communal issues to gain support. Leaders of all parties, especially those who are in government, should not play with the fire of narrow ethnic politics to win Malay support and remain in power. It appears that racial politics is being deliberately perpetuated so that the masses in the lower strata of society will never be united as a force to alter the *status quo*, which at present greatly benefits the upper class and also the foreign monopoly-capitalists who are actually in close cooperation with one another.

At present, political parties that raise political, economic, social and cultural issues on the basis of class differences between the rich and the poor have not proven to be successful. They have not been able to unite the various sectors in the lower class of all ethnic groups. The PKR, led by Anwar is firmly opposed to UMNO's narrow ethnic politics, and abuse of power, corruption and cronyism to enrich only a small group of political and economic elite in the country. They cannot be accused of being communist or Muslim extremists and so the ethnic or racial card is raised against them. Such actions will only worsen the trend of ethnic or communal politics among the people and this will not auger well for the future of united and prosperous Malaysia where justice is for all.

By way of conclusion it may be said that in this country, there is little political space for democratic activism, and civil society is severely restricted. Several draconian laws and regulations have been passed and implemented that allow for detention without trial, impose restrictions on freedom of the press. It is not being suggested here that these laws have been deliberately used to divide ethnic groups, but they do stifle change, which consequently create social and ethnic animosities.

Ethnic differences and similarities are often opportunistically used in political processes for determining, perpetuating or capturing power and influence in the economic and political fields. The present BN ruling coalition appears to be multi-ethnic, but in fact most of its thirteen component members represent particular ethnic groups and interests. In several elections, the ruling coalition has been known to resort to ethnic fears and threats to win the general support of the electorate.

Conflicts and killings can occur when one group tries to use race in order to perpetrate racial superiority and control economic and political power. We do not know of any easy solutions to these problems. Nevertheless, in the context of Malaysia, the establishment of social justice and democracy can go a long way to improve the situation. Social justice must mean a more equitable distribution of wealth. Democracy must mean broader civil liberties, greater freedom, more people's participation in decision-making processes, and a check against any growing authoritarian state.

There is a need to promote ethnic cooperation and interdependence in economic and political activities and the establishment of institutions cutting across ethnic barriers at all levels. It is also necessary to disseminate universal values and attitudes, which can help people so that they do not succumb easily to racial or ethnic appeals. There is also a need to overcome 'false consciousness' caused by ethnicity. At the same time, the state should not be allowed to legitimise ethnic violence to perpetrate itself. Until racial and ethnic harmony comes naturally, it must be strived for. ❁

9
CONCLUSION

This book tries to narrate and analyse important changes and serious problems relating to the Malays in Malaysia. The Malays as an ethnic group has been defined on the basis of both legal-constitutional and historical-cultural factors. It is difficult to speculate or visualise correctly the future of the Malays, for that matter any country or people. Nevertheless, it is possible to provide a general outline of the trends of the past and present, and probably attempt to at least indicate what should be avoided and promoted to ensure a better future for the Malays. Many types of changes and problems have been discussed in detail or mentioned only in passing in the various chapters of this book. Some of the main features may be summarised as follows:

a. *History:* The Malays have a long history as the original settlers of this country. They experienced a number of colonial rules, the longest and most effective being the British. With the help of the British colonialists who imprisoned or killed genuine liberation fighters, the country's independence was passed to those willing to collaborate with colonial power. Therefore British heritage in this country remained strong in many areas. During fifty years of UMNO-BN rule, a number of problems have arisen.

b. *Economy:* As part of the colonial heritage there are still elements of dual economy and economic specialisation along ethnic line, with Britain together with the US now playing dominant role. The dominating *laissez faire* system allows for concentration of wealth in the hands of a few (multi-ethnic with non-Malay majority) that results in poverty of the many (also multi-ethnic but with Malay majority). Although absolute poverty has been reduced, relative poverty (widening of the socio-economic gap) has increased. NEP helps to sponsor Malay rich and have resulted in nepotism and cronyism.

c. *Politics:* Traditional political system and institution exist under the symbol of the constitutional monarchy. Effective power lies in the hands of politicians elected often through unfair methods and they have remained in power for half a century. With each successive prime minister there has been increasing authoritarian tendency – draconian laws used, media controlled, the police not neutral and many judges not independent. Emphasis on Malay unity and Malay power *(ketuanan Melayu)* are political ploys used to continue remaining in power and concentrating more wealth.

d. *Social:* In more traditional sectors of society, family and local community ties are still strong, but are weakening in the face of growing social stratification system based on social classes that strengthen shared interests cutting across family and locality. Many social problems such as corruption, crime, unemployment and slums are linked with uneven changes in the economy, politics and social stratification system. The stratified structure of society with inequitable distribution of income results in difficulty to access good health, education and housing for the lower class.

e. *Religion:* Traditional beliefs and practices are still strong among the Malays. As Muslims the Malays are stronger in performing rituals than mastering the doctrines and practising the jurisprudence *(shariah)*. Administration of Islam is beginning to be bureaucratised which, together with the symbolic headship of the sultan, has been resistant to progressive change. Religion has also formed the ideological basis of Muslim political parties and social movements, which in a multi-ethnic society are limited in success and sometimes create sources of conflict.

f. *Ethnic relations:* Different factors such as the economy, politics, religion, culture and language tend to separate the various ethnic groups. Generally there have been harmonious relationships, but inter-ethnic tensions caused by conflicts of values and interests have sometimes erupted into open clashes. The politics of divide and rule and ethnic fear are still widespread and threaten national unity. After fifty years of *Merdeka* the national unity agenda has not shown any sign of success. New issues are used to mobilise support but cause ethnic tension.

g. *Development:* Government policies and plans focus more on promoting the interests of a selected few. The NEP objective of restructuring society has concentrated on creating Malay capitalist businessmen and industrialists. Several policies and plans initiated and carried out under Dr Mahathir's premiership further strengthened the creation of a small coterie of Malay capitalists and exacerbated cronyism and corruption. Socio-economic inequity among the Malays has become more marked and the *laissez faire* system further strengthened.

Turning to the future, there seems to be growing clamour among the people for change. As in many other Third World countries, there is a strong desire to develop this country into a modern society. But what type of modernisation do we want to achieve? Dr Mahathir's idea of modernising the Malays through capitalism has still a great influence over the present government leaders and policies of the country and probably will remain for quite some time more. What effects will this type of modernisation have on the Malays? What form of society and what type of social values should be encouraged? These are interesting questions that need to be answered. They can serve as useful pointers for the future.

The process of modernisation is often mistakenly regarded as synonymous with westernisation. Unfortunately, for a long time the Western elements that have spread in the society are not really those determined by the people themselves, but instead those determined by the colonial masters. The decision to modernise was made by them, as was the case in many other countries that have been colonised. They have practically forced upon the people the values, systems and life styles of the West. What followed was more in the nature of westernisation rather than modernisation. But to be fair it must be admitted that under the five prime ministers there were different degrees of attempts to introduce or to revive elements of local as opposed to foreign identity.

But these were mainly in the linguistic, educational, cultural and religious spheres.

The economic, political, administrative, legal and educational systems that have been established here during the last hundred years are based on the Western pattern, mainly the British one. The Western systems and values, or for that matter anything Western, have been revered to such an extent that the indigenous systems and values have often been ignored, despised if not destroyed. This is not to deny that there are some aspects of Western systems and values that are positive and have been beneficial to the Malays.

Although these Western systems, values and lifestyles are disseminated throughout the country, their influences are greatest among individuals and groups in the upper and middle classes, especially those in the urban areas. During the colonial days, members from these classes were the first ones used by the colonial rulers to strengthen their position. But undoubtedly these influences were more clearly perceived after independence.

Although some changes occurred during colonial rule, they were rather limited. For instance, within the economic sphere there were many changes which were deliberately not introduced into the rural areas. As already noted, the British encouraged the Malay peasants to continue their traditional occupations of *paddy* planting and fishing and, by encouraging foreign immigrants into the Peninsula, they were at the same time stopping the Malays from being absorbed into new economic activities such as business and industry. Thus the process of modernisation was slowed down for them.

In the field of education, schools were built and opportunities for education were extended to more Malays than before, especially those from the upper class who could be recruited into the administration; but for the common people, particularly children of the peasants, the opportunities were limited. Good schools were not built in the rural areas, and even if some were built, they were only for the primary level. It was clear that the colonial rulers wanted to limit the education made available to the villagers only up to the level of being able to read, write and do some calculations, so that they would not easily be cheated in their daily lives.

It appears obvious why the colonial masters did not want to encourage development in the economy and education among the people. In the economy, it was not the intention of colonialism to develop those whom they colonised, but to harvest as much from the colonies as possible. For the British colonialists opening estates and mines was more beneficial than improving the conditions of agriculture and the peasants in the villages, for clearly estates and mines could be exploited for larger profits. Furthermore, the colonial rulers knew that if education were extensively encouraged then their very position could be threatened.

If many schools were built and the doors opened to allow higher education to a large number of local children, then there would emerge a group of educated people who could challenge the colonial power. This had happened in many other colonies, where a small number of western-educated individuals succeeded with the help of their education to challenge colonialism. By limiting the opportunity for education, the colonialists would delay somewhat the process of social and political consciousness and the emergence of leadership that could challenge them.

Since the modernising influence of colonialism was limited, it was therefore not able (or had no intention) to eradicate or replace all elements of traditional society, which have continued till this day. As an example, in the economic sphere many of the old agricultural methods are still practised in the villages; in politics the old symbols of power such as the sultan and *penghulu* still persist; and in culture many of the old beliefs are still widespread among a large number of people. The old traditional systems and values exist side by side now with the new systems and values which were encouraged by colonialism. They do not coexist in a stable equilibrium.

Admittedly, the process of modernisation introduced by the government after independence and continuing at higher speed and greater intensity now, has brought positive changes in various fields. While Western elements become stronger, the traditional elements tend to get correspondingly weaker. This occurs from food and attire to economy and politics. Indeed Malay society is now in transition. To a great extent it can be said that many changes that have occurred since independence follow the patterns that had already been set during the colonial days. This can be seen most clearly in economic, educational, administrative and also legal spheres. In this country the influence and effects of westernisation since colonialism are still strong and significant, but they have been generally and inevitably accepted as part of the so-called modernisation process.

How could this happen? This is connected with the history of national struggle in this country, which, as was explained in earlier chapters, followed two different and opposite traditions. First, there is the tradition of cooperation or collaboration between local leaders and the colonialists. Second, there is the tradition of opposition or resistance. Both these traditions were found in the 19th century, following British intervention in this country and in the 20th century during the struggle to achieve independence.

In the 19th century the local leaders who collaborated were willing to accept British rule as long as their own positions were safeguarded. Those who opposed carried on with their resistance, although many of them were imprisoned, hunted or killed. In the 20th century the group that cooperated was ready to compromise with what was alleged as "half-baked independence" which would allow the colonialists to retain their economic control over the country. Those who opposed wanted all forms of colonialism to end, so that genuine independence could be achieved.

The difference and contradiction between these two traditions are found not only in this country, but also in several other countries that have experienced colonial rule. In many countries it is the first tradition of cooperation or collaboration that initially won. But eventually the people became politically aware, and they began to realise that the independence they fought for did not bring much benefit to the majority of people. This awareness is already taking place among the people of various ethnicities in this country, and this could probably bring about new changes for the future.

When political consciousness is again aroused and becomes widespread among the majority of people, then they will not want to be deceived anymore by leaders and policies that betray their own interests. They would act in different ways and their actions might initially cause problems or disruptions. Some people say that this cannot be avoided because as one revolutionary leader was claimed to have said, "You cannot eat an omelette unless you break the egg first". Ultimately the demands and struggles of the people themselves, under the leadership of genuine nationalists, would achieve victory. Being an optimist, I believe this country and the Malays will certainly witness this change or development ultimately.

The true leaders and champions of the people generally show two characteristics in their policies and actions. First, they give priority to the interests of their own country and people and not the interests of the foreign powers and the ruling elites. Second, they emphasise greater concern for and show more commitment to the poor and weak who form the majority of people in the lower class, and not for the rich and strong, especially the limited few in the upper class who monopolise political and economic powers. These two characteristics can serve as useful guides or principles for the people in this country, particularly for the Malays, if they want a better future for themselves.

In this country there still exist systems and values which are contrary to the interests of its own people. As a result of colonial control and of the lack of courage found among the country's leadership, who have failed to change the economic system and structure inherited from colonialism, part of the sources of wealth of this country continue to be controlled by a handful of monopoly-capitalists. Year in and year out they keep draining out enormous profits.

The first Prime Minister Tunku Abdul Rahman was weak in both aspects of the above characteristics. His policies and plans were pro-Western or more clearly pro-British. As for Dr Mahathir Mohamad, judging from his anti-Western particularly anti-American stance and rhetoric, he was much stronger in the first aspect, but he did not show enough strength in the second. His internal policies and plans tended to favour the rich cronies and kins close to him more than the poor, and favouring more the ruling elites rather than the masses. It may be said that during the time of Mahathir's premiership, concentration of wealth among the few became very intensive and extensive. Nothing has really changed under the leadership of Abdullah Badawi.

It is ironical that a rather rich country well blessed with natural resources such as ours has to beg and borrow all over the world, especially in the West, in order to finance some of the development projects and for investments. In 2005 public debts incurred by the government totaled about RM228.7 billion, of which RM198.7 were local while more than RM30 billion were foreign debts. In some newly emerging states, the disadvantages of colonial economic structures and systems have been realised. That is why many such states have taken firm action to retrieve all their sources of wealth that were controlled by the colonialists. That is the reason why many of the Middle Eastern and Latin American states, for example, have nationalised their oil industries. In this way they have placed the interests of their own people and country above the interests of the foreigners. But the tragedy is that the ruling elites (many of them feudalistic or authoritarian) have put their own and family interests above the interests of the ordinary people.

There was some significant change in the approach towards development following the May Thirteenth Incident in 1969. The NEP was introduced the following year and much development occurred. According to figures from the International Monetary Fund, the per-capita income of Malaysia rose from US$1,100 in 1975 to US$4,300 in 1990 and US$8,970 in 2003. The objective to alleviate poverty irrespective of ethnicity promised more focus and attention on the poor. Of course there was more financial allocation to achieve this, and in fact the incidence of absolute poverty steadily decreased from 49.3 per cent in 1957 to just around 5.7 per cent in 2005.

But on the other hand relative poverty increased, with the socio-economic gap between the poor and the rich widening. A handful few have become very wealthy, but absolute poverty in the rural areas is still high at 2.9 per cent, considering the wealth of the country. In other words, a just and equitable distribution of wealth has not taken place. The values of social justice and egalitarianism do not seem to be upheld and practised. At the same time, although the objective specifically emphasises on a multi-ethnic approach and greater attention on the Malays in the rural areas involved in agriculture, yet rural incidence of poverty remained quite high at 11.9 per cent in 2005. The Indians have complained that almost no substantial allocation has been given especially to the poor estate workers.

One of the reasons why the socio-economic gap increased was partly because of the very nature of the second objective of the NEP and the way it was implemented. The objective was to restructure society by overcoming identification of occupations according to ethnicity, but instead of implementing it overall, the government has concentrated on the limited target of increasing the number of Malays in industry, business and certain professional fields. The idea was to reach a balance between Malay and non-Malay capital and also the top positions in these fields. All kinds of sponsorship – grants, loans, training, education and quotas – were provided or determined by the government to uplift the Malays. Admittedly, the net was cast wide open, but only a small minority of those close to the most powerful in government were in the position to get much more privileges than the others.

In the name of the people and the country, a handful from the upper class who have the power and influence can always grab the country's wealth to satisfy their own selfish ends. They operate through their families and cronies. This being so, there is need for effective guarantee to ensure that the country's wealth should be redistributed fairly, and that the benefit of development projects would really filter down to the bottom, so that they could be enjoyed by the poor people too, irrespective of ethnicity and whether they are peasants in the rural areas or workers in the towns. Economically, there are two things that can give rise to this handful of individuals monopolising the country's wealth and obstructing the majority of the poor people from achieving development. The first is the *laissez faire* system, under which the NEP operates and is still firmly entrenched, and the second is the present nature of stratification in the society.

A *laissez faire* or free enterprise economy is an aspect of the capitalist system which was encouraged by the colonial rulers in this country for its economic and social development, so that the country and its people would be modernised along the Western pattern. Although there are some leaders who deny it, the fact is that capitalism gets the full blessing and support of the government. It is true that, within the framework of this system, development efforts can also be carried out to benefit the people. As always claimed by some leaders, development in this country has raised the incomes of the peasants, especially those in the land schemes, and increased the number of villagers who can afford to own scooters, motorcycles and even cars or vans.

But surely they overlook more important things. Are not the profits gained by the contractors, middlemen, businessmen, entrepreneurs, capitalists and corrupt politicians much greater? If the poor people can get a piece of land or a small shop, it is much easier for the rich to get logging areas and permits or licenses for all kinds of business and industry. If the poor can buy a scooter, it is a lot easier for the rich to buy a number of Mercedes because they can afford it. In fact, while it is true that incomes of the lower class have increased, those of the upper class have increased much faster; therefore, the economic gap between these two classes of people is getting wider. Worse still, there is a tendency for concentration of wealth in the hands of a sprinkling few that results in the rich becoming richer and the poor poorer.

The effects of the free enterprise economy will grow worse in a stratified society which inherently perpetuates socio-economic inequity. Different classes in the society differ greatly from one another in the political, economic and social positions – the position of the upper class is much more strong, stable and influential than that of the lower class. Actually the differences between the classes correspond with the differences between the rich and the poor. The rich upper class normally controls positions of economic influence, and often plays roles that are looked up to in society. The reverse is quite true of the lower class. At the same time, a stratified society creates unequal opportunities not only in the economic fields, but also in access for good education, health and housing.

Social classes have long existed in human society. Many modern societies today continue to reflect traditional class differences between the rulers and the ruled, and alongside these emerge differences between the capitalists and workers. Historical changes often change only the form of classes.

Dr Mahathir, during his time as Deputy Prime Minister, has written that "... in Muslim societies there are no classes. There are the rich and poor people, but class divisions do not exist." Furthermore, according to him kinship ties are so strong that they cannot be severed by economic class differences.[37] Evidently the good doctor is confused. First, it is necessary to distinguish between 'Islamic teachings' and 'Muslim society'. It is true that, according to Islamic teaching, those who are considered to be honoured before God are the ones who show *taqwa*, which means fear of God. The degree of *taqwa* is not determined by one's social status, whether rich or poor, ministers or peasants.

But it is different with Muslim society, which may be interpreted strictly as one where most of the people practise all aspects of Islamic

---

37. Mahathir Mohamad, 1976.

teachings, or loosely as a society that consists mainly of Muslims, but is not necessarily governed on the basis of Islamic teachings. In any Muslim society, following these two interpretations, there exist different social categories that can be considered as classes. During the Umayyad and Abassid periods in early Muslim history, there were social classes; for example, the feudal ruling class stood out clearly above the common people who formed the majority of the ruled. Such class categories exist up to this day in Muslim countries like Arabia, Jordan and Egypt, although they have taken somewhat different forms.

Second, when a person like Dr Mahathir admits that in a particular society there exists groups of rich and poor people, he is in fact also admitting the presence of an important factor which determines the formation and existence of classes. Admittedly, there are many factors that can make a person rich, such as his education, occupation and his own diligence. But usually the very rich in society control capital or land or other assets, either inherited or acquired. With these they can embark on various enterprises such as opening plantations or factories and controlling labour.

The wealthy usually live opulently in exclusive areas and maintain social relations and a style of life that differentiate them from the poor people. With their wealth they can 'buy' political influence and social prestige. So, once we admit the existence of the rich and poor in society, then we must admit that classes and class differences also exist.

Third, the former prime minister contended that in a Muslim society kinship ties are strong and cannot be severed by class differences. This contention shows an utter ignorance even of traditional folk tales and contemporary events. It is true that kinship ties are strong in traditional societies, whether Muslim or non-Muslim. Tribes or clans are forms of extended families found all over Asia and Africa. But owing to different political, economic, social and educational changes, these kinship ties have been considerably weakened, perhaps even broken asunder, giving way to new ones based on common class or status ties.

In Malay society, such a folk tale as *Hikayat Si Tenggang* shows that when Tenggang succeeded in becoming a rich sea trader, his class position changed. With this new position he became a snob and was even unwilling to acknowledge his poor peasant parents in front of his wife. As the story went, his mother was so angry that she cursed

Tenggang and his wife. Immediately both of them and their ship turned into stone. The story implied that he was willing to break his kinship ties and take whatever consequence.

We can find even today instances which show basic similarities with the story of Tenggang. There are many young men, who, after receiving higher education and its accompanying status, refuse to go back to their families and home villages, and try to conceal their origins because they are ashamed of them. But undeniably there are others who shower their love and responsibility on their poor parents. It only shows that the stratification system is still quite fluid and not fully crystalised. But it does not mean there are no different class or status groups.

In politics there are those who practise nepotism and tend to favour some of their kith and kin. Although generally speaking this tendency seems to be waning as a result of new changes taking place in Malay society, yet specifically in the arena of politics and economy the practices of nepotism together with cronyism have been on the increase and sometimes practised blatantly among a handful that constitute the most powerful. True, it is not always possible or beneficial for a successful politician to continue favouring his relatives because of likely unpopular consequences. But some of them have become so powerful that they are able to defy it in the full knowledge that the media under their control or influence are not free to expose them. The powers that be are able to widen their political base and strengthen their economic control by having fully trusted kindreds and also fully trusted cronies or nominees, who need not be their close family members.

Malay society may be said to be made up entirely of Muslims, although there are a sprinkling few who have embraced other religions. But the fear of God *(taqwa)* is seldom applied as an important factor in determining the prestige of individuals or groups. Even in the villages, where religion is more strongly rooted, the power of wealth and politics is often given great respect. Of course a religious person who is also wealthy would be accorded much more deference than others.

As already noted, the traditional class structure still persists, though in a modified form. The middle class is a new reality. But the existence of a big middle class group could also possibly act as economic and social leveler, although it would not erase the wide socio-economic gap between the very rich and the very poor. It is possible that with the present trend of greater economic inequality, class formations will become more distinct and crystalised in Malay society.

One of the factors that can influence the class formation among the Malays is the present government economic development policies, particularly the NEP. In the name of the NEP, strengthened further by the article on special position of the Malays in the Constitution, a small group of those in power as well as those close to them, corner whatever opportunities available to enrich themselves. This is quite easy to do because the government policy encourages the emergence and growth of Malay businessmen and industrialists. Some of them form joint ventures with their non-Malay counterparts. Enjoying unstinted support from the powerful politicians, these select multi-ethnic capitalist groups find it easy to cooperate with one another efficiently to enrich themselves by practically plundering the wealth of the country.

Of course joint ventures are also encouraged with the argument that it helps to promote and strengthen inter-ethnic cooperation and integration especially among members of the upper class. They too will be capable of exploiting the poor peasants, and workers who are multi-ethnic in composition, although a big majority of the peasants are Malays. Concentration of wealth among the very rich few is one of the strongest factors causing extreme poverty and widening the socio-economic inequity.

As a result, we have now the situation of intra-ethnic inequality being as serious if not more serious than inter-ethnic inequality. Thus a large group of poor Malays together with poor non-Malays in the country are getting poorer, while a small group of wealthy Malays together with equally or more wealthy non-Malays are getting even wealthier. Thus class differences will become more marked and crystalised among them. This tendency is certainly happening among the Malays too.

Poverty is indeed a serious problem in newly emerging nations. In the Peninsula, many plans and projects have been carried out to eradicate poverty. Following the NEP, expenditure allocated for them has been much bigger and there was significant success in the efforts to reduce the incidence of poverty. But less attention was focused in agriculture following the policies and projects initiated by Dr Mahathir.

The Fifth, Sixth and Seventh Malaysia Plans under Mahathir showed decrease of allocations on agricultural and rural development to RM7.3 billion, RM6.3 billion and RM4.5 billion respectively. It went up slightly to RM6.2 billion under the Eighth Malaysia Plan and more significantly to RM11.4 billion for the Ninth Malaysia Plan under Abdullah Badawi, who had pronounced that he would concentrate more on agriculture and rural development. During Mahathir's period it appeared that the rate of decrease in poverty incidence was slower than before. But it has been argued that this tendency is to be expected as poverty nears the point of total eradication.

Admittedly, there are sections of the peasantry which have benefited from the policies and plans for eradicating poverty, but on the whole incomes of the majority of the poor people in the lower class have not improved very much. The hard core poor is still there. This group and the others who continue to be under the poverty line have been left lagging very far behind the rich members of the upper class, whose incomes have increased much faster.

To make their plight worse, inflation over the years has caused the prices of their daily needs to soar upwards, sometimes beyond the means of the majority poor. Official figures show the inflation rate to be around 3.6 per cent in 2007. But during that year, as in many years before, prices of food and other daily needs of people have gone far higher than what is officially shown as the overall price index. This affected even the middle class badly.

The NEP has not really succeeded in uplifting the socio-economic life of the Malays and at the same time it has caused three types of dissatisfaction. Firstly, it has opened the chance for a small circle of Malay and also non-Malay 'new rich' who have political and family links with the powerful in the country to collaborate to acquire more wealth in the quickest time possible. This leads to dissatisfaction of even the Malays (not to say the non-Malays) outside this circle, who are not accorded the same opportunity and left only with the crumbs.

Secondly, although the fight to eradicate poverty should override ethnic considerations, yet on the basis of the NEP and the Constitution, Malays are given priority for most programmes of socio-economic upliftment of the poor, to the extent that non-Malays find or regard themselves as being deliberately excluded. Obviously this creates anger and disappointment among the non-Malays.

Thirdly, as has been repeatedly mentioned earlier, despite or perhaps because of the NEP, concentration of wealth has happened, which leads to the widening of the socio-economic gap of inequity. This economic trend can have far-reaching political and social consequences that could cause more harm than good. This and the other two types of dissatisfactions described above would obviously be of no help in the effort to forge national unity.

There are more than enough reasons to replace the NEP with a Malaysian Economic Agenda (MEA) as urged and envisioned by Anwar Ibrahim on behalf of the People's Justice Party (PKR). He correctly argues that NEA should be based on the dictum or principle of "concern for and commitment to the people" or more precisely expressed in the Malay language as *"kepedulian rakyat"*.

This principle emphasises on: (a) concentrating efforts, programmes and financial allocations on the socio-economic upliftment of the poor and disadvantaged irrespective of ethnicity, (b) ensuring that the article on special position in the Constitution will stop to be used by a small group of Malays to take personal advantage of projects, loans, shares, contracts and so forth, all in the name of the Malays and Bumiputera but without improving the conditions of the ordinary Malays as a whole, and (c) speeding up the economic development of Malaysia so that it can catch up with countries like Singapore, Korea and Taiwan which are far ahead, although all of them were almost on par about 50 years ago.

As mentioned earlier, a multi-ethnic approach to combat poverty will not mean neglecting the plight of the Malays. In fact it will be no loss to the Malays because they form the majority of the poor who will be the first above others to benefit from this agenda anyhow. At the same time it would be welcome by the poor non-Malays who feel that they have been discriminated by the NEP all this while.

In terms of the macro-economic performance, Singapore and Korea have done much better than Malaysia. Without the help of anything equivalent to the NEP, Singapore and Korea have done much better in terms of their per-capita GDP; according to an IMF report in 2006 they were to the tune of US$34,152 and US$19,624 respectively. In comparison, Malaysia had a mere US$6,146. Obviously the NEP has not been of great help to Malaysia's economic performance.

It is true that the NEP has succeeded in creating a few Malay millionaires and even billionaires, but in the event corruption, cronyism and nepotism have become rampant. There are more non-Malay billionaires than Malay billionaires and although they have not benefited from the NEP directly they certainly have made much gains in their enterprise through the practices of corruption and cronyism. It needs to be repeated that concentration of wealth in the hands of a few multi-millionaires and billionaires made up of different ethnic groups has caused socio-economic gap to widen at inter- and intra-ethnic levels as well as between the rural areas (especially the hinterland) and the urban centres. Will this trend be checked in the future? To overcome the problems of increasing relative poverty and concentration of wealth that have continued under the NEP and to ensure that the NEA is effective in promoting and achieving its goals, perhaps an alternative approach is needed for development. Much of the socio-economic woes suffered particularly by the poor and others in the lower class have largely been caused by the dominance of the *laissez faire* or capitalist system. It is not suggested here that to succeed in future, Malaysia has to abandon immediately this system in its entirety and adopt something completely different, including socialism and central planning, for example.

Under the present stage of development and the level of people's political consciousness, it is unrealistic, unpractical and even unwise to put socialism in the agenda now. In fact, many will argue that in Russia, socialism failed and China is slowly following the capitalist road. Further, after all, it can be easily argued too that Singapore and South Korea still manage to succeed with the capitalist system. But in the context of Malaysia, this system has brought in its wake many problems and disadvantages that have already been explained earlier quite extensively. What is needed now is more social justice and egalitarianism that cut across ethnic lines.

A certain amount of state control through nationalisation and more than a certain amount of planning are needed so that the future for just development leading to ethnic integration and unity could be more guaranteed. It must be remembered that PETRONAS is already a state or nationalised institution that controls petroleum in this country. Why cannot water, energy, education, health and other key social services be nationalised instead of being privatised? In this country some of these industries and services that have been privatised have not proven to be more efficient, but instead have become more costly and a heavier burden on the people.

If nationalisation of some of the key industries and services is the alternative choice, the most important thing is that they should be used to serve the people and their accruing profits should not be squandered on mega projects that are uneconomic but would provide cronies with big contracts and enormous commissions. What has happened to PETRONAS and its earnings, whereby almost all its accumulated savings have been squandered without any annual account presented even to Parliament, is a good lesson to learn and should not be repeated.

Further, industries and services put under state control should never be used as a means to further enrich the rich, especially the politically powerful and their cronies and families. If profits accrued from state owned enterprises are used for the benefit of the poor and underprivileged, for free education and healthcare as well as cheap housing, surely their livelihood could be improved and the socio-economic gap can be reduced.

Indeed the prospect of eradicating poverty, closing the socio-economic gap, fighting corruption and cronyism in the near future is dim, as long as the *laissez faire* system is perpetuated. This system contains inherent elements that are unjust and can only burden the poor people much more than the other groups. It is clear that poverty can be more easily eradicated if there is structural change in the land tenancy and tenure systems at the production level and the marketing system at the distribution level. But this depends almost entirely on government leadership that has genuine concern for the poor.

Poverty and concentration of wealth have serious implications on a ramification of social problems. Two such problems are corruption and crimes. As described earlier corruption is of great concern and it is sad if the present trend of deterioration continues to persist. It cannot be fought just by rhetoric and going only for the small fish as is happening now. The sharks, especially those who have power or who are close to the centre of power can quite easily go scot free. Corruption is most dangerous when it goes hand in hand with cronyism. The greatest worry is that Malays from policemen to ministers are involved with corruption and they do not seem to care (despite 'Islam Hadhari') about the Islamic teaching that condemns both the giver and taker in corruption. Countries and nations can be destroyed by corruption.

As for crimes, it is an irony that as the economy develops and leaders speak louder about Islam, violent crimes grow more. But of course, despite the development recorded, poverty is still widespread and this is one of the factors that cause criminal activities. Besides, some of the leaders who talk about Islam do not practise many of its principles. They may pray or fast, but they condone and participate in corruption, and use draconian laws that can detain people without trial, although they know that this is against the teaching of Islam.

From 2003 to 2007, cases of crimes have risen by 45 per cent from 156,315 to 224,298. There have been increases for almost all crimes – violent and non-violent – in 2007 compared to the previous year. Just to take four types of crimes and their increase in absolute number and percentage we get the following: rape increased by 29.5 per cent to 3,177 cases, night-time break-in by 21.7 per cent to 24,440, car theft by 11.4 per cent to 12,427 and motorcycle theft by 3.2 per cent to 12,427 cases.

Granted criminal acts involve various ethnic groups, but some available figures suggest that the involvement of Malays to be higher than others. This happens also in drug abuse, where statistics show that most of them are Malays. All these do not augur well for the Malays as well for Islam in the future (*see Table 13*). Urgent actions are needed, not just platitudes from leaders whose sincerity is questionable. For the economic and social systems to change and their problems overcome, we need radical political actions. Whether this will happen or not depends on the level of consciousness among the people and the type of effective leadership that will emerge from them. The signs are quite clear that the majority of people desire these changes, and desire them immediately, but the ruling elites seem to prefer defending the political and economic *status quo* that have provided them with enormous privileges.

In order to determine the direction of these major changes the Malays now need to give the correct answers to the following questions:

Do they want the people and the country to continue being dominated by the remnants of colonial systems, structures and values?

Do they want the people to uphold commercial cultural values that degrade the morals and place individual self-interests before collective welfare?

Do they want the people to allow the economic gaps between different classes to grow wider, and only a handful of people are able to enjoy fully the benefits of development?

Do they want the people to allow exploitation, manipulation, cronyism and corruption to become rampant and humanitarian relationships to disappear?

Do they want people to continue being subjugated to feudal influences which create fear for truth and encourage superstition, fatalism, slavish mentality and blind following?

Do they want the people to be chained to outdated values and beliefs as well as anachronistic political systems and structures that obstruct progress?

Do they want to allow democratic values, institutions and practices to be eroded and authoritarianism to get worse?

Do they want the people to allow religion to be degraded by those groups which want to use it as a tool for advancing self-interest and obstructing change and liberation?

Do they want to perpetuate economic, political and religious structures and values that create tensions and conflicts along ethnic lines and undermine national unity?

There are other questions that can be asked, which need the right answers to serve as guides for action. There is also a need for a major revivalist movement that can develop the highest level of consciousness among the majority of people so that they will strive for a progressive new life. The changes envisaged should embrace every sector: politics, economics, education, law, culture and religion. It is to be expected that such changes and a revivalist movement that follows will be opposed by groups and leaders ready to continue cooperating or collaborating with the collapsing imperial powers and the anachronistic feudal elements. That is why the people must develop the right attitudes and carry out the struggle, imbued with a courageous spirit ever marching forward and never retreating, realising how important it is to achieve liberation and progress, justice and democracy.

The Malays have to stop the rot and choose change. Their future is in their own hands.

APPENDIX

1. Distribution of Population by Ethnic Group
2. Population of Ethnic Group and State
3. Urban and Rural Populations by Ethnic Group
4. Number of Poor Households by Sector
5. Incidence of Poverty and Hardcore Poverty, 1999 and 2004
6. Incidence of Poverty by Ethnic Group
7. Household Income
8. Employment by Ethnic Group
9. Ownership of Shared Capital of Limited Companies by Ethnic Group
10. Professionals by Ethnic Group
11. Enrolments in Primary and Secondary Education by Ethnic Group
12. Enrolments in Tertiary Education by Ethnic Group
13. Number of Drug Addicts at Pusat Serenti by Ethnic Group and Sex, 2000, 2002 and 2004
14. Farming Operators by Ethnic Group

1. Distribution of Population by Ethnic Group

TABLE 1.1 - 1970 (Peninsula Malaysia)

Ethnic Group	Total	Percentage
Total	8,810,348	100
Malay	4,685,838	53.2
Chinese	3,122,850	35.4
Indians	939,629	10.6
Others	69,531	0.8

Source: R. Chander, Golongan Masyarakat - Banci Penduduk dan Perumanhan Malaysia 1970, Jabatan Perangkaan Malaysia, Kuala Lumpur, 1972, p.6, Table VI

TABLE 1.2 - 2007

Ethnic Group	Total (`000)	Percentage
Total	27,173.6	100
Malaysian citizens	25,265.8	92.97
Bumiputera	16,768.0	61.7
Malays	13,773.1	50.68
Other Bumiputeras	2,994.9	11.02
Chinese	6,287.9	23.13
Indians	1,883.9	6.93
Others	326.1	1.2
Non-Malaysian citizens	1,907.8	70

Source: Social Statistics Bulletin, Malaysia 2007, Department of Statistics

2. Population of Ethnic Group and State

TABLE 2.1 - 1970 (Peninsula Malaysia)

State	Malay	Chinese	Indian
Terengganu	93.9	5.4	0.6
Kelantan	92.8	5.3	0.8
Perlis	79.4	16.2	2.0
Kedah	70.7	19.3	8.4
Pahang	61.2	31.2	7.3
Johore	53.4	39.4	6.7
Melaka	51.8	39.6	7.8
Negeri Sembilan	45.4	38.1	16.1
Perak	43.1	42.5	14.2
Selangor	34.6	46.3	18.3
Penang	30.7	56.1	11.5

Source: R. Chander, Golongan Masyarakat - Banci Penduduk dan Perumahan Malaysia 1970, Jabatan Perangkaan Malaysia, Kuala Lumpur, 1972, p.32, Table XIV

2. Population of Ethnic Group and State (continued)

TABLE 2.2 - 2007

State	Total	Bumiputera	Malays	Other Bumiputeras	Chinese	Indians	Others	Non-Malaysian Citizens
Malaysia	27,173.6	1,678.0	13,773.3	2,994.9	6,287.9	1,883.9	326.1	1,907.8
Johor	3,240.9	1,756.5	1,714.9	41.6	1,034.4	214.6	19.9	215.5
Kedah	1,918.6	1,448.9	1,445.1	3.7	261.8	128.3	32.6	47.1
Kelantan	1,560.5	1,455.9	1,442.9	13.0	52.9	4.0	15.2	32.5
Melaka	738.8	462.8	452.9	9.9	193.6	44.0	5.0	33.4
Negeri Sembilan	978.2	556.3	542.1	14.2	228.6	147.9	4.2	41.2
Pahang	1,483.6	1,094.6	1,022.2	72.4	234.7	67.9	10.6	75.8
Perak	2,314.6	1,275.4	1,218.6	56.8	682.2	285.6	8.4	63.0
Perlis	231.9	195.7	195.0	0.7	22.1	2.9	6.8	4.4
Pulau Pinang	1,518.4	631.2	625.3	5.9	639.8	149.3	6.3	91.8
Sabah	3,063.6	1,853.5	351.3	1,502.2	292.7	11.4	135.8	770.2
Sarawak	2,404.2	1,692.8	534.6	1,158.2	611.9	4.5	5.0	90.0
Selangor (incl. Putrajaya)	4,961.6	2,612.0	2,537.3	74.7	1,366.0	657.0	51.1	275.5
Terengganu	1,067.9	1,011.7	1,008.3	3.4	26.4	2.3	2.8	24.7
W.P. Kuala Lumpur	1,604.4	667.7	652.2	15.5	630.0	163.3	20.2	123.2
W.P. Labuan	86.4	53.1	30.6	22.5	10.7	0.9	2.2	19.5

Source: Social Statistics Bulletin, Malaysia 2007, Department of Statistics

3. Urban and Rural Populations by Ethnic Group

TABLE 3.1 - 1970 (Peninsula Malaysia)

	Urban		Rural	
	No.	%	No.	%
Total	2,530.433	28.7	6,279,915	71.3
Malay	699,372	14.9	3,986,466	85.1
Chinese	1,479,225	47.4	1,643,125	52.6
Indian	323,435	34.7	609,194	65.3
Others	28,401	40.8	41,130	59.2

Source: R. Chander, Golongan Masyarakat - Banci Penduduk dan Perumanhan Malaysia 1970, Jabatan Perangkaan Malaysia, Kuala Lumpur, 1972, p.32, Table XIV

4. Number of Poor Households by Sector

TABLE 4

	1970				1975				1980			
	Total households (000)	Total poor households (000)	Incidence of poverty (%)	Percentage among poor	Total households (000)	Total poor households (000)	Incidence of poverty (%)	Percentage among poor	Total households (000)	Total poor households (000)	Incidence of poverty (%)	Percentage among poor
AGRICULTURE												
Rubber smallholders	350.0	226.4	64.7	28.6	396.3	233.8	59.0	28.0	423.4	169.4	40.0	22.0
Oil palm smallholders	6.6	2.0	30.3	0.3	9.9	0.9	9.1	0.1	24.5	2.0	8.2	0.3
Coconut smallholders	32.0	16.9	52.8	2.1	34.4	17.5	50.9	2.1	34.0	16.0	47.1	2.1
Padi farmers	140.0	123.4	88.1	15.6	148.5	114.3	77.0	13.7	150.1	109.6	73.0	14.2
Other agriculture	137.5	126.2	91.8	16.0	157.4	124.1	78.8	14.9	171.5	110.3	64.3	14.4
Fishermen	38.4	28.1	73.2	3.5	41.6	26.2	63.0	3.1	42.5	22.1	52.0	2.9
Estate workers	148.4	59.4	40.1	7.5	127.0	59.7	47.0	7.1	111.5	42.4	38.0	5.5
Agricultural total												
NON-AGRICULTURE	852.9	582.4	68.3	73.6	915.1	576.5	63.0	69.0	957.5	471.8	49.3	61.4
Mining	32.4	11.1	34.3	1.4	31.8	10.1	31.8	1.2	32.4	9.6	29.6	1.3
Manufacturing	150.2	48.5	32.3	6.1	206.9	59.6	28.8	7.1	299.3	75.2	25.1	9.8
Construction	35.0	12.8	36.6	1.6	44.0	13.4	30.5	1.6	56.0	14.5	25.9	1.9
Utilities	12.8	4.7	36.7	0.6	16.4	4.8	29.3	0.6	20.5	4.8	23.4	0.6
Commerce	162.3	49.2	30.3	6.2	209.4	55.6	26.6	6.7	265.1	60.9	23.0	7.9
Transport	61.3	22.4	36.5	2.8	91.7	24.2	26.4	2.9	115.9	29.5	25.5	3.8
Services	229.1	60.7	20.3	7.7	386.1	90.9	23.5	10.9	523.8	102.0	19.5	13.3
Non-agricultural total	753.1	209.4	27.8	26.4	986.4	258.6	26.2	31.0	1,313.0	296.5	22.6	38.6
TOTAL	1,606.0	791.8	49.3	100.0	1,901.5	835.1	43.9	100.0	2,270.5	768.3	33.8	100.0

1. Two target groups namely, residents of New Villages and agricultural labourers are included among these households, especially in other agriculture, rubber and padi.
2. (%) refers to the percentage of poor households in the total.

Source: *Third Malaysia Plan*, Government Printers, Kuala Lumpur, 1976, p. 163, Table 9-3.

5. Incidence of Poverty and Hardcore poverty, 1999 and 2004

TABLE 5

		1999				2004		
		Malaysia	Urban	Rural	Malaysia	Urban	Rural
Hardcore Poverty							
Incidence of Hardcore Poverty[1]	(%)	1.9	0.5	3.6	1.2	0.4	2.9
Number of Hardcore Poverty Households	('000)	91.7	11.9	79.8	67.3	14.1	53.2
Poverty Gap[2]	(%)	0.4	0.1	0.8	0.2	0.1	0.6
Overall Poverty							
Incidence Poverty[3]	(%)	8.5	3.3	14.8	5.7	2.5	11.9
Number of Poor Households	('000)	409.3	86.1	323.2	311.3	91.6	219.7
Poverty Gap	(%)	2.3	0.8	4.0	1.4	0.6	3.0
Total Households	('000)	4,800.0	2,612.5	2,187.5	5,459.4	3,605.9	1,853.5

1. *Refers to households with monthly gross income of less than the food PLI.*
2. *Refers to the total income shortfall (expressed in proportion to the poverty line) of poor households.*
3. *Refers to households with monthly gross income below PLI.*

Source: *Economic Planning Unit and Department of Statistics - Household Income Surveys, 1999 and 2004.*

6. INCIDENCE OF POVERTY BY ETHNIC GROUP

TABLE 6.1 - 1970 (Peninsular Malaysia)

	All households (000)	Poor households (000)	Poverty incidence (%)	Percentage of total poor households
Malay	901.5	584.2	64.8	73.8
Chinese	525.2	136.3	26.0	17.2
Indian	160.5	62.9	39.2	7.9
Others	18.8	8.4	44.8	1.1
TOTAL	1,606.0	791.8	49.3	100.0
All Rural	1,166.7	683.7	58.6	86.3
All Urban	439.3	108.1	24.6	13.7

Source: Third Malaysia Plan, Government Printers, Kuala Lumpur, 1976, p. 180, Table 9-6.

TABLE 6.2 - 2004

	1999			2004		
	Bumiputera	Chinese	Indian	Bumiputera	Chinese	Indian
Hardcore Poverty	**2.9**	**0.2**	**0.3**	**1.9**	**0.1**	**0.3**
Urban	0.7	0.1	0.2	0.7	neg. 1	0.2
Rural	4.4	0.4	0.5	3.3	0.3	0.5
Overall Poverty	**12.4**	**1.2**	**3.5**	**8.3**	**0.6**	**2.9**
Urban	5.1	0.8	2.4	4.1	0.4	2.4
Rural	17.5	2.7	5.8	13.4	2.3	5.4
Poverty Gap	**3.3**	**0.2**	**0.7**	**2.1**	**0.1**	**0.6**

Source: Economic Planning Unit and Department of Statistics - Household Income Surveys, 1999 and 2004.

Appendix

7. Household Income

TABLE 7.1 - 1970 (Peninsular Malaysia)

Income Range (per month)	Malay	Chinese	Indian	Others	Total
$ 10-99	84.5	9.6	4.9	1.0	100.0
$ 100-199	60.8	24.9	14.0	0.3	100.0
$ 200-399	40.3	46.0	13.5	0.2	100.0
$ 400-699	31.6	55.7	12.1	0.6	100.0
$ 700-1499	23.2	61.4	12.5	2.9	100.0
$ 1500-2999	14.0	62.1	13.6	10.3	100.0
$ 3000 and above	12.1	52.0	17.3	18.6	100.0

Source: Raymond Lee, Study of Interaction and Integration Among Some Malay and Chinese Students, M.A. Thesis, University of Malaya, 1975, p. 33, Table 2.7. (Adapted from Mid-Term Review of the Second Malaysia Plan, p. 4, Table 1.2)

TABLE 7.2 Mean Monthly Gross Household Income and Gini Coefficient by Ethnic Group and Strata, 1999 and 2004

Ethnic Group and Strata	In Current Prices (RM)		Average Annual Growth Rate (%)	In Constant 1999 Prices (RM)		Average Annual Growth Rate (%)	Gini Coefficient	
	1999	2004	2000-2004	1999	2004	2000-2004	1999	2004
Bumiputera	1,984	2,711	6.4	1,984	2,522	4.9	0.433	0.452
Chinese	3,456	4,437	5.1	3,456	4,127	3.6	0.434	0.446
Indians	2,702	3,456	5.0	2,702	3,125	3.5	0.413	0.425
Others	1,371	2,312	11.0	1,371	2,150	9.4	0.393	0.462
Malaysia	2,472	3,249	5.6	2,472	3,022	4.1	0.452	0.462
Urban	3,103	3,956	5.0	3,103	3,680	3.5	0.432	0.444
Rural	1,718	1,875	1.8	1,718	1,744	0.3	0.421	0.397

Source: Department of Statistics - Household Income Survey, 1999 and 2004

8. EMPLOYMENT BY ETHNIC GROUP

TABLE 8.1 Employment by Race and Sector, Peninsular Malaysia 1970
(000)

Sector	Malays	% of sector total	Chinese	% of sector total	Indians	% of sector total	Others	% of sector total	Totals	% of total employment
Agriculture, forestry and fisheries	925.4	67.6	293.0	21.4	138.3	10.1	12.3	0.9	1,369	49.1
Mining and quarrying	21.1	24.8	56.1	66.0	7.1	8.4	0.7	0.8	85	3.1
Manufacturing	84.4	28.9	191.0	65.4	15.5	5.3	1.2	0.4	922	10.5
Construction	16.9	21.7	56.2	72.1	4.7	6.0	0.2	0.2	78	2.8
Electricity, water and sanitary services	10.2	48.5	3.8	18.0	6.8	23.3	0.3	1.4	21	0.8
Transport, storage and communication	49.0	42.6	45.5	39.6	19.7	17.1	0.8	0.7	115	4.1
Commerce	69.3	23.5	192.6	65.3	31.6	10.7	1.5	0.5	295	10.6
Services	256.1	48.5	188.5	35.7	73.9	14.0	9.5	1.8	529	100.0
Total	1,432.4	51.5	1,026.7	36.9	297.6	10.7	26.5	0.9	2,783	100.0
LABOUR FORCE	1,557.0	1,108.9		334.4		3,026				
%	51.5	36.6		11.1		100				
UNEMPLOYMENT	124.6	82.2	36.8	26.0		0.8				
%	8.0	7.4	11.0	0.8	243	8.0				
POPULATION	4,841.3	3,285.6	981.5	73.0	9,181					
%	52.7	35.8	10.7		100					

1. Totals do not add because of rounding.
Source: Mid-Term Review of the Second Malaysia Plan, Government Printers, Kuala Lumpur, 1973, p. 77, Table 4·4.

8. Employment by Ethnic Group (continued)

TABLE 8.2 EMPLOYMENT BY OCCUPATION AND ETHNIC GROUP, 2000 AND 2005

Occupation	2000 Bumiputera '000	%	Chinese '000	%	Indians '000	%	Others '000	%	Total '000	%	2005 Bumiputera '000	%	Chinese '000	%	Indians '000	%	Others '000	%	Total '000	%
Senior Officials & Managers	230.8	4.8	351.8	12.7	41.9	5.4	5.6	3.3	630.1	7.4	278.2	5.4	413.6	14.0	53.4	6.3	5.4	3.3	750.6	8.2
% of Total	36.6		55.8		6.6		0.9		100.0		37.1		55.1		7.1		0.7		100.0	
Professionals	298.1	6.2	174.5	6.3	41.1	5.3	6.8	4.0	520.5	6.1	314.2	6.1	171.3	5.8	44.1	5.2	7.1	4.3	536.7	5.9
% of Total	57.3		33.5		7.9		1.3		100.0		58.5		31.9		8.2		1.3		100.0	
Lecturers, Pre-University & Secondary School Teachers and Writers & Artists	158.6	3.3	38.8	1.4	12.4	1.6	3.4	2.0	213.2	2.5	164.8	3.2	38.4	1.3	13.6	1.6	3.3	2.0	220.1	2.4
% of Total	74.4		18.2		5.8		1.6		100.0		74.9		17.4		6.2		1.5		100.0	
Technicians & Associate Professionals	649.0	13.5	329.7	11.9	103.2	13.3	8.0	4.7	1,089.8	12.8	752.1	14.6	375.2	12.7	126.3	14.9	9.7	5.9	1,263.3	13.9
% of Total	59.6		30.2		9.5		0.7		100.0		59.5		29.7		10.0		0.8		100.0	
Primary School Teachers and Nurses	230.8	4.8	69.3	2.5	20.9	2.7	3.4	2.0	324.4	3.8	252.4	4.9	76.8	2.6	24.6	2.9	3.8	2.3	357.6	3.9
% of Total	71.1		21.4		6.5		1.1		100.0		70.6		21.5		6.9		1.1		100.0	
Clerical Workers	495.2	10.3	310.3	11.2	65.2	8.4	4.8	2.8	875.3	10.3	546.0	10.6	330.8	11.2	81.4	9.6	5.1	3.1	963.4	10.6
% of Total	56.6		35.4		7.4		0.5		100.0		56.7		34.3		8.4		0.5		100.0	
Service Workers and Shop & Market Sales Workers	610.5	12.7	484.8	17.5	86.9	11.2	10.6	6.2	1,192.8	14.0	721.2	14.0	555.3	18.8	112.8	13.3	12.3	7.5	1,401.6	15.4
% of Total	51.2		40.6		7.3		0.9		100.0		51.5		39.6		8.0		0.9		100.0	

8. Employment by Ethnic Group (continued)

	2000										2005									
	Bumiputera		Chinese		Indians		Others		Total		Bumiputera		Chinese		Indians		Others		Total	
Occupation	'000	%	'000	%	'000	%	'000	%	'000	%	'000	%	'000	%	'000	%	'000	%	'000	%
Craft & Related Trade Workers	379.8	7.9	398.9	14.4	58.2	7.5	10.1	5.9	846.9	9.9	448.2	8.7	434.2	14.7	79.7	9.4	11.3	6.9	973.4	10.7
% of Total	44.8		47.1		6.9		1.2		100.0		46.0		44.6		8.2		1.2		100.0	
Plant & Machine Operators & Assemblers	774.0	16.1	324.1	11.7	161.3	20.8	26.4	15.5	1,285.8	15.1	798.4	15.5	327.9	11.1	170.4	20.1	24.9	15.2	1,321.7	14.5
% of Total	60.2		25.2		12.5		2.1		100.0		60.4		24.8		12.9		1.9		100.0	
Elementary Occupations	461.5	9.6	232.7	8.4	153.6	19.8	56.1	32.9	903.9	10.6	510.0	9.9	236.3	8.0	138.2	16.3	52.5	32.0	937.0	10.3
% of Total	51.1		25.7		17.0		6.2		100.0		54.4		25.2		14.7		5.6		100.0	
Total	4,807.3	100.0	2,770.2	100.0	775.6	100.0	170.5	100.0	8,523.6	100.0	5,151.2	100.0	2,954.0	100.0	847.9	100.0	164.1	100.0	9,117.2	100.0
% of Total	56.4		32.5		9.1		2.0		100.0		56.5		32.4		9.3		1.8		100.0	
Labour Force	5,036.6		2,813.8		793.8		176.4		8,821.6		5,441.4		3,025.1		875.2		171.2		9,512.9	
% of Total	57.1		31.9		9.0		2.0		100.0		57.2		31.8		9.2		1.8		100.0	
Unemployment	229.3		43.6		18.2		5.9		297.0		290.2		71.1		27.3		7.1		395.7	
% of Total	77.2		14.7		6.1		2.0		100.0		73.3		18.0		6.9		1.8		100.0	
Unemployment Rate (%)	4.6		1.5		2.3		3.4		3.4		5.3		2.4		3.1		4.1		4.2	

1. Excludes non-citizens.
Source: Department of Statistics - Labour Force Surveys, 2000 and 2005.

9. Ownership of Shared Capital of Limited Companies by Ethnic Group

TABLE 9.1 PENINSULAR MALAYSIA: OWNERSHIP OF SHARE CAPITAL IN LIMITED COMPANIES, 1970-90

	1970[1] $ million	%	1975[2] $ million	%	Average annual growth rate (%) 1971-75	1980[3] $ million	%	1990[4] $ million	%	Average annual growth rate (%) 1976-90
Malays and Malay interests	125.6	2.4	768.1	7.8	43.6	3,284.3	16.0	24,009.7	30.0	25.8
Malay individuals[5]	84.4	1.6	227.1	2.3	21.9	695.4	3.4	5,914.2	7.4	24.3
Malay interests[6]	41.2	0.8	541.0	5.5	67.4	2,588.9	12.6	18,095.5	22.6	26.4
Other Malaysians[7]	1,826.5	34.3	3,687.3	37.3	15.1	8,290.5	40.4	32,012.9	40.0	15.5
Foreign[8]	3,377.1	63.3	5,434.7	54.9	10.0	8,952.2	43.6	24,009.7	30.0	10.4
Total private sectors[9]	5,329.2	100.0	9,890.1	100.0	13.2	20,527.0	100.0	80,032.3	100.0	15.0
Gross domestic product (In 1970 prices)	9,038.0		12,914.0		7.4	19,487.0		42,462.0		8.3

1. Actual.
2. Estimated.
3. Targets.
4. Totals for 1970 differ from those presented in the SMP and its Mid-Term Review because of the exclusion of the Government, the re-classification of the trust agencies as Malay interests and the re-allocation of most of the shares previously categorised as "held by other companies" to the shareholders of these companies.
5. Includes institutions channelling private Malay funds such as Amanah Saham MARA and Lembaga Urusan dan Tabung Haji.
6. Shares considered to be held in trust by agencies such as MARA (excluding Amanah Saham MARA), PERNAS, UDA, SEDCs, Bank Bumiputra and Bank Pembangunan.
7. Includes nominee companies and third-company minority holdings.
8. Non-residents.
9. Excludes the Government and its agencies except trust agencies.

Source: Third Malaysia Plan, Government Printers, Kuala Lumpur, p. 86, Table 4-16.

9. OWNERSHIP OF SHARED CAPITAL OF LIMITED COMPANIES... (CONTINUED)

TABLE 9.2 OWNERSHIP OF SHARE CAPITAL¹ (AT PAR VALUE) OF LIMITED COMPANIES BY ETHNIC GROUP AND SECTOR, 2004
(%)

Ownership Group	Agriculture	Mining	Manufacturing	Utility	Wholesale & Retail Trade	Construction	Transportation	Finance	Services	Others	Total
Bumiputera	16.4	12.3	8.1	6.3	35.2	20.4	26.7	12.5	18.7	24.3	18.9
Non-Bumiputera	54.0	39.8	25.3	9.2	44.0	53.3	30.6	10.5	40.9	48.6	40.6
Chinese	52.9	39.5	24.5	8.9	42.6	50.7	27.7	10.2	39.5	45.7	39.0
Indians	0.8	0.2	0.6	0.2	1.1	2.0	2.5	0.3	1.1	1.8	1.2
Others	0.2	0.1	0.1	0.1	0.3	0.6	0.4	0.04	0.2	1.1	0.4
Nominee Companies	6.6	25.4	1.9	17.2	5.9	0.7	11.4	17.5	10.9	3.9	8.0
Foreigners	23.0	22.5	64.7	67.3	14.9	25.6	31.3	59.5	29.5	23.2	32.5
Total	100.0	100.0	100.0	100.0	100.0	100.0	100.0	100.0	100.0	100.0	100.0

1. Excludes shares held of Malaysia by Federal and State Governments.
Source: Companies Commission

10. Professionals by Ethnic Group

TABLE 10.1
MALAYSIA: MANPOWER SURVEY RESULTS, 1973 AND ESTIMATED[1] REQUIREMENTS, 1976-80 MANPOWER SURVEY, 1973

	Total Employed	Malay and other indigenous people	Chinese	Indian	Others	Total	Vacancies	Estimated[2] requirements, 1970-80
		Racial distribution (%)						
	(1)	(2)	(3)	(4)	(5)	(6)	(7)	(8)
Professional and Technical	145,517	48.9	39.3	10.5	1.3	100.0	10.4	65,309
Chemists and Physical Scientists	354	11.6	76.8	11.3	0.3	100.0	20.6	327
Laboratory and Science Technicians	3,824	48.2	37.3	13.9	0.6	100.0	27.8	2,137
Architects and Town Planners	353	21.0	71.4	2.5	5.1	100.0	22.4	180
Engineers	2,244	13.5	69.9	12.8	3.8	100.0	22.4	2,764
Engineering Assistants and Technicians	11,824	46.1	34.9	16.4	2.6	100.0	24.0	5,538
Surveyors	168	19.1	58.0	13.7	9.2	100.0	19.6	346
Draughtsman	2,979	39.0	53.4	6.6	1.0	100.0	9.1	2,041
Agronomist	652	39.1	49.7	8.7	2.5	100.0	38.0	540
Life Science Technicians	2,070	76.9	20.6	2.0	0.5	100.0	29.1	1,396
Veterinarians	162	30.8	24.1	42.6	2.5	100.0	19.8	95
Veterinary Assistants	352	62.7	27.6	8.8	0.9	100.0	15.6	127
Medical Doctors	1,915	7.6	49.5	36.7	6.2	100.0	24.0	728
Medical Assistants	2,323	35.3	34.6	28.1	2.0	100.0	16.4	2,414
Professional Nurses	5,623	33.7	55.1	9.0	2.2	100.0	19.4	5,297

10. Professionals by Ethnic Group (continued)

	Total Employed	Malay and other indigenous people	Chinese	Indian	Others	Total	Vacancies	Estimated[2] requirements, 1970-80
	(1)	(2)	(3)	(4)	(5)	(6)	(7)	(8)
Dental Assistants	1,030	24.4	72.1	3.0	0.5	100.0	10.1	578
Accountants	1,774	17.9	70.3	11.0	0.8	100.0	19.1	1,971
Lawyers	809	20.3	46.8	29.9	3.0	100.0	5.2	284
Higher Education Teachers	1,844	37.5	34.8	16.2	11.5	100.0	50.9	286
Primary and Secondary Teachers	79,527	49.5	40.4	9.4	0.7	100.0	3.1	19,872
Other Professional and Technical	20,353	68.0	24.6	6.4	1.0	100.0	16.7	18,183
Administrative and Managerial	22,605	35.4	55.5	7.3	1.8	100.0	8.6	12,264
Managers	12,535	13.0	81.5	3.7	1.8	100.0	3.3	10,472
Clerical	129,374	39.9	48.6	10.4	1.1	100.0	7.1	58,755
Sales	54,041	10.5	82.9	5.9	0.7	100.0	1.7	31,776
Services	64,917	70.4	20.2	8.0	1.4	100.0	6.3	145,300
Agricultural	105,742	37.9	18.0	43.5	0.6	100.0	3.1	142,309
Farm Managers and Supervisors	7,238	30.4	29.2	38.8	1.6	100.0	3.2	13,701
Production	210,331	39.2	47.7	12.4	0.7	100.0	4.4	190,123

1. Data refer to Survey results and therefore are not adjusted for undercoverage and exclusions.
2. Estimated from output and employment targets of the Plan and adjusted for undercoverage and exclusions.
Source: *Third Malaysia Plan*, Government Printers, Kuala Lumpur, 1976, p. 153, Table 8-11.

10. Professionals by Ethnic Group (continued)

TABLE 10.2 REGISTERED PROFESSIONALS BY ETHNIC GROUP, 2000 AND 2005

Profession	2000					2005					Net Increase, 2001-2005				
	Bumiputera	Chinese	Indians	Others	Total	Bumiputera	Chinese	Indians	Others	Total	Bumiputera	Chinese	Indians	Others	Total
Accountants	2,673	11,944	883	178	15,678	4,498	15,892	941	258	21,589	1,825	3,948	58	80	5,911
% of Total	17.1	76.2	5.6	1.1	100.0	20.8	73.6	4.4	1.2	100.0					
Professionals						961	13,541	798	102	15,402					
% of Total						6.2	87.9	5.2	0.7	100.0					
Architects	1,152	1,539	41	6	2,738	1,358	1,594	43	6	3,001	206	55	2	0	263
% of Total	42.1	56.2	1.5	0.2	100.0	45.3	53.1	1.4	0.2	100.0					
Professionals	450	1,034	23	4	1,511	557	1,066	26	4	1,653	107	32	3	0	142
% of Total	29.8	68.4	1.5	0.3	100.0	33.7	64.5	1.6	0.2	100.0					
Doctors	4,570	3,855	3,697	306	12,428	5,720	4,657	4,142	1,055	15,574	1,150	802	445	749	3,146
% of Total	36.8	31.0	29.7	2.5	100.0	36.7	29.9	26.6	6.8	100.0					
Dentists	790	952	460	43	2,245	1,159	920	480	49	2,608	369	-32	20	6	363
% of Total	35.2	42.4	20.5	1.9	100.0	44.4	35.3	18.4	1.9	100.0					
Veterinary Surgeons	428	284	281	33	1,026	522	431	332	54	1,339	94	147	51	21	313
% of Total	41.7	27.7	27.4	3.2	100.0	39.0	32.2	24.8	4.0	100.0					
Engineers	15,334	18,416	1,864	405	36,019	22,623	23,432	2,648	498	49,201	7,289	5,016	784	93	13,182
% of Total	42.6	51.1	5.2	1.1	100.0	46.0	47.6	5.4	1.0	100.0					
Professionals	2,461	6,536	636	198	9,831	3,326	7,283	726	188	11,523	865	747	90	-10	1,692
% of Total	25.0	66.5	6.5	2.0	100.0	28.9	63.2	6.3	1.6	100.0					
Surveyors	1,298	1,426	97	56	2,877	2,069	2,017	136	68	4,290	771	591	39	12	1,413
% of Total	45.1	49.6	3.4	1.9	100.0	48.2	47.0	3.2	1.6	100.0					
Professionals	713	876	58	30	1,677	975	989	70	31	2,065	262	113	12	1	388
% of Total	42.5	52.2	3.5	1.8	100.0	47.2	47.9	3.4	1.5	100.0					
Lawyers	3,111	3,860	2,586	76	9,633	4,465	4,354	2,834	97	11,750	1,354	494	248	21	2,117
% of Total	32.3	40.1	26.8	0.8	100.0	38.0	37.1	24.1	0.8	100.0					
Total	29,356	42,276	9,909	1,103	82,644	42,414	53,297	11,556	2,085	109,352	13,058	11,021	1,647	982	26,708
%of Total	35.5	51.2	12.0	1.3	100.0	38.8	48.7	10.6	1.9	100.0					

Source: Professional associations and institutions covering both public and private sectors such as Malaysian Institute of Accountants, Board of Architects Malaysia, Malaysian Medical Council, Malaysian Dental Council, Board of Engineers Malaysia, Bar Council Malaysia, The Institution of Surveyors Malaysia and Malaysia Veterinary Surgeons Council

11. ENROLMENTS IN PRIMARY AND SECONDARY EDUCATION BY ETHNIC GROUP

TABLE 11 - 1970 (Peninsular Malaysia)

	1970					1975				
	Malay	Chinese	Indian	Others	Total	Malay	Chinese	Indian	Others	Total
Primary	759,064	511,729	142,147	8,529	1,421,469	875,975	550,064	151,744	9,126	1,586,909
%	53.4	36.0	10.0	0.6	100.0	55.2	34.7	9.6	0.5	100.0
Lower secondary	193,054	146,872	36,339	2,270	378,535	305,700	198,493	54,290	2,988	561,471
%	51.0	38.8	9.6	0.6	100.0	54.4	35.4	9.7	0.5	100.0
Upper secondary	43,627	38,800	6,258	715	89,400	101,486	54,095	10,420	1,108	167,109
%	48.8	43.4	7.0	0.8	100.0	60.7	32.4	6.2	0.7	100.0
Post secondary	4,609	5,267	637	106	10,619	8,817	6,617	804	97	16,335
%	43.4	49.6	6.0	1.0	100.0	54.0	40.5	4.9	0.6	100.0

Source: Third Malaysia Plan, Government Printers, Kuala Lumpur, 1976, p. 40, Table 22-6.

12. Enrolments in Tertiary Education by Ethnic Group

TABLE 12 - 1970-75[1]

	1970					1975				
	Malay	Chinese	Indian	Others	Total	Malay	Chinese	Indian	Others	Total
Diploma and certificate courses[2]										
Universiti Malaya	-	-	-	-	-	61	5	3	132	63
Universiti Pertanian Malaysia	458	72	3	12	545	1,691	139	27	1	1,858
Universiti Teknologi Malaysia	390	198	23	7	618	1,557	118	9	12	1,696
Institiut Teknologi MARA	1,801	-	-	-	1,801	7,524	-	-	-	7,524
Politeknik Ungku Omar	216	267	10	-	493	744	341	51	-	1,136
Kolej Tunku Abdul Rahman	-	-	-	-	-	-	1,151	46	4	1,201
Sub-total	2,865	537	36	19	3,457	11,579	1,810	138	20	13,547
%	82.9	15.5	1.0	0.6	100.0	85.4	13.4	1.0	0.2	100.0
Degree courses										
Universiti Malaya	3,005	3,861	559	302	7,727	3,590	3,515	504	122	7,731
Universiti Sains Malaysia	68	144	35	5	252	1,205	1,361	179	14	2,759
Universiti Kebangsaan Malaysia	164	4	1	-	169	2,337	126	35	4	2,502
Universiti Pertanian Malaysia	-	-	-	-	-	538	135	22	-	695
Universiti Teknologi Malaysia	-	-	-	-	-	483	80	3	1	567
Sub-total	3,237	4,009	595	307	8,148	8,153	5,217	743	141	14,254
%	39.7	49.2	7.3	3.8	100.0	57.2	36.6	5.2	1.0	100.0
Preliminary and pre-university courses										
Universiti Malaya	28	14	6	2	50	190	3	-	-	193
Universiti Sains Malaysia	16	3	-	-	19	92	-	-	-	92

12. Enrolments in Tertiary Education by Ethnic Group (continued)

	1970					1975				
	Malay	Chinese	Indian	Others	Total	Malay	Chinese	Indian	Others	Total
Universiti Teknologi Malaysia..	..	74	-	-	-	74	-	-	-	-
Institiut Teknologi MARA	341	-	-	-	341	348	-	-	-	348
KolejTunkuAbdulRahman	30	1,122	41	2	1,195	32	2,739	157	4	2,932
Sub-total	520	1,141	47	11	1,719	815	2,751	157	5	3,728
%	30.3	66.4	2.7	0.6	100.0	21.9	73.8	4.2	0.1	100.0
TOTAL...	6,622	5,687	678	337	13,324	20,547	9,778	1,038	166	31,529
%	49.7	42.7	5.1	2.5	100.0	65.1	31.1	3.3	0.5	100.0

1. Figures refer only to enrolments in local universities and colleges.
2. Does not include enrolments in domestic private institutions.
Source: Third Malaysia Plan, Government Printers, Kuala Lumpur, p. 401. Table 22-7.

13. NUMBER OF DRUG ADDICTS AT PUSAT SERENTI[1] BY ETHNIC GROUP AND SEX, 2000, 2002 AND 2004

TABLE 13.1
Number of Drug Addicts at Pusat Serenti by Ethnic Group and Sex 2002, 2002 and 2004

Ethnic Group	2000				2002				2004			
	Jumlah	M	F	%F	Jumlah	M	F	%F	Jumlah	M	F	%F
Malay	9,986	9,888	98	1.0	10,633	10,455	178	1.7	9,860	9,722	138	1.4
Chinese	2,428	2,395	33	1.4	1,994	1,967	27	1.4	1,960	1,924	36	1.8
Indian	1,517	1,501	16	1.1	1,362	1,337	25	1.8	1,479	1,454	25	1.7
Bumiputera (Sbh/Swk)	90	84	6	6.7	107	100	7	6.5	288	268	20	6.9
Others	73	69	4	5.5	67	62	5	7.5	108	108	0	0.0
Total	**14,094**	**13,937**	**157**	**1.1**	**14,163**	**13**	**242**	**1.7**	**13,695**	**13,476**	**219**	**1.6**

M - Male F - Female
1. Rehabilitation centre for drug addicts.
Source: National Anti-Drug Agency, Ministry of Internal Security.

14. Farming Operators by Ethnic Group

CHART 1

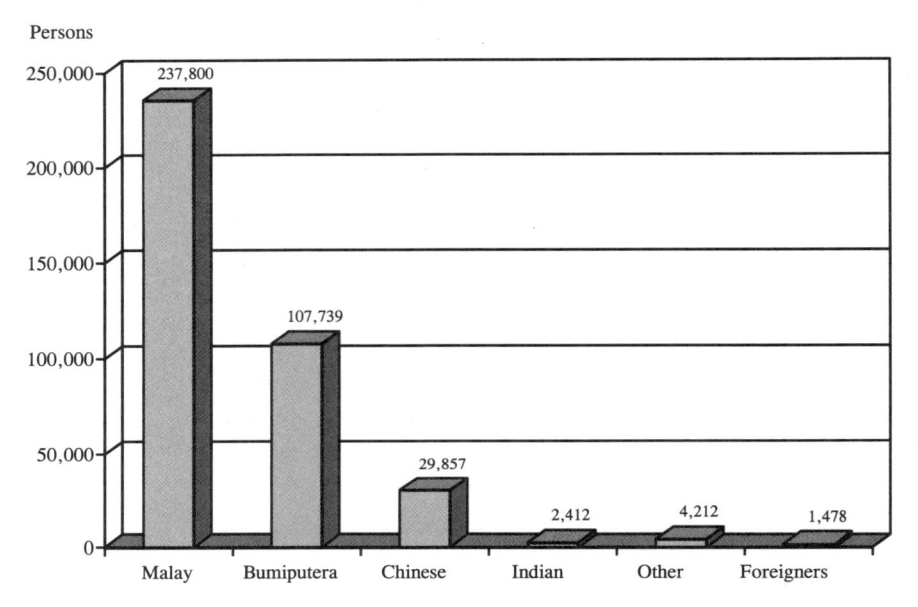

Persons

Ethnic Group	Number
Malay	237,800
Bumiputera	107,739
Chinese	29,857
Indian	2,412
Other	4,212
Foreigners	1,478

Source: Banci Pertanian 2005, Jabatan Perangkaan Malaysia p.59, Fig.14

BIBLIOGRAPHY

Anand, Sudhir, *The Size and Income in Malaysia*, (Mimeograph), 1973.

Callis, H.G., "Foreign Capital in Southeast Asia", Institute of Pacific Relations, New York, 1972.

Chander, R., *Socio-economic Sample Survey of Households 1967-68: Employment and Unemployment in East Malaysia*, Statistics Department, Kuala Lumpur, 1970.

Chander, R, *Banci Penduduk dan Perumahan Malaysia 1970*, Jabatan Perangkaan, Kuala Lumpur, 1972.

Furnivall, J.S., *Colonial Policy and Practice*, London, 1948.

Husin Ali, S., *Apa Erti Pembangunan*, Dewan Bahasa dan Pustaka, Kuala Lumpur, 1976.

Husin Ali, S., *Kemiskinan dan Kelaparan Tanah di Kelantan*, Karangkraf Sdn Bhd, Kuala Lumpur, 1978.

Husin Ali, S., *Isu Raja dan Pindaan Perlembagaan*, SHA, Petaling Jaya, 1993.

Husin Ali, S., *Merdeka, Rakyat dan Keadilan*, SIRD, Petaling Jaya, 2004.

Husin Ali, S., ed., *Pembangunan di Malaysia: Perencanaan, Perlaksanaan dan Prestasi*, PSSM, Kuala Lumpur, 1987.

Jomo, ed., *Mahathi's Economic Policies*, Insan, Kuala Lumpur, 1988.

Mahathir Mohamad, *Menghadapi Cabaran*, Pustaka Antara, Kuala Lumpur, 1976.

Malaysian Government, *Second Malaysia Plan*, Government Printers, Kuala Lumpur, 1971.

Malaysian Government, *Mid-Term Review of Second Malaysia Plan*, Government Printers, Kuala Lumpur, 1973.

Malaysian Government, *Third Malaysia Plan*, Government Printers, Kuala Lumpur, 1976.

Malaysia, *Rangka Rancangan Jangka Panjang Kedua*, 1991-2000, Jabatan Percetakan Negara, Kuala Lumpur, 1991...

Malaysia, *Rancangan Malaysia Ketujuh*, 1996-2000, Unit Perancang Ekonomi, Jabatan Perdana Menteri, Kuala Lumpur, 1996.

Malaysia, *Rancangan Separuh Penggal Rancangan Malaysia Ketujuh*, 1996-2000, Percetakan Nasional Malaysia Berhad, 1999.

Malaysia, *Rancangan Malaysia Kesembilan*, 2006-2010, Unit Perancang Ekonomi, Jabatan Perdana Menteri, Putrajaya, 2006.

Puthucheary, Mavis C, Administration, *Politics and Development: A Case Study of West Malaysia*, Ph.D. Thesis, University of Manchester, 1973.

Ragayah Hj Mat Zain, "Explaining the Trend in Malaysian Income Distribution" (Memeo), Institute of Malaysian and International Studies and Faculty of Economics, University Kebangsaan Malaysia.

Shamsul Amri Baharuddin, *RMK: Tinjauan dan Perlaksanaannya*, Kuala Lumpur 1977.

Shibutani, T. & Kwan, K.M, *Ethnic Stratification*, Macmillan, London, 1965.

INDEX

Abdul Aziz Ishak 23, 24

Abdul Halim Saad 114

Abdul Rahim Noor 52

Abdul Razak Hussein 21, 25, 26, 42, 49, 106, 124, 125

Abdullah Ahmad Badawi 28, 29, 53, 54-56, 76, 77, 119, 148, 149, 150, 152, 187, 194; attacked by Mahathir 53; 'Mr Clean' 28; not as firm as Mahathir 29; weak leader 55

ABIM, *see* Muslim Youth Movement of Malaysia

aborigines 4, 5, 6

Abu Bakar Bakir 71

Aceh 13

Acehnese 5, 62, 159

ADIL 28, 52, 76

Advisers 15, 33, 34, 35

Africa 13, 169, 191

African 8

AFTA, *see* Asian Free Trade Agreement

Agong 3, 54

agriculture 101-104, 106-108, 115, 116, 119, 127-129, 132, 140, 143 144, 149, 150, 162, 185, 188, 193, 194; emphasis under Abdullah 149; less importance under Mahathir 193

Ahmad Fuad, Haji 23

Ali Baba 43, 172

American(s) 113; anti- 187

animism 58

animists 5, 6

Anwar Ibrahim 28, 51-56, 76, 144, 150-151, 176, 177, 178, 179, 195; accused of corruption and sodomy 51; beaten up 52; released from prison 53; sacked by Mahathir 76; wants NEP replaced 150, 176

Apartheid 169

API 18, 20, 39

Approved Permits 4; scandal 53

Arab(s) 3, 6, 7, 17, 72, 138, 152; states 152

Arabic 60, 72, 85; -educated 86

Asia 191; Minor 13; South 71

Asian 8, 18, 28; Southeast 28, 77

Asian Strategy and Leadership Institute 120

Asian Free Trade Agreement 116, 117

ASLI, *see* Asian Strategy and Leadership Institute
Asri Muda 45, 49, 75
Attorney General 55
Australian(s) 113 171
AWAS 18, 20, 39

❁

Baba Melaka 4, 7
Bahaman, Datuk 15
Bali 57
Baling 22; hunger march in 26
Bangkok 15
Bangladesh 93
bangsa 7, 8
bangsawan 81
Banjarese 5, 159
Bar Council 54
Barisan Nasional 26, 29, 45, 49, 50, 53, 73-75, 151, 165, 172-174, 178-181; big victory in 1974, 26; spin doctors 51
Barisan Alternatif 53
batin 31
Batu Kikir 171
Batu Malim 171
Batu Pahat 13, 171
Bendahara 31
Bernard Shaw 9
bersanding 58
BERSIH 54, 55
bilal 66, 67
Birch, W.W. 15
BN, *see* Barisan Nasional

Boestamam, Ahmad 18, 23
bomoh 60, 61
Borneo 2, 5, 6, 11
Britain 2, 16, 112, 141, 181; nationalisation 137
British 1, 3, 8, 14-24, 33-39, 42, 55, 57, 65-71, 81-85, 91, 93, 102-105, 112, 113, 119, 159, 160, 169, 171, 181-187; buy British last 141; collaboration with 16, 21; Empire 39; strong influence 14
Buddhism 161
Bugis 5, 159, 161
Bukit Mertajam 171
Bukit Semanggol 71
Bumiputera 1-6, 92, 99, 105, 109, 110, 116, 120, 158, 163, 195; legal meaning 6; special position to all – 6
Burhanuddin Helmi 7, 18, 23, 71
Burma 160

❁

Candi Batu Pahat 13
capitalism 28
capitalists 16, 17, 34, 39, 40, 43, 47-49, 70, 94, 102, 106, 112, 115, 116, 120, 130-146, 149, 150, 154-156, 166, 175, 178, 183, 187, 189, 190; British 102, 112; Chinese 16, 39, 43, 143, 166, 172; foreign 34, 40, 49, 106, 120, 133-137, 141, 154, 175, 178, 187; Malay 120, 133, 140, 142, 143, 146, 166, 183; non-Malay 134
Ceylonese 160
Chettiars 175
Chin Peng 22
China 11, 13, 104, 159, 196

Index

Chinese 1, 3, 4, 6, 7, 8, 17, 19, 23, 25, 34, 39, 40-43, 46, 50, 57, 101-111, 116, 126, 128, 129, 133, 142, 143, 150, 151, 158-178; capitalists 16, 43, 166, 172; convert to Islam 3; DAP voice of 41, 43; different clans among 161; education 163-164, 174; Malay stereotypes of 172, 175-176; more outspoken 25; not strict to beliefs 161; participate in politics 43, 165; position of – language 50, 174; poverty among 108-109, 169; pro- 25, 41; sold out to 40; towkays 166; urban 23, 40

Christian(s) 6, 161; missions 57

Christianity 4, 57

civil service 3, 22, 36, 37, 38, 85, 91, 92, 167; Malayan 35, 36

Clifford School, 85

colonialism 7-10, 14, 18, 27, 30, 49, 62, 69, 70, 117, 136, 137, 154, 160, 185-187; arrival of 2; introduced segregation 2, 7; neo– 49, 137; struggle against 8; threat to Islam 18

Commonwealth 22

communal clashes 171; politics 24, 41, 179; tensions 24

Communist Party of Malaya 46

Communist 8, 20, 39

Confrontation 23, 24, 41

Constitution 2, 22, 58, 72, 92, 174, 178, 193, 194, 195; for Malaya 22; special position of Malays in, 193

corruption 26, 28, 29, 45, 50-55, 77, 94, 138, 141, 147, 148, 179, 182, 183, 196-199; due to failure of the PM 94

crime(s) 28, 198; criminal activities 147

cronyism 28, 29, 51, 53, 179, 182, 183, 192, 196, 197, 199

culture 46

❈

da'wah 73, 78

Danaharta 114, 142

DAP, *see* Democratic Action Party

Datuk (title) 4, 166

Dawn Raid, the 105

democracy 25, 179

Democratic Action Party 25, 41, 43, 50, 53, 165, 174

Denmark 156

divide and rule 183

dondang sayang 4

Dongson culture 12

dukun 59

Dutch 2, 14, 70, 138, 160

❈

East India Company 14

East Indies 160

education 3, 16, 36, 39, 40, 41, 45, 46, 50, 57, 65, 67-69, 83, 85, 89, 90, 95, 97-99, 125, 127, 152, 154, 163, 171-177, 182, 184, 185, 189-191, 196-199; higher 85, 88, 91, 97, 98, 185, 192; lack of 89; Malay nobles given 16, 85; Malay teachers unhappy with policy on 39, 40; more opportunities for Malays 184; religious 67-68; secular 69

Emergency 8, 71

Employees' Provident Fund 114

English (language and people) 2, 4, 40, 57, 68, 85, 163-164, 167; schools 163

EPF, *see* Employees' Provident Fund

Eric Chia 114, 144

ethnic, inter– integration 165, 168; jobs according to 168, 181; politics 50, 147, 174, 176, 178, 179

ethnocentric 9

Eton 85

Europe 13, 159

Eusoff Chin 54

exploitation 130

❀

farmers 82, 104, 127, 132

fatwa 66

Federated Malay States 14, 15, 34, 107

Federation Agreement 20, 36

Felda 49

feudal 27

Filipinos 2

financial crisis 51, 142

fishermen 13, 82, 108, 126, 127, 155

foreign investors 106, 112, 113, 114, 115, 121, 153

foreign investments 107, 112, 122, 149, 153

Furnivall, John Sydenham 160

❀

general elections 22, 174; eleventh 53; in 1999, 52; in 2008, 148

Georgetown 84, 89

Gerakan 26, 165

Germany 107

Gestapu 24

Ghazali Shafie 27

ghosts 61

GLC 120

Golden Hope 106

government servants 20, 21, 22, 45, 66, 76, 85, 92

Guthrie 105, 106

❀

Hadith 75, 78

Hajj 161

Hamzah Haji Taib 19

Hang Li Po 159

hantar belanja 58

hardcore poor 111

Hari Raya 87

hartal 41

Harun Idris 26

headscarf 72

Hikayat Si Tenggang 191

HINDRAF, *see* Hindu Rights Action Force

Hindu Rights Action Force 55, 56, 176, 177, 178

Hindu(s) 57, 161; influence 12, 13; priests 12, 13

Hinduism 13, 159

Hizbul Muslimin 71

Hoabinh 11

Hoabinhian culture 11

Holland, *see* Netherlands

Hussein Onn 21, 25-27, 42, 49, 106, 125, 143

❀

Ibans 6, 111, 178

ijab kabul 59

imam 60, 66, 67

IMF, *see* International Monetary Fund

immigrants 1, 5, 6, 159, 184; descendants of 5

Independence for Malaya Party 21, 144

Independent Power Producers 143

Indians 1, 7, 17, 19, 57, 103, 104, 106, 108-111, 126, 128, 129, 148, 158-178, 188; accepted as Malays 6, 7; convert to Islam 3; devout Hindus 161; encouraged by British to migrate 104; labourers 55, 104, 128, 168; marginalised 173, 178; Muslims 3, 7, 161; poverty among 148, 169, 177-178, 188; stereotypes of 172, 175-176; sepoys 15; traders 12; weak leadership 174

Indochina 11, 12, 125

Indonesia 1, 2, 7, 14, 18, 20, 23, 24, 28, 41, 51, 57, 70, 71, 93, 160; nationalisation policy 138

Industrial Master Plan 144

industrialisation 27, 83, 140, 144-146; Malaysia is late-comer to 144

inflation 111, 112, 148, 175, 194

Internal Security Act 24, 26, 29, 50, 52, 77

International Monetary Fund 188

International Islamic University 76

Ipoh 84, 89

Iran 78

Iranian revolution 75

Iraq 138

ISA, *see* Internal Security Act

Ishak Haji Muhammad 18, 23

Islam Hadhari 76, 77, 197

Islam 3, 4, 6, 7, 13, 14, 18, 19, 23, 44, 46, 57-78, 153, 159, 161, 164, 182, 198; bureaucratisation 182; closely linked with Melaka kingdom 62; converts to 3; fundamentals of 63; history of 62; important factor for social relations 63; Malays ignorant of its tenets 72

Islamic State 71

Islamic, jurisprudence 67; political agenda 49; rituals 64

Islamic Councils 65

Ismail Abdul Rahman, Dr 19, 25, 26

Jakun 5

Jamaluddin al-Afghani 18, 70

Japan 107, 141, 144

Japanese 113; occupation by 18

Java 12, 13, 57, 158

Javanese 5, 7, 159, 161

Jemaah Islah Malaysia 76

Johor 8, 15, 67, 68, 107, 170

Johor Bahru 84, 89

Johor Malay Union, *see* Kesatuan Melayu Johor

Johor-Riau Sultanate 32

Kadazandusun(s) 6, 51, 111, 178

kadi(s) 66, 67

Kampung Baru 50

Kampung Medan 171, 177

Kampung Rawa 171

Kaum Muda 70
Keadilan, *see* Parti Keadilan Nasional
Kedah 12, 13, 14, 23, 47, 64, 71, 107, 108, 119, 131
Kelantan 14, 23, 44, 45, 47, 49, 64, 67, 68, 71, 74, 107, 108, 119, 128, 168
keris 50
Kesatuan Melayu Johor 19
Kesatuan Melayu Muda 18, 19
ketua 31
ketuanan Melayu 45, 56, 182
Khir Johari, Mohd 40
King Edward VII School 85
King George V School 85
kingdoms 2, 12, 31, 32, 33, 39, 62, 101
KMM, *see* Kesatuan Melayu Muda
Korea 107, 141, 195, 196
Kuala Lumpur 22, 25, 26, 50, 54, 84, 85, 89, 94, 95, 145, 167, 171, 177
Kuala Lipis 85
Kwan, E.M. 160

❖

Labour Party of Malaya 23, 24
laissez faire 39, 112-123, 130, 133-134, 136, 139, 153-156, 181, 183, 189, 196-197; disadvantage to poor 133; not desirable 153; obstacle to Malay progress 118
Lake Club 95, 166
Laksamana 31
landlessness 175
Langkasuka Empire 12
Latin 13

Latin American 188
Libya 138
Lim Chong Yew 23
Lingam, V.K. 54
lingua franca 13
LLN, *see* National Electricity Board
Look East policy 140, 141
Lord Reid 22
LPM, *see* Labour Party of Malaya
LPN, *see* National Padi Board

❖

Mahakuwasa Scandal 114
Maharaja Lela 15
Mahathir Mohamad, Dr 25-29, 49-54, 76, 77, 114, 119, 124, 140-150, 153, 172, 187, 190-194; accused Anwar of sodomy 51; anti-American rhetoric 187; as authoritarian 28, 49; challenged as UMNO president 27; concentrated more on industrialisation 144; crony capitalism under 172; declared "Islamic state" 76-77; expelled from UMNO 25; forced to give way to deputy 52; introduced modernisation plans 27; introduced new electoral procedures 51; outmaneuvered Hussein 27; reaccepted into UMNO 26; revived UMNO 50
Majapahit 2, 12
makan beradap 59
Malay, customs 3, 4, 65; economy dependent on agriculture and trade 102; elite 44, 176; entrepreneurs 116; equity not met 121; legal definition 2-5; feudal system 13; kingdoms 31; language 3, 5, 6, 13, 39, 40, 85, 163,

195; middle class 4, 43; participation in business/industry 118, 134, 153; privileges 3, 22, 25, 48, 73, 98, 175; pro- 42, 44, 55, 174; Proto- 12; social and cultural definition 1; traditional beliefs strongly rooted in – society 62; traditional economy 27; traditional political system 30; unity 41-47, 49, 56, 182; urban population 84; women 84

Malays, almost all Muslims 57; ancestors of 12; anti- 56, 150, 176, 178; descendants in the Philippines 2; deutero- 13; English-educated 85; new rich (*nouveaux riche*) 134; ignorant of Islamic tenets 72; take another religion 4, 57; have lowest incomes 110; mostly in rural agriculture 115; do not own big estates 128; quota reserved for 3; reluctant to send their children to English schools 57; rural 17, 86, 103, 104, 107, 148; type of jobs monopolised by 128; special position in Constitution 193; urban 4, 17, 84

Malay Administrative Service 35

Malay Annals, *see* Sejarah Melayu

Malay Dilemma, The 140

Malaya 2, 7, 21, 22, 24, 46

Malayan Communist Party 20, 22

Malayan Chinese Association 22, 23, 25, 41, 165, 172, 174

Malayan Nationalist Party 18, 19, 20, 23, 36, 39, 71

Malayan People's Party, *see* Partai Rakyat Malaya

Malayan Union 19, 20, 21, 36, 42, 45, 46, 47

Malayanisation 22, 37, 91

Malayo-Indonesians 1

Malaysia 7, 23, 24, 51, 77, 78, 84, 94, 102, 107, 110, 117, 139, 140, 141, 144, 147, 157, 170, 171, 176, 177, 188, 196; first advocated by Tunku 23; formation 2, 6, 24; opposition to 24; ousting of Singapore from 24

Malaysia Day 5

Malaysia Incorporated 140, 141, 142

Malaysia Plan, First 118; Second 118, 119, 124, 125; Third 73, 118, 119, 122, 124-127, 130, 131, 135, 140; Fourth 119; Fifth 119; Sixth 119; Seventh 119; Eighth 119, 194; Ninth 119, 149, 194

Malaysian Economic Agenda 56, 150, 176, 177, 195

Malaysian Indian Congress 22, 165, 174, 178

MARA 139, 164

Marxist 18

MAS 35, 36

Mat Kilau 15

Matsushita Electronics 115

May Thirteenth Incident 23, 24, 25, 41, 42, 43, 47, 56, 73, 118, 125, 134, 165, 188

MCA, *see* Malayan Chinese Association

McDonald, Malcolm 21, 23

MCKK 35, 85

McMichael, William 19

Mecca 161

mega projects 27

Melaka 2, 4, 7, 13, 14, 23, 31, 32, 57, 62, 65, 81, 82, 101, 103, 107, 158, 159; Baba 4; Chinese 4; kingdom closely linked with Islam 62

Melanesian islands 11
Melayu 7, 8
Melayu Raya 18, 19
meminang 58
Menteri Besar 8, 21, 25, 49, 50
Merdeka 2, 3, 19, 21, 40, 71, 147, 151, 183
merisik 58
Mesolithic 10, 11, 30, 81
MIC, *see* Malaysian Indian Congress
Middle East 18, 70, 71, 86
Middle Eastern 139, 188
migrant workers 93
Minangkabau 5, 159, 161
MNP, *see* Malayan Nationalist Party
modernisation 14, 27, 141, 183, 184, 185, 186; Islam introduced – among Malays 14; not westernisation 183; slowed down for Malays 184
money economy 17, 103, 104
money politics 50, 94, 146
morality 72
mufti(s) 66, 67
Muhammad Abduh 18, 70
Muhammad Muhammad Taib 50
Multimedia Super Corridor 145
Multimedia University 145
Musa Hitam 50
Muslim 2-4, 6, 14, 18, 40, 57-78, 153, 182, 190, 191; aborigines 6; almost all Malays are 57; extremists 179; Indian 3, 161; law of inheritance 131; modernists 18; NGOs 76; not same as 'Malay' 3; reformists 18,70; society 190-192; terrorists 77

Muslims 6, 7, 13, 51, 58, 67, 68, 70, 72, 74, 75, 76, 77, 78, 161, 175, 182, 191, 192
Muslim Youth Movement of Malaysia 76
MSC, *see* Multimedia Super Corridor

❖

Najib Abdul Razak 50
Naning, Datuk 15
national identity 7
National Agricultural Policy 143, 144
National Alliance 22-26, 40, 41, 73, 165
National Convention Party 24
National Electricity Board 139, 143
National Front, *see* Barisan Nasional
National Justice Party, *see* Parti Keadilan Nasional
National Padi Board 132
National Operations Council 25, 41, 42, 44, 73, 124
National Schools 163
National-type Schools 163
nationalisation 123, 136-139, 152-154, 196, 197; opposite of 142; Iraq, Libya and Arabia's oil 138
nationalism 8, 18, 164
Negeri Sembilan 14, 15, 161
neo-colonialists 48
Neolithic 10, 11, 12, 30, 81, 100
NEP, *see* New Economic Policy
nepotism 28, 51, 87, 182, 192, 196
Netherlands 2, 107
New Economic Policy 26, 55, 84, 118, 124; abused by Malay elite 176;

appeared attractive 130; created few Malay millionaires 196; has not helped economy 195; resulted in nepotism and cronyism 182; to promote National Unity 125

New Development Policy 140, 146-148

Newbolt, A 20

NOC, *see* National Operations Council

noja 66

non-governmental organisations 165

North Africa 13

oil palm 84

Onn Jaafar 8, 19, 21, 36, 49

Operasi Lalang 50

Orang Asli 5, 126

orientalists 9, 10

Pacific War 18, 102

paddy 59, 83, 92, 96, 98

Pahang 14, 15, 19

Pakistan 78

Pakistanis 7

Palestinian 72

Pan-Malayan Islamic Party, *see* PAS

Pangkor 171

Pangkor Agreement 14

Parliament 22, 25, 40, 41, 42, 44, 106, 124, 125, 136, 142, 152, 197

Parti Rakyat Malaysia 23, 24, 28, 49, 50, 53, 164

Partai Rakyat Malaya 23

Parti Keadilan Nasional 28, 52

Parti Negara 21, 36

Parti Keadilan Rakyat, 150; formed 52; promotes multi-ethnic appeal 174

PAS 22-26, 40-50, 53, 67, 71-76, 86, 164, 165, 174, 178; conflict with UMNO 45; failure to bring changes in Kelantan 74; participated in struggle for independence 71; pressured into joining BN 45; pulled out of BN 49

pawang 59

peasantry 47, 130, 143, 150, 156, 175, 194

peasants 13, 17, 26, 59, 92, 93, 96, 99, 117-120, 128, 130-134, 149, 150, 154, 156, 168, 175, 176, 184, 185, 189, 190, 193

Penang 14, 65, 171

penghulu 31, 185

Pension Trust Fund 114

People's Manifesto 7

Perak 14, 15, 18, 25, 41, 71, 101, 104, 107, 161

Perlis 14, 23, 47, 106, 107, 108, 119

Permaisuri Tun Fatimah 83

Permodalan Nasional 84

PERNAS 84, 121, 139

persalinan 82

Persatuan Guru-Guru Melayu Semenanjung 40

Perwaja Steel 114, 144

Petaling Jaya 95

petroleum 113, 139, 151, 152, 154, 196

PETRONAS 119, 139, 149, 151, 152, 196, 197

Philippines 1, 2, 7, 11

PKR, *see* Parti Keadilan Rakyat

Police Act 29

pondok school 64, 71

Portugal 2

Portuguese 2, 101; captured Melaka 14; influence on Malay society 14

poverty 26, 48, 88, 108-118, 123-136, 146-152, 156, 162, 169, 175, 182, 188, 193-198; a problem of Malays 126; among Malays 109; eradication of 26, 118, 123-126, 130, 136, 146, 153, 156, 193, 194, 197; in towns 109; not entirely Malay problem 135; rampant in villages 88, 108, 131, 188; result of *laissez faire* economy 112

PPP 26, 43

Printing and Publications Act 29

Privatisation 140-143, 154

PRM, *see* Parti Rakyat Malaysia

Prophet Muhammad 59, 74; birthday celebration 64

Proton 53, 144, 145

Province Wellesley 14, 106

PSM 164

PUTERA-AMCJA 7

Putrajaya 145

❁

Qur'an 60, 62, 75, 78; recital competitions 64

❁

Raja Mahadi 15

Raja Chulan 36

Raja Mohar Raja Badiozzaman 106

Raub 171

Razaleigh Hamzah, Tengku 27; challenged Mahathir 50; Malays turned against 51

Red Book 125

Reformasi 28, 52

reformists 18

Religious Council 66, 67

Residents 15, 33, 34, 35

Royal Commission of Inquiry 54

Royal Golf Club 95, 166, 167

rubber 16, 17, 26, 84, 92, 96, 102-108, 126-128, 131, 132, 161, 62

❁

Sabah 2, 5, 6, 24, 51, 56, 108, 109, 151, 158, 169

Sarawak 2, 5, 6, 24, 108, 109, 158, 169

sarung 4

Saudi Arabia 78

scholarships 3, 4, 98, 164, 173

SEDC, *see* State Economic Development Cooperation

Sejarah Melayu 159

Sekolah Agama Rakyat 67

Selangor 14, 15, 25, 26, 41, 50, 89, 94, 101, 107, 161, 167

Semang 5

Semangat Melayu '46, 27, 50

Senoi 5

Seremban 84, 85

Seychelles 15

SF, *see* Socialist Front

Shamsiah Fakeh 18

Shariah 75, 182
Sheikh Tahir Jalaluddin 18, 70
Shibutani, T. 160
Siam 13
Siamese 14, 15
Sikhs 175
Sime Darby 105, 106
Singapore Journalists Union 23
Singapore 2, 13, 14, 19, 20, 23, 85, 107, 176, 195, 196; ousted from Malaysia 24
slum 86, 87, 182; encouraged by UMNO 89
smallholders 126
SNAP 26
social, classes 191; control 90; mobility 82, 97; problems 28, 29, 86, 88, 89, 182, 197; scientists 10, 79, 93, 172; stratification 80, 90, 93, 169, 182
socialist 25
Socialist Party 164
Socialist Front 23, 24, 40, 41
South Africa 169
South China 11
South Korea 147, 150, 176, 196
Spain 2
Sri Rama 12
Sriwijaya 2
State Economic Development Cooperation 84, 122, 139
Stone Age 10
Straits Settlements 14, 19, 20, 34, 91
Sufism 13
Suharto 24; downfall 28, 51
Sukarno 24

Sulaiman Abdul Rahman 19
Sultan(s) 3, 20, 31-32; no real power 93; of Johor 19; of Kedah 14; of Melaka 31; of Perak 14; position of 25
Sultan Abdullah 15
Sumatra 11, 13
SUPP 26
surau(s) 63, 67
Sutan Djenain 18
Syahbandar 31, 101
Syariah courts 67
Syed Mashur 15
Syed Sheikh Alhady 18, 70

Tabligh 74
tahlil 64
Taiping 85
Taiwan 141, 176, 195
taklid 63
Tan Cheng Lock 7, 21
Tan Sri (title) 4, 166
Taoism 161
technological gap 145
Telekom Malaysia 143
Temasik 13
Temenggung 31
Temiar 5
Tenaga Nasional 143
Tengku Adnan 54
Terengganu 14, 23, 47, 49, 71, 107, 108, 119, 151
terrorism, war against 77

Thailand 15
Third World 27, 136
Thuraisingam, S. 21
Time.com 114
tin mining 16, 84
Tok Gajah 15
Transparency International 94
tudung 72
Tunku Abdul Rahman 21-25, 42, 187; liberal towards Chinese 25; resigned as Prime Minister 25
Tunku Abdul Rahman University 164

❂

UDA 122, 139
UiTM 164
UKM 164
ulama 75
UMNO 8, 19-28, 36-56, 67, 71, 76, 77, 85, 89, 117, 140, 145-148, 151, 152, 164, 165, 173, 174, 177-181; as quickest means to reach top 44; conflict with PAS 45; crisis within leadership 27; declining popularity of 47; formed 19; hegemony 25; integrate Islamic values 76; New 27; presents itself as champions of Malays 174; success of 20
unemployment 85, 86, 89, 97, 113, 125, 126, 175, 182; among graduates 85; gives rise to social problems 89
Unfederated Malay States 3, 15, 34, 107

United States 2, 27, 107, 116, 169; 9/11 attack 77; interests in Malaysia 107; assets in Malaysia 171
Universiti Putra Malaysia 164
Universiti Teknologi Mara 164
universities 26, 43, 85, 86, 88, 99, 139, 164, 173
University of Malaya 85, 164
urbanisation 83, 90; faster among Malays 162

❂

Victoria Institution 85
Vincent Tan 54

❂

Wan Azizah Wan Ismail, Dr 52
Western, pro- 39, 187; culture 72; values 74
westernisation 72, 183
Westernised 7
women 43, 72, 82-84, 87-90, 115, 159, 165, 168; change of position 87; continue to be objects and symbols 88; degradation of 88; do domestic work 87; in higher education 88; left villages to work in factories 90; outnumber men in universities 88; sexually exploited 90
World War II 7, 104

❂

Zionism 72